# The Old Dominion at War

George Washington in the uniform of a colonel in the Virginia Regiment, from a portrait by Charles Willson Peale, 1772 (courtesy Washington/Custis/Lee Collection, Washington and Lee University, Lexington, Va.).

# THE OLD DOMINION AT WAR

*Society, Politics, and Warfare*
*in Late Colonial Virginia*

*James Titus*

*University of South Carolina Press*

# AMERICAN MILITARY HISTORY
## Thomas L. Connelly, Editor

*Travels to Hallowed Ground*
By Emory M. Thomas

*Forged by Fire:*
*General Robert L. Eichelberger*
*and the Pacific War*
by John F. Shortal

*War and Society in Revolutionary America:*
*The Wider Dimensions of Conflict*
by Don Higginbotham

*Soldiers Blue and Gray*
by James I. Robertson

*Diary of a Confederate Soldier:*
*John S. Jackman of the Orphan Brigade*
edited by William C. Davis

*The Old Dominion at War:*
*Society, Politics, and Warfare in Late Colonial Virginia*
by James Titus

Copyright © 1991 University of South Carolina

Published in Columbia, South Carolina, by the
University of South Carolina Press

Manufactured in the United States of America

Library of Congress Cataloging-in-Publication Data
Titus, James.
    The Old Dominion at war : society, politics, and warfare in late
colonial Virginia / James Titus.
        p.      cm. — (American military history)
    Includes bibliographical references and index.
    ISBN 0–87249–724–0 (hard : alk. paper)
        1. Virginia—History—French and Indian War, 1754–1763.
I. Title. II. Series: American military history (Columbia, S.C.)
E199.T63 1990
973.2'6–dc20                                                90-20880

*For Suzanne*

# CONTENTS

# ILLUSTRATIONS

Frontispiece.   George Washington in provincial uniform

Robert Dinwiddie, Lieutenant Governor of the colony of Virginia, 1751–1758   18

## MAPS

## TABLES

# PREFACE

This is a study of how the largest colony in English North America waged the French and Indian War. Its major themes are formed by the answers to three questions: What kind of military policy did Virginia leaders devise to guide and direct their colony's mobilization for the war? What political and military problems did the war create and how did Virginians attempt to solve them? What social and political implications may be discerned in Virginians' military behavior? As the foregoing suggests, my principal aim is to place Virginia's military experience in its wider social and political setting and to determine whether the conduct of those caught up in the toils of war has anything important to tell us about the nature of Virginia society in the late colonial period. I argue that it does.

Virginia's military needs changed over time between 1754 and 1763. But for almost half that period the colony's basic military policy was remarkably consistent. It called for fighting the war with a homegrown European-style army, an army of men drawn largely from the mudsill of provincial society. The members of that army were called provincial troops; collectively they composed an armed force known as the Virginia Regiment. In theory, the policy of imposing the war's heaviest burdens on the "lesser sort" appeared militarily sound and politically and economically expedient. Yet by 1758 that policy had failed almost completely. Essentially, it failed because the "lesser sort" of men singled out for service refused to cooperate in their own exploitation. Midway through the war colonial authorities abandoned compulsion and replaced conscripts with men induced to volunteer by generous enlistment bounties. In effect, only by allowing Virginians to soldier on close to their own terms could the colonial government raise the numbers of men it needed.

The "lesser sort" were unwilling to soldier except on their own terms for a variety of reasons. Suffice it to say here that their military behavior contrasted sharply with the customary conception of the Old Dominion as a place where subordination and deference were the orders of the day. Put another way, in the process of organizing their human and material resources for war, the people of the Old Dominion acted in ways that throw unfamiliar light on the social order and political culture of mid-eighteenth-century Virginia. That light reveals that Virginia was not a placid society. It also discloses that when it came to questions involving war and military service, popular support for official policy would be forthcoming voluntarily or not at all.

# ACKNOWLEDGMENTS

This book grew out of a dissertation, and writers of dissertations and books accumulate numerous debts. Many people helped me along the way but none more than Richard H. Kohn. It was he who originally suggested this topic, and he has been a constant source of inspiration as the manuscript passed through successive drafts. All who know him can attest that Dick Kohn possesses remarkable creativity, energy, and intelligence. He has shared all those gifts with me for over a decade, and his friendship besides.

A number of other scholars read the manuscript at various points and furnished much good counsel. I am especially grateful to Fred Anderson, Don Higginbotham, and Douglas Edward Leach. Each offered a wealth of useful ideas and learned criticism. To the extent that I followed their advice, a much better book resulted; to the extent I did not, I have only myself to blame. Edward M. Coffman, John M. Thompson, and Charles P. Carroll were also of great assistance and I deeply thank them for it. Thanks are due as well to George M. Curtiss III and Harold B. Gill. Both proved expert tutors in Virginia history. They also gave me a firsthand taste of Virginia hospitality during the four delightful months that I lived in Williamsburg. So did Marguerite Winn-Roberts, a charming Southern gentlewoman who graciously permitted me to stay in her beautiful Williamsburg home. The archivists and librarians at the Colonial Williamsburg Research Library, The Swem Library at the College of William and Mary, and the Virginia State Library were unfailingly polite and exceedingly helpful. Ken Scott and David Caffry of the University of South Carolina Press deserve special thanks for their encouragement, patience, and thoughtful criticism. Kathie Martin contributed her superlative word-processing skills. Lisa Cardio drew the maps.

It is appropriate to record here my abiding gratitude to John T. Horton and the late Milton Plesur of the State University of New York at Buffalo, Bradley Chapin of the Ohio State University, and the late Max M. Moorhead of the University of Oklahoma. Each taught me about the past and much else. I am equally grateful to Colonel Philip D. Caine, USAF, and Brigadier General Alfred F. Hurley, USAF, Retired, for their unswerving support and for showing me in their own lives what professional officership is all about.

Others sustained me in more personal ways. I am endebted to my parents, Florence M. and Russell P. Titus, Jr., for countless reasons but mostly for always having faith in their son. My own sons, Ethan, Luke, Michael, and Matthew, were full of understanding for ones so young. My wife, Suzanne, was there when the going was worst. She always is.

# The Old Dominion at War

They were soldiers, when they chose to be so, and when they chose, laid down their arms.

JOSEPH DODDRIDGE,
*Notes on the Settlement and Indian Wars of the Western Parts of Virginia and Pennsylvania*

# · 1 ·

# "I FOUND THE MILITIA
# IN VERY BAD ORDER"
## The Old Dominion on the Eve of War

*On my arrival at my Gov't, I found the Militia in very bad Order.*
*GOVERNOR ROBERT DINWIDDIE, 1756*

In the midst of the French and Indian War, Colonel George Washington of Virginia described his native colony as "a Country young in War. Untill the breaking out of these Disturbances [it] has Lived in the most profound and Tranquil Peace; never studying War nor Warfare."[1] The characterization offered by the young commander of Virginia's provincial army was apt and ironic. In fact, Virginia had played a crucial part in the events that led to the final armed encounter between British North America and France. When hostilities began in 1754, the Old Dominion was at the very center of military activity, and the colony continued to play an active part in military affairs even after the main theater of operations had shifted northward.[2] This prominent role notwithstanding, the war with France had been neither courted nor desired by most Virginians, and the people and institutions of the Old Dominion were sadly unprepared for the military responsibilities that conflict thrust upon them.

## THE VIRGINIA MILITIA SYSTEM
Since the founding of the colony in 1607, the people of Virginia had relied for their defense on the militia—an armed citizenry formed into military units that could be mobilized to ward off foreign invasion or to quell internal insurrection. Militia duty was the one military obligation that theoretically touched the lives of all men in colonial Virginia, and the militia system was the subject of an elaborate body of colonial law. Detailed legislation periodically enacted by the general assembly addressed almost all conceivable aspects of militia training, organization, and equipment.

In a report submitted to the Board of Trade in 1750, Thomas Lee, a member of the Virginia Council then serving as the colony's acting lieutenant governor, stated that the militia consisted of all free white male residents between the ages of twenty-one and sixty.[3] In truth, however, the militia system was by no means universal. When the French and Indian War began, the militia was regulated under an act of 1738 that granted exemptions to Anglican ministers; the president, faculty, and students at the College of William and Mary; overseers of slaves; mill keepers; and those employed in iron, copper, or lead foundries or in the mines from which such ores and minerals were extracted. The list of those enjoying partial exemption was even longer. Although their names were carried on the militia rolls, persons who fell into this category were excused from all military training on condition that they provide an able-bodied man to be trained in their stead. This list included past and present members of the council; speakers of the House of Burgesses; the secretary, receiver-general, and auditor of the colony; judges of the vice-admiralty court; attorneys-general; past and present clerks of the council, House of Burgesses, and secretary's office; justices of the peace; clerks of any county court; all persons who once had held a military commission as a captain or higher ranking officer; and "any of the people commonly called Quakers."[4] One historian claims that by 1749 these exemptions served to excuse as many as eight thousand men from militia duty.[5] The following year Thomas Lee reported that the Virginia militia totaled approximately fourteen thousand men organized into 176 foot companies and 100 cavalry troops.[6]

According to the militia statutes, the military chain of command in each county was to consist of a county lieutenant who exercised overall control over the local militia forces, a colonel, at least two men in the grades of lieutenant colonel and major, and a sufficient number of company officers to supervise the men in the ranks. Commanders of militia companies were required to hold monthly training sessions, and the laws specified that each county was to conduct a general muster of its forces once a year.[7] The designated commander in chief of the Virginia militia was the colonial governor, although that authority was increasingly delegated to others as the eighteenth century progressed.[8] In 1742 a new staff position in the militia hierarchy was established when an adjutant general was appointed to oversee the training of Virginia's citizen-soldiers. The first incumbent was George Washington's elder half-brother, Lawrence, who had held a regular British commission and commanded an infantry company in the Cartegena expedition of 1740–41.[9]

The militia principle was an integral part of the colonial inheritance from England. The militia had existed for centuries in the mother country and had formed the basic element in England's military structure from the days of the Saxons to those of the Stuarts.[10] By the seventeenth century, however, the English militia system was in an advanced state of decay.[11] But for a time at least, this ancient institution gained new life by being transplanted to the American colonies. The early colonists lived in a dangerous world, and the need for mutual protection was of primary importance. In Virginia and in other English colonies, the militia system was established as the basis for colonial defense, and invigorated by the hostile environment, it soon became a reasonably effective, well-functioning institution. But over the years as the immediate Indian threat declined and life became more secure, the colonial militia began to lose its vigor and to molder after the manner of the English archetype.[12]

Such was the fate of the militia system in Virginia. During the first half of the eighteenth century, Virginia had no serious military problems, and her forces were seldom employed.[13] No urgent Indian threat had confronted the colony since well before the end of the seventeenth century, and by 1735 Governor William Gooch could report that the nearest Indian neighbors of any consequence lived three hundred to four hundred miles from the settled portions of the Old Dominion.[14] Nor had Virginia been much affected by the three French wars that preceded the climactic struggle begun in 1754. The colony's participation in King William's War (1689–1697) was limited to modest financial support, and the impact of Queen Anne's War (1702–1713) on the lives of most Virginians was no more significant.[15] Down to the middle of the eighteenth century, Virginia's greatest military effort occurred in 1740–41 during the so-called War of Jenkins' Ear.[16] Beginning in 1739 as an Anglo-Spanish conflict, the War of Jenkins' Ear subsequently developed into the broader struggle between Britain and France known as King George's War (1744–1748).

British strategy in 1739 called for an amphibious descent on Spain's possessions in the Caribbean. Accordingly, the War Office issued a call for American volunteers to augment the king's regular troops in an attack on Cartagena, the principal Spanish port on the northern coast of South America. Although one historian has written that "many" Americans volunteered for the expedition, "glad of a chance to exchange the broom and the hoe for the fancied rewards of military conquest," the number of Virginians willing to participate in the assault fell far short of official expectations.[17] In spite of the fact that enlistment bounties were offered by the Virginia assembly, at least half of the four hundred men eventually raised in the Old Dominion had to be conscripted.[18] Employing criteria it would use again during

the French and Indian War, the assembly voted to make only poor
men liable for compulsory military service by limiting eligibility for
the draft to "able-bodied persons, fit to serve his majesty, who follow
no lawful calling or employment."[19] The attack on Cartagena was a
disaster, and the combined Anglo-American invasion force suffered
huge losses. Most of the Virginians who participated in the ill-fated
venture never returned.[20] In the war with France that followed (King
George's War), Virginia contributed but one company of 136 volunteers, none of whom saw any action.[21]

Although the Cartagena invasion represented the colony's only significant military involvement in the eighteenth century prior to the
French and Indian War, the practical effects of the expedition on
military preparedness in Virginia were negligible. The expedition
was a British project undertaken for purposes of foreign military conquest; it had no bearing on the defense of the Old Dominion, and
the Virginia militia played no part in it. Perhaps that was just as
well, for there is ample reason to believe that by the 1740s the Virginia
militia had become enervated by lack of use and popular indifference.
Writing shortly after the Cartegena episode, one contemporary
penned the following description of Virginia's citizen-soldiers:

> Your Ears are constantly astonished at the Number of Colonels, Ma-
> jors, and Captains that you hear mentioned: In short, the whole Coun-
> try seems at first to you a Retreat of Heroes; but, alas! to behold the
> Musters of their Militia, would induce a Man to Nauseate a Sash and
> hold a Sword forever in Derision. Diversity of Weapons and Dresses,
> Unsizeableness of the Men, and Want of the least Grain of Discipline
> in their Officers or them, make the whole Scene little better than
> Dryden has expressed it... "And raw in fields the rude militia
> swarms; ... Of seeming arms, they make a short essay, then hasten to
> get drunk the bus'ness of the day."[22]

Moreover, in at least one Virginia county during this period, there
was no militia organization at all. Responding in December 1750 to
an official letter addressed to the county lieutenant of Cumberland
County, a local resident reported that "we have neither County Lieutenant nor any other Military Officer amongst us and Consequently
no Soldiers, for no Commission has ever appeared amongst us, Since
we were in the County of Cumberland."[23]

In sum, the Virginia militia system—the colony's principal means
of military protection—deteriorated during the first half of the eighteenth century because throughout those decades the people of the
Old Dominion enjoyed an almost unbroken period of peace and sub-

stantial security. From one decade to the next, her leaders dismissed the existence of any military threat to the colony.[24] Barely ten years before the climactic struggle for North America began, Governor Gooch was still reporting to London on the remoteness and lack of communication between the Virginia backcountry and the nearest French and Indian settlements.[25] The colony's traditional security was soon to contribute to the generally apathetic response that greeted the first alarms raised over French penetration of the Ohio Valley at the end of the 1740s.

## THE VIRGINIA FRONTIER

A principal source of the French and Indian War involved the assertion of conflicting claims to the Ohio Valley by Frenchmen and Virginians. Virginians based their pretensions to western empire on the colony's royal charter of 1609. By virtue of that document, Virginians laid claim to a vast territory that reached two hundred miles north and two hundred miles south of Point Comfort and extended westward from the Atlantic coast to the Pacific Ocean. Making the most of the colony's vaguely defined borders, Virginians further asserted a claim to territory that stretched northwestward from the Blue Ridge to the shores of the Great Lakes, an area that encompassed the lands drained by the Ohio River.[26]

Official interest in peopling the western borderlands of Virginia long predated the rise of large-scale land speculation in the middle of the eighteenth century. The beginnings of Virginia's drive toward the trans-Allegheny west usually are associated with the administration of Governor Alexander Spotswood (1710–1722).[27] But even before Spotswood's time, Virginia authorities had come to view frontier settlements as military barriers that would strengthen the colony's western defenses. It was with this end in mind that the Virginia assembly had voted in 1701 to grant two hundred acres of land to every man willing to join with others in forming a society organized to settle and defend the colony's frontiers. According to the act of assembly, candidates for this enterprise were to be "Christian warlike men between sixteen and sixty years of age, perfect of limbs, able and fitt for service."[28] This particular project seems to have stirred little interest, for nothing more was to be heard of it in later years. Another measure designed to promote frontier settlement was enacted in 1738. In this instance the assembly was seeking to attract newcomers to the area of southwest Virginia that later became Halifax County. For that purpose the legislators voted to exempt those who would settle in the region from all taxes for ten years. In the same year the assem-

bly provided for the establishment of Frederick and Augusta counties
on lands west of the Blue Ridge Mountains. To promote settlement in
the new counties, the legislature once again voted to waive all levies
for a ten-year period. The stated purpose of this enactment was to
increase the king's quitrents and to strengthen the colony's western
defenses.[29]

The timing of these inducements to settlement was propitious. Until 1730 few settlers had ventured as far west as the Blue Ridge, and
none had crossed it; after that date, increasing numbers of people
began moving into the area immediately behind that barrier. In most
cases these venturesome folk were not Virginians who had decided to
quit the tidewater or piedmont for fresher fields in the west. The
overwhelming majority of the newcomers were outsiders from Pennsylvania, Germany, or Northern Ireland who were drawn to the Virginia frontier by the promise of low taxes, cheap land, and the chance
to preserve their cultural identity.[30] Following the line of least resistance, these immigrants entered Virginia via the Appalachian Valley,
the long and fertile depression extending from the Hudson River into
the Cherokee Indian country below the Old Dominion's southwest
corner. In the Old Dominion this valley ran in a southwesterly direction from the upper Potomac to the present-day Tennessee-Carolina
border; it is known now as the Valley of Virginia. Bounded in the
east by the Blue Ridge, the valley's outer limits were set by the Allegheny Mountains, which rose up some thirty miles to the west.[31]
Thus, during the several decades preceding the French and Indian
War, the principal movement of population in Virginia was not push-
ing westward toward the Ohio but flowing southward down the
valley toward the Carolinas.[32]

By the mid-1750s three Virginia counties had been established on
the far side of the Blue Ridge: Hampshire, Frederick, and Augusta.
During the 1740s and 1750s, these three westernmost counties, together with Bedford and Halifax counties in the far southwest, constituted the Virginia frontier. Hampshire, Frederick, and Augusta
bore the brunt of the French and Indian War from 1754 until the
winter of 1758–59; Bedford and Halifax became scenes of major military activity after 1758 when the powerful Cherokee nation took up
the hatchet against their one-time Virginia allies.

The migrants who streamed into the Valley of Virginia during the
1730s and 1740s were culturally different. The Germans were the
first to arrive, and these folk came to constitute the major ethnic
group in Hampshire and Frederick counties at the lower (or northern)
end of the valley.[33] They were followed after 1740 by the Scotch-Irish,

who soon held sway in sprawling Augusta County.[34] Persons of English ancestry were present on the frontier in significant numbers, but only in Bedford and Halifax counties did they constitute a majority of the population. Smaller numbers of people of Scots, Irish, Welsh, Dutch, Swedish, and Swiss descent were also resident on the Virginia frontier.[35]

In the main, those who settled on the frontier made their livelihood in agriculture. Most were self-sufficient farmers, producing little beyond what they and their families could consume.[36] Given the essentially noncommercial nature of agriculture in the Virginia backcountry, the slave population there was extremely small, although an appreciable number of blacks did live in Bedford and Halifax, where tobacco growing was an important activity.[37] Religious affiliation among the frontiersmen was generally determined by national origin. The English were mostly Anglicans, and the Scots and Scotch-Irish were overwhelmingly Presbyterian. There was greater diversity among the Germans, who divided themselves into Lutherans, German Reformed, Mennonites, and Dunkers. Although Baptists drew from various national groups, only a small and inconsequential scattering lived on the frontier before the 1760s.[38]

The original occupants of North America, the Amerindians, customarily are represented as a principal roadblock to the advance of European civilization. But during the first half of the eighteenth century at least, white settlers living on the western frontier of Virginia enjoyed generally peaceful relations with their Indian neighbors.[39] Although Indian raids did take place from time to time, armed conflict between red and white men was limited and sporadic. The earliest recorded clash during the decade preceding the war occurred in the southern portion of the Valley of Virginia on 18 December 1742. In this incident a thirty-four-man unit from the Augusta County militia was pitted against a mixed band of about forty Onondagas and Oniedas, member tribes of the powerful Iroquois confederation. After each side had suffered a number of casualties, the Indians broke off the engagement and retreated northward. The Six Nations of the Iroquois at that time claimed the valley as a tribal preserve by right of conquest and subsequently petitioned the governor of Pennsylvania to adjudicate their dispute with the Virginians. This particular quarrel was one of the issues resolved in 1744 by the Treaty of Lancaster, an important compact in which, among other things, the Six Nations agreed to give up their claim to the valley.[40]

In the years that followed the Lancaster agreement, such Indian depredations as occurred in Augusta seem to have been minor. Returning in July 1750 from a surveying trip to the New River country in southwestern Virginia, Dr. Thomas Walker, physician, prominent land speculator, and later commissary general to Virginia's provincial army during the French and Indian War, noted that families living on the eastern edge of the Alleghenies in southern Augusta were subject to frequent thefts committed by Indians.[41] Three years later a large band of Indians from the "Norward" burned the house and stable of one Augusta resident and killed two horses belonging to a neighbor.[42] Perhaps other unfortunate episodes occurred and went unreported. In retrospect what was important was not that these incidents took place but that they were so few in number.

If the residents of Augusta had relatively few problems with the Indians, Indian-white relations in nearby Frederick and Hampshire were positively cordial by comparison. The only Native Americans resident within the boundaries of these counties were a small group of Shawnee who owed fealty to the pro-English Iroquois.[43] The main body of the Shawnee nation had long since removed to the banks of the Scioto River in the Ohio country, where they quickly had come under French influence. After 1754 the Shawnee were among the most feared and active of Virginia's Indian enemies.[44] The Delawares were another important tribe that once had been reasonably well disposed toward the British. Originally inhabitants of New Jersey and eastern Pennsylvania, the Delawares by 1754 had seated themselves in what is now southeastern Ohio. Like the Shawnee, the Delawares threw in with the French when the war began and became a source of much woe to Virginia frontiersmen.[45]

Below Virginia's southwest border in the mountainous up-country along the Tennessee and Savannah rivers lived the Cherokee, another powerful Indian nation that eventually would descend in fury upon the Virginia frontier. However, before relations turned sour in 1759, the Cherokee were allies of the Old Dominion and periodically sent war parties down the valley to join the Virginians on campaigns against the French and the northern tribes who were aligned with them.[46] Other southern tribes favorably disposed toward the British were the Catawbas, the Chickasaws, and the Creeks.[47]

Virginians could best insure continued peace with neighboring Indian tribes by taking part in that complicated process known as Indian diplomacy. Although Virginia had not maintained steady diplomatic relations with any Indian nation prior to the French and Indian War, beginning in the mid-1740s the colony did participate in several Indian conferences that had a significant bearing on the outbreak of hostilities with the French ten years later.[48]

The first of these conferences was convened in the summer of 1744 at Lancaster, Pennsylvania. At issue was a controversy over lands west of the Alleghenies involving the Iroquois and the colonies of Virginia, Maryland, and Pennsylvania. Representing the Old Dominion were Thomas Lee and William Beverley, both members of the Virginia Council. In the treaty that came out of this conference, the Six Nations agreed to cede to the British their nominal rights to the Valley of Virginia and other western lands, including territory along the Ohio River. On the basis of her original sea-to-sea charter, Virginia quickly asserted a claim to these lands even though no one, the Iroquois included, was certain of the exact boundaries of the cession.[49] Subsequent disagreement over the provisions of the Treaty of Lancaster and the destabilizing activities of Virginia land speculators led to another conference in 1752. Meeting at Logstown, an Indian village on the Ohio River about twenty miles south of present-day Pittsburgh, the Iroquois, Delaware, Shawnee, and Wyandot representatives in attendance reluctantly consented to a treaty that gave the Virginia-based Ohio Company tentative permission to build a fort at the confluence of the Allegheny and Monongahela rivers—the forks of the Ohio—and to take up lands south and east of that point for white settlement.[50]

The Virginians sought to win confirmation of the Logstown agreement at another conference held the following year in Winchester. Unfortunately, by 1753 French aggressiveness in the Ohio region had weakened the generally pro-British orientation of the Ohio tribes nominally subservient to the Iroquois. Thus, despite its importance to Virginians with an interest in the vast trans-Appalachian area, no final resolution of the western lands question was reached at the Winchester conference. The Indians were unenthused with the prospect of losing their hunting grounds and let it be known that neither French nor British settlements would be particularly welcome in the Ohio Valley. After a week of feasting and drinking, all the Virginians could obtain was the Indians' grudging consent to construction of a fort and trading post on the Ohio.[51] In any event, the Indians' chilly response to possible white encroachment in the trans-Allegheny, and the contingent and controversial nature of the agreements struck at Lancaster, Logstown, and Winchester, failed to deter men of affairs and vision in the Old Dominion. Virginia politicians preferred to believe that these conferences had the effect of confirming the colony's long-held pretensions to dominion over the trans-Allegheny west; to Virginia land speculators these shaky diplomatic agreements served to open dazzling possibilities for personal enrichment.[52]

## THE LURE OF THE WEST

Men of means in eighteenth-century Virginia had relatively few
alternatives for investment open to them. Speculative purchases of
slaves, luxury imports, bills of exchange, or land constituted the primary outlets for surplus capital.[53] Investment in land was a particularly attractive alternative for several reasons. In the Old Dominion,
as in early modern Europe, land ownership was a fundamental
source of social prestige. Land ownership was also a primary meas-
urement of wealth in the agrarian world of the eighteenth centry.[54]
Moreover, as Rhys Isaac has pointed out in his studies of cultural
change in late colonial Virginia, the importance of land as a com-
modity of trade and speculation steadily increased during the second
half of the eighteenth century. Even as that period began, acquisitive
and calculating men concluded that decreasing soil fertility and growing population pressure in the older sections of Virginia clearly had
increased the value of unsettled lands at the back of the colony. No
matter that for twenty years after 1730 the direction of setlement on
the Virginia frontier had been pointed toward Carolina rather than
the Alleghenies. To Virginia gentlemen who commanded the resources necessary to explore and survey the trans-Allegheny wilderness, the lure of the west was virtually irresistible. Notwithstanding
the southward orientation of settlement in the 1730s and 1740s, men
with money and foresight believed that future expansion was sure to
be tilted in the direction of the rich and open lands that stretched to
the Ohio and beyond. Western lands were known to be fertile and
so, it was imagined, were the prospects for a lucrative trade with the
Indians who roamed them. For men of boldness and enterprise in
mid-eighteenth-century Virginia, the west was the future.[55]

The involvement of Virginians in large-scale speculation in trans-
Allegheny lands began within months of the Lancaster conference,
where, as noted above, it was deemed that the Iroquois had conveyed
to the British their pretended sovereignty over the Ohio country.[56]
Beginning in the spring of 1745 and during the nine years that followed, the governor and Council of Virginia, in whom was vested
the authority to pass on such matters, authorized a total of thirty-six
grants of land in the trans-Allegheny west. Well over 2,000,000 acres
were conveyed by these grants, most of them to corporate interests.
Only six grants went to individuals, and these assigned but 10,000
acres to each recipient. The balance of the land, some 2,614,000
acres, came under the control of twenty-two separate companies or
partnerships. The membership of these organizations was drawn primarily from three groups: wealthy individuals from the Virginia tide-

water and piedmont, leading inhabitants of the Virginia frontier, and influential British businessmen.[57]

The earliest of the large grants was issued in April 1745 to the Greenbrier Company, a twelve-man group headed by John Robinson, Sr., the president of the Virginia Council. This organization was authorized to take up 100,000 acres along the Greenbrier River in southwest Virginia and was given the right to survey and sell its holdings to settlers or to other speculators. Robinson's fellow councillors also saw to it that the Greenbrier Company was excused from paying the traditional "head-right" duties of fifty shillings on each 50 acres of land until the time the land actually had been sold. It was a cozy arrangement and spared the company's members from virtually all financial risk. The grant given to Robinson and his associates was renewable after four years, and at their request it was renewed in 1749.[58]

A second 100,000-acre grant was made in April 1745 to the Wood's River Company. This twenty-member partnership was led by James Patton, the leading citizen of Augusta County. The grant assigned to this organization was located on the western slope of the Alleghenies in southwest Virgnia, where it bordered a stream known as "Wood's River."[59] Before the close of 1745, the government of Virginia made its third large grant to private interests when it conveyed 100,000 acres along the Potomac and Youghiogheny rivers to John Blair, a member of the Virginia Council, and seventeen associates.[60]

The 100,000-acre tracts assigned to the Greenbriar Company, the Wood's River Company, and to Blair and his friends were by no means ungenerous, but they appeared puny indeed when compared to the tremendous grants allocated to two new organizations in the summer of 1749. Acting on instructions from the Crown, the Virginia Council on 12 July conveyed 200,000 acres to the Ohio Company and on the same day approved a grant of 800,000 acres to the Loyal Company. The sprawling territory assigned to the Loyal Company was located along the western end of the Virginia-North Carolina border, a portion of it extending into what is now the state of Kentucky.[61] Although its grant was only one-fourth that received by the Loyal Company, the Ohio Company was to exert a much more potent influence on developments in the trans-Allegheny west. Simply put, it was the activities of the Ohio Company that brought to a head the conflicting claims of France and Britain to dominion over the Ohio Valley and in so doing served to spark the French and Indian War.

The 200,000-acre grant assigned to the Ohio Company in 1749 was the fruit of almost two years' labor. The company's first petition for

a trans-Allegheny grant was submitted to the governor and Council
of Virginia shortly after the company was organized in the fall of
1747 by thirteen investors from the Northern Neck of Virginia.[62] Action on the petition was postponed by Governor William Gooch's
decision to refer the politically sensitive question of further western
expansion to the Board of Trade. King George's War was coming to
an end in 1747, and by approving additional transmontane grants,
Gooch was afraid that he might jeopardize the chances for securing
a general peace with France.[63] But the promoters of the Ohio Company were powerful men, determined and persistent. Upon learning
of Gooch's intention to seek a decision in London, the company's
stockholders quickly invited an influential English merchant named
John Hanbury to join their number with the understanding that he
would use his influence in Whitehall on the company's behalf.[64] They
also took it upon themselves to appeal over Gooch's head directly to
the authorities at home.

The Ohio Company petition referred by Gooch to the Board of
Trade was important for a number of reasons. First, the petitioners
themselves were overwhelmingly rich, prominent, and powerful
men. Concluding an examination of the company's membership roll,
one historian has stated simply that "it would be difficult to assemble
a more formidable roster of men of colonial business and politics."[65]
And, in addition to the wealthy planters who dominated its ranks
numerically, the company's members included by the early 1750s two
leading London merchants, the governor of Virginia, three members
of the Virginia Council, and the future governor of North Carolina.[66]
No wonder that contemporaries came to believe the Ohio Company
enjoyed sufficient influence in both Williamsburg and London to
command special advantages in the drive to open and exploit the
trans-Allegheny west.[67] In requesting a 500,000-acre grant in the
Ohio Valley, the petitioners promised to construct and garrison a fort
on their lands and to settle one hundred families on the tract within
seven years. Having thus sweetened their request, the petitioners then
asked that 200,000 of the 500,000 acres by conveyed to them immediately.[68] The point to be emphasized here is that the provision of a
fort, garrison, and settlement was proposed by the company itself.
Rather than being imposed by the Crown as historians have sometimes maintained, this stipulation, devised by a small group of Virginia land speculators, was merely endorsed by the Privy Council.[69]
Finally, although the division of interest went largely unnoticed until
1760, the wording of the Ohio Company's petition made it clear that
British authorities on the one hand, and westward-looking Americans

on the other, were pursuing conflicting goals from the very beginning of Britain's transmontane advance.

The petition sent to London by the Ohio Company was couched in the language of mercantilism and stressed the economic dimension of western expansion. The petitioners pointed out the commercial advantages that would result from settling British subjects in the Ohio country and put particular emphasis on the economics of winning a monopoly over the lucrative fur trade with the western Indians. According to the company's sponsors, western settlement and an expanded Indian trade could be expected to increase the demand for British manufactures and stimulate British shipping. While the petitioners predicted that the company's activities would benefit colonial security as well, the strategic significance of a British presence west of the Alleghenies received only secondary notice.[70] To policymakers in London, however, the company's potential usefulness as an instrument for checking French penetration of the Ohio Valley was the most compelling argument in its behalf. And with good reason. If the French secured the Ohio country for themselves, the British would be confined to the Atlantic seaboard; if the area was gained by Britain, it would provide access to the continent while serving as a wedge to separate France's strongholds in Canada and Louisiana. From either a French or British perspective, control of the Ohio country was vital.[71]

Believing that possession of the Ohio region constituted a strategic imperative, the Board of Trade, which at the request of the Privy Council had reviewed the case for granting the Ohio Company's petition, argued strongly that the company's western design should be approved because it would create a protective barrier against French encroachment. The Privy Council endorsed this view, and in March 1749 directed that Governor Gooch be instructed to grant the Ohio Company 200,000 acres of land in the vicinity of the forks of the Ohio, with the understanding that the company was responsible for building a fort and settling one hundred families on its tract within seven years.[72] The instructions were prepared and transmitted by the Board of Trade, which added its own assurance to Gooch that settlement of the Ohio country would be in the king's interest. Leaving no doubt of what it expected from the governor, the board went on to "recommend" that he do all he could to "promote" support for this important enterprise among members of the Virginia assembly.[73] In obedience to these instructions, the governor made the required grant in July, stipulating that the company would receive an additional

300,000 acres as soon as it met its obligations in regard to a fort and settlers.[74]

Obviously, the conflicting purposes latent in the Ohio Company venture were little short of explosive. The home government's chief interest was to hinder French expansion into the vast central region in back of the Alleghenies. Concern for the geopolitical interests of the Crown, soon informed by growing awareness that the disposition of the Indians was the real key to a stable and secure frontier, continued to be the guiding principle of British policy in the years ahead.[75] The goals of the Ohio Company, on the other hand, were fixed on the profits that might be made from the Indian trade and land speculation. Interestingly enough, even the Ohio Company's objectives were mutually contradictory. The rub was that white settlement would jeopardize trading prospects since the Indians were of no mind to suffer the loss of their lands for cheaply priced manufactured goods. Moreoever, land speculation also threatened to tilt Indian sympathies in the direction of the French, who did not propose to populate tribal hunting grounds with white settlers. The activities of the Ohio Company, in short, could serve to imperil British control of the Ohio country, the very objective that the home government prized most and thought the company would help to deliver.[76]

More was involved in the competition for the Ohio country than the conflicting goals of British ministers and Virginia land jobbers. At stake also were the interests of the "common" people of Virginia, the ordinary folk whose attitudes about these western schemes would become increasingly important once the French and Indian War had begun. As later events were to demonstrate, the average Virginian felt little enthusiasm for the French and Indian War and the objectives for which it was fought. The people at large certainly had no interest in the speculative activities of the Ohio Company, nor did they expect to derive any benefit from them. Indeed, from the ordinary Virginian's point of view, the Old Dominion had no need for the Ohio country in the first place. Virginians were not confronted by a shortage of land in the mid-eighteenth century, and even if they had been, the Ohio country would not have been a prime objective for land-hungry pioneers. The principal stream of population movement was flowing southward down the colony's fertile lateral valleys rather than west through the Alleghenies. Moreover, the major north-south corridor—the Valley of Virginia—was only thinly settled by 1750, and even at that date much vacant land still existed in the more accessible piedmont region on the eastern side of the Blue Ridge. In short, the lands in the distant Ohio country had little appeal for most

Virginians. Even the Ohio Company would recognize this fact within a few years of being organized. By the early 1750s it was weighing the possibility of colonizing its grant with Pennsylvania Dutch and German immigrants due to the lack of interest in western settlement among Virginians.[77]

Furthermore, only a handful of Virginians had any concern with the Indian trade. Because they lived in a producer economy devoted to the cultivation of tobacco and cereal crops, the faces of most Virginians were turned toward Europe and the West Indies rather than the western wilderness where markets did not exist. The relative unimportance of the Indian trade in Virginia's economic life was reflected in a report on commerce prepared in 1755 by Governor Robert Dinwiddie. According to Dinwiddie, less than 17 percent of the Old Dominion's total export trade was derived from deerskins and furs, the articles of exchange received from the Indians.[78] Moreover, the western tribes provided few of these goods; most were obtained in the Cherokee country that lay to the south.[79] In sum, if the economic stakes at issue were worth a war with France, they seem to have involved the economic interests of a distinct minority of Virginians.

If the economic purposes of the war impinged on the interests of few Virginians, the people of the Old Dominion also found it difficult to translate reports of French activity on the Ohio into fear that these movements posed an imminent threat to their lives and property. The French and their Indian allies were too far away, and the region they prized too distant from the settled part of Virginia, to give real cause for alarm. Even the small clusters of settlement beyond the Blue Ridge on Virginia's western frontier were separated from the Ohio country by formidable mountains, trackless forests, and many days of travel. The trans-Allegheny area simply was very remote from the concerns of all but a handful of Virginians, and it was only those few who were ready to support a confrontational western policy. Significantly, even within the ranks of the colony's elite, there were many who disagreed with such a course.

As noted above, most Ohio Company investors were well-to-do residents of the Northern Neck, an area adjoining the eastern reaches of the Ohio country. The facts of geography and personal financial interest induced this group to urge an aggressive approach to western expansion. But other leading men, for reasons that also were rooted in geography and calculations of personal advantage, preferred a less belligerent course. Drawn from the older, more settled portions of the colony, the speculators among this group generally owned tracts well south of the contested lands in the Ohio country and consequent-

ly saw no reason to provoke the French. As we shall see, the existence
of these opposing factions complicated considerably the task of raising
a provincial army in 1754. George Washington, for one, attributed
the antiwar sentiment that later came to plague Virginia's mobilization efforts to the widespread belief that the struggle with France
had been joined in the first place merely to further the schemes of the
Ohio Company.[80] His appraisal of popular sentiment was remarkably
accurate. Rich or poor, the majority of Virginians were understandably reluctant to sacrifice their money and blood for the sake of an
exclusive group of speculators seeking to engross a huge expanse of
trans-Allegheny land in which the people as a whole had little
interest.[81]

Among the small group of men actively concerned with the fortunes of the Ohio Company, none was more important than Robert
Dinwiddie, a fifty-eight-year-old Scotsman who arrived in Virginia
as the colony's new governor in November 1751. An earnest, industri-
ous, and conscientious administrator, Dinwiddie was also tactless
and, perhaps, a bit too anxious to prove himself the king's good servant.[82] His administration represented something of a watershed in
Virginia political history, for it marked the end of a quarter-century
of generally harmonious relations between his predecessors and the
colonial legislature.[83]

Dinwiddie received his appointment as governor in July 1751. During the period between the departure of Governor William Gooch in
mid-1749 and Dinwiddie's arrival in Williamsburg over two years
later, Virginia was governed by Thomas Lee, president of the council,
and on Lee's death in November 1750, by Louis Burwell.[84] (Conveniently enough, Thomas Lee was also president of the Ohio Company
and in his official correspondence with the home government used
the opportunity of his office to extol the cause for western expansion.[85]) After Dinwiddie had assumed his new position, he was quite
prepared to reiterate in his own writings the need for a forward
western policy. The governor was an ardent imperialist to begin with,
and his zealous backing for western expansion was heightened by
membership in the Ohio Company.[86] One historian has suggested
quite openly that affairs in the Ohio Valley were close to Dinwiddie's
heart because they were close to his pocketbook.[87]

While it would be difficult to prove that Dinwiddie's promotion of
an aggressive western policy was motivated by the hope for personal
gain, it was certainly possible. Soon after arriving in Virginia, Dinwiddie declared that he had "the Success and Prosperity of the Ohio
Company much at Heart" and that he maintained a strong interest

in projects that would redound to the company's advantage.[88] Writing to the Secretary of State for the Southern Department on the eve of the outbreak of hostilities in 1754, the governor remarked that "the Settling and securing the Lands in the interior Parts of this large Cont't, particularly those on the back of this Dom'n, has been much in my Thoughts ever since my arrival at my Gov't."[89] Certainly Dinwiddie's motives were questioned by some of his contemporaries. Governor James Glen of South Carolina, for example, called Dinwiddie's handling of western affairs unnecessarily provocative to the French.[90] Dinwiddie was aware of these suspicions and staunchly denied that personal interest was guiding his official actions. In one indignant letter to his South Carolina colleague, Dinwiddie declared, "I am sure there is no secret Designs or private Advantages in my View. No, Sir, my Endeavours are with Diligence and Assiduity to comply with the Com'ds I have from home."[91] Notwithstanding Dinwiddie's pronouncements on behalf of his own probity, Virginians also were inclined to doubt that their governor's great zest for western expansion was entirely selfless.[92] On the other hand, Dinwiddie did not lack defenders, and a number of highly respected students of Virginia history have argued strongly in behalf of his personal integrity.[93] Perhaps the most that could be said was that Dinwiddie's interest in the Ohio Company furnished him with, as one scholar put it, "a peculiar, if sincere view of what was required for the public good."[94]

Dinwiddie most assuredly did strive to make Virginia's claims to the Ohio country an urgent matter of public interest. In his first formal address to the Virginia Assembly, the new governor warned that the French were attempting to stir up neighboring Indian tribes in order to seize the "interior parts of America, the back of our frontier Settlem'ts to the Westward." The legislators' "own good Sense," Dinwiddie was certain, would "soon discover what bad Consequences such Settlem'ts wou'd be to us and our Posterity."[95] To strengthen Virginia's ability to defend its western interests, Dinwiddie urged the lawmakers to cultivate good relations with the Ohio tribes and to enact an effective militia law.[96] Clearly, by 1752, as far as Robert Dinwiddie was concerned, the rivalry with France for control of the great central region behind the Alleghenies had become an issue of paramount importance.

Although his relations with the legislature were soon poisoned by animosity and mutual suspicion, Dinwiddie's dealings with the assembly at the outset of his administration seem to have been congenial enough. At the end of Dinwiddie's first session with the general assembly, the members of the House of Burgesses even felt moved to

Robert Dinwiddie, lieutenant governor of the colony of Virginia, 1751–1758 (courtesy National Portrait Gallery, London).

present the new chief executive with a gift of five hundred pounds as a token of their "esteem."[97] Significantly, however, the members' initial regard for Dinwiddie did not lead them to share his perception of the French threat. The assembly's response to Dinwiddie's call for strengthening Virginia's frontier defenses was limited to passage of a measure that reinstituted the old policy of exempting those who settled in the colony's far western reaches (in this case the trans-Allegheny) from payment of taxes for a ten-year period.[98] The governor's recommendations for promoting good relations with the Indians and for improving the readiness of the militia were simply ignored.[99]

Dinwiddie met with even less success when his second assembly convened in Williamsburg in November 1753. Called specifically to affirm Virginia's claim to the Ohio country, this session instead attacked the governor's decision to charge the sum of one pistole for placing his seal and signature on land patents. Similar charges were levied in other colonies, but this particular fee had never before been imposed in Virginia, where such exactions were deemed the prerogative of the House of Burgesses.[100] In renouncing the governor's action, the lower house declared that the fee represented nothing less than a move to deprive British subjects of their property without their consent and therefore was contrary to the rights of Englishmen.[101] The controversy over the pistole fee dragged on for months and became a fiercely argued constitutional issue. Its chief significance in this instance was the rupture it caused in Dinwiddie's relations with the House of Burgesses and its hampering of his efforts to resolve by military means Virginia's dispute with France over possession of the Ohio country.[102] Primarily for this reason, Dinwiddie later came to regret his part in precipitating this drawn-out political conflict.[103]

Although much caught up in the furor of the pistole fee, the lower house, while meeting in the fall of 1753, also found time to demonstrate hostility to the Ohio Company and thus managed to assail Dinwiddie indirectly from another quarter, by petitioning the king to limit the size of future consignments of land beyond the Allegheny divide. The burgesses urged that subsequent grants be restricted to parcels of one thousand acres because the conveyance of large tracts into private hands effectively deterred the westward movement of "poorer people" out of "fear they should be taken in by these Grants."[104] Despite the influence and prestige of the Ohio Company, which at this very time was seeking an enlargement of its original grant, the Board of Trade remained true to its belief that a well-populated frontier would provide the best security for the English colonies. The Privy Council considered the burgesses' petition in mid-1754 and on the board's recommendation, ordered that future grants in the Ohio country be limited to one thousand acres.[105] Coinciding as it did with the opening rounds of the controversy over the pistole fee, the immediate effect of the burgesses' petition was to widen the estrangement between Governor (and Ohio Company stockholder) Dinwiddie and a majority of Virginia's lawmakers. Dinwiddie angrily adjourned the assembly in December 1753, but the rapidly escalating crisis over the Ohio country was to force him to recall it only two months later.[106]

## THE GATHERING CRISIS

At the same time that Virginians were beginning to penetrate the Ohio Valley from the south, the French were moving down into that region from the north. French claims to the territory between the Alleghenies and the Mississippi reached back to the explorations made by the Sieur de La Salle in the 1670s, but prior to the 1740s French authorities did not show much interest in the area. However, soon after the end of King George's War in 1748, the French became alarmed over the intrusion of British-Americans into lands they insisted were unquestionably those of his most Christian majesty. From the French point of view, the English intruders were a dangerous threat to the security of the vital midsection of France's North American empire.[107]

The French attempted to stem the English advance by means of a coordinated plan that called for the reassertion of French claims to sovereignty over the Ohio country, the intimidation and ejection of British subjects from the region, and the establishment of a line of forts along the upper reaches of the Allegheny River.[108] In 1749 the Marquis de la Jonquière, governor of New France, began putting this plan into effect by dispatching a mixed force of 230 French and Indians under the command of Captain Pierre-Joseph Céloron de Blainville on an expedition through the Ohio country to proclaim formally that title to the region still resided with Louis XV. Céloron was also instructed to win over the Indians of the area to the French interest and to expel any British subjects that he encountered along his route. Setting out in June, Céloron made his way south from Lake Erie to Lake Chautaugua and then down the Allegheny to the forks of the Ohio. From that point the expedition made its way south on the Ohio River, thence up the Miami, and after completing an overland trek to the Maumee, followed that stream back to Lake Erie. Along the way the French officer posted metal plaques emblazoned with the Bourbon crest and buried lead markers recording that the King of France had "renewed" his possession of the Ohio country.[109]

Much more serious than Céloron's ceremonious "repossession" of the Ohio country was the surprise destruction in 1752 of the Miami (or "Twightee") Indian village at Pickawillany by some 240 Chippewas and Ottawas under the command of Charles Michael Langlade, a half-blood French trader.[110] The Twightees were led by a strongly pro-British chief known to the English as Old Briton, and their community at Pickawillany was an important Anglo-Indian trading center on the Miami River deep within the area recently traversed by Céloron. The fierce attack on Pickawillany constituted something of a turning point in the early struggle for domination of the Ohio country. It marked the first resort to real violence by an official French force and succeeded in terrorizing those Ohio tribes with pro-British leanings. Many of the Twightees who survived the attack quickly forsook their English trading connections, and news of the French strike generally disrupted, when it did not ruin altogether, the activities of British traders elsewhere in the trans-Allegheny region. Even more important, the attack so impressed and frightened the Indians of the Ohio country that they began to fall rapidly within the French orbit. By 1753 the French seemed to be well on their way toward alienating British influence everywhere west of the mountains.[111]

Early that same year the French began to implement the final element in their anti-British strategy by constructing a series of forts that would enable them to dominate the upper Ohio Valley. The first of these posts was established at Presque Isle (now Erie, Pennsylvania); the second, known as Fort Le Boeuf, was located at the head of French Creek (now Waterford, Pennsylvania); the third was situated at Venango, where French Creek joins the Allegheny (now Franklin, Pennsylvania).[112] It was Dinwiddie's confirmation of these French moves that finally prompted the British government to intervene in the deteriorating situation. On 28 August 1753, the earl of Holderness, Secretary of State for the Southern Department, issued a circular letter to all colonial governors in North America instructing them how to deal with French encroachment on British territory. Holderness directed that the withdrawal of any French intruders was to be obtained by peaceful means if possible, but if a warning did not suffice, the governors were authorized to mobilize their provincial forces and "repel Force by Force."[113] With these orders Holderness included additional and more specific instructions to Virginia empowering Dinwiddie to treat as hostile acts either French moves to erect forts on the king's lands or French interference with fort-building projects on the Ohio undertaken by Virginians.[114]

Acting on the basis of the instructions received from Holderness and their own awareness that the French were constructing forts on the upper Allegheny, Dinwiddie and the Virginia Council decided to send the senior officer at Fort Le Boeuf a formal demand for the withdrawal of French forces.[115] Dinwiddie's letter to M. de St. Pierre, commander of the French garrison at Le Boeuf, claimed that:

the lands upon the River Ohio, in the western parts of the Colony of
Virginia, are so notoriously known to be the property of the Crown of
Great Britain that it is a matter of equal concern and surprise to me,
to hear that a body of French forces are erecting fortresses and making
settlements upon that river, within his Majesty's dominions.[116]

Dinwiddie closed his missive by requiring the "peaceable departure"
of the French.[117]

To deliver his warning to St. Pierre, Dinwiddie selected Major
George Washington, a twenty-one-year-old adjutant in the Virginia
militia who had volunteered for the job.[118] Washington left Williamsburg for Fort Le Boeuf on 31 October 1753. After making a hazardous
nine hundred-mile midwinter journey through the wilderness with a
half dozen companions, Washington returned to the Virginia capital
in January 1754 with news that the French were determined to remain in the Ohio country and planned to enlarge the area under their
control during the approaching spring.[119] At Dinwiddie's request
Washington prepared a report of his journey for presentation to the
Virginia Council.[120] Washington's journal, which set forth the ada-
mant refusal of the French to withdraw from the disputed territory,
made it clear that a crisis was at hand. Now convinced that there
was no recourse but war, Dinwiddie saw to it that the journal was
published in both Virginia and London.[121]

Dinwiddie clearly sought to employ Washington's report as evidence of French determination to remain on the Ohio. His intention
in doing so was to convince Virginians in general and the House of
Burgesses in particular of the danger of permitting the French to
penetrate further into the Ohio Valley. As the governor knew, without
the cooperation of the lower house, it would be next to impossible to
mount an offensive against the French. But on the threshold of war,
Dinwiddie's misfortune was to have so antagonized the House over
the pistole fee that his influence was virtually nonexistent.[122]

Alienated by Dinwiddie's impolitic behavior and skeptical about
his motives, doubtful that possession of the Ohio country was something worth fighting and dying over, and perhaps lulled in any case
by the colony's traditional security, most Virginians were feeling decidedly unwarlike on the very eve of the final struggle with France.
By and large, the people of Virginia were simply unpersuaded that
the presence of Frenchmen in a remote valley beyond the Alleghenies
presented a serious threat either to their colony or to themselves as
individuals. And they were notably suspicious of those who contended

that a French menace did exist. Even after he had returned from his journey to Le Boeuf with confirmation of French intentions to seize the Ohio Valley, George Washington found that most Virginians treated this news as "a fiction, and a scheme to promote the interest of a private company."[123]

# · 2 ·

# "THE DISAGREEABLE
# SUBJECT OF DEFENCE"
## *The Politics of Mobilization*

*. . .it was so disagreeable a Subject that much art was used to get
one penny raised for the defence of the Country.*

LANDON CARTER, 1755

In 1754 Virginians went to war blithely unaware that they were
precipitating a great international conflict that would last (in America) for nine years. On the contrary, Virginia's war leaders initially
had anticipated a quick campaign and an easy victory. The men in
Williamsburg were confident that a modest show of force at the forks
of the Ohio would intimidate the French and insure Virginia's control
over the gateway to the Ohio Valley and the rich hinterland that lay
beyond. They were all the more surprised and dismayed, therefore,
when the campaign proved a disaster. It ended a few months after it
had begun in the rout of the Old Dominion's expeditionary force and
with the French in secure possession of the forks.

The campaign of 1754 was poorly conceived and executed, but it
did embody in a rudimentary way what eventually became for Virginia a notably successful military policy. Put simply, that policy
called for delegating the Old Dominion's military problems to a
homegrown armed force that in certain ways resembled a European-
style army. The members of that force were called provincial troops;
collectively they formed an organization known as the Virginia Regiment. As it happened, the decision to rely on provincials rather than
militia, the traditional mainstay of colonial defense, was dictated less
by design than by a set of peculiar social, political, and military
circumstances that conspired to make a provincial army the only
practical answer to Virginia's difficulties with the French.

## STEERING A COLLISION COURSE

The Old Dominion had no military problems at the beginning of
1754, and most Virginians knew it. The colony was at peace with its

Indian and European neighbors. No flying parties of French and Shawnees were slaughtering Virginia residents and laying waste their homes and fields. Even on the colony's western fringes, settlers on the slopes of the Blue Ridge and in the Shenandoah Valley went about their daily lives untroubled and unthreatened by groups who soon would become their enemies. What were threatened, however, were the interests of a handful of land speculators and the expansionist designs of Governor Robert Dinwiddie.

The sources of the French and Indian War involved a number of potentially explosive issues of which control over the Ohio Valley was only one. By the mid-eighteenth century, Britain and France were at odds over places as diverse as the Netherlands, Africa, and the Indian subcontinent. Three areas were in dispute in North America: the Ohio Valley, the region south and west of Nova Scotia known as Acadia, and the long frontier line dividing Canada from New York and New England. Impressed by the continuing Anglo-French rivalry for commerce and colonies and the serious issues left unresolved by the Peace of Aix-la-Chapelle (1748), historians sometimes have read a kind of inevitability into the coming of the climactic struggle between Britain and Fance. Accordingly, the period from 1748 to 1754 is often characterized as an intermission in the continuing imperial contest, a breathing space needed by both sides for licking their wounds and rebuilding their forces before resuming hostilities.[1]

Unlike later historians, the Virginians who actually lived through the war were not inclined to see it as an irreconcilable conflict. In their view, impersonal political forces unleashed by a far-flung international rivalry had little to do with the shooting that broke out in the spring of 1754. A much more simple explanation was at hand. Most Virginians believed that hostilities had been triggered by the readiness of Ohio Company stockholders to secure their interests on the frontier even at the risk of war with the French. One contemporary described those who advocated an aggressive western policy as "blades" who were positively anxious to "go to the French & provoke them." Adopting the language of the common man to underscore his point, the same writer stated bluntly: "Iduzzent like such proceedings, nor [does] no buddy else."[2]

Such "unfavorable Surmises" were of crucial importance, for they accounted for much of the indifference and even outright opposition with which Virginians greeted the subsequent call to arms. Popular suspicion that public policy had been manipulated for private advantage centered primarily on the activities of Governor Dinwiddie.[3] And in Dinwiddie's case, there is some reason for supposing that these suspicions were justified. Indeed, nothing better illuminates the process by which the Anglo-French conflict in the Ohio Valley was, in a sense, manufactured, than a study of the militant and enterprising behavior of Virginia's chief executive.

Policymakers in London certainly recognized the strategic importance of the Ohio Valley by the end of the 1740's. That recognition dovetailed nicely with the personal inclinations of Virginia's pugnacious governor. As an ardent imperialist, Dinwiddie was disposed to inflate the territorial claims of his government; as an Ohio Company stockholder, he also had, as he once put it, "the Success and Prosperity of the Ohio Company much at heart."[4] It is difficult to say which motivation was paramount. Perhaps the most that can be said is that for reasons that combined calculations of personal advantage with the extravagant goals and fears of hyperpatriotism, Dinwiddie reinforced the Francophobic tendencies of the Newcastle ministry and effectively steered the British government into a collision course with the French.

During the gathering crisis over the Ohio country, Dinwiddie steadfastly maintained that title to that region resided in the British Crown because of its alleged special relationship with the western Indians. The governor rested his case on the Treaty of Utrecht (1713), which had recognized Britain as guardian of the Six Nations of the Iroquois. The Iroquois subsequently had come to assert a loose suzerainty over tribes living in the Ohio area. This claim had little real substance, but it did furnish Dinwiddie (and British colonial officialdom in general) with a theoretical basis for asserting that the English protectorate over the Iroquois also included the Iroquois' supposed tributaries in the Ohio country. The governor further buttressed his claims on behalf of British jurisdiction on the shaky agreements negotiated with the Indians at Lancaster (1744) and Logstown (1752).[5]

The French were notably unimpressed by Dinwiddie's arguments. Annoyed by the Ohio Company's erection of a storehouse on Redstone Creek in 1752, they had lost little time in constructing a line of forts along the northern approaches to the upper Ohio Valley (the same outposts visited by George Washington during the winter of 1753).[6] This French countermove was, in turn, greeted by Dinwiddie with an alarm that verged on panic. By the summer of 1753, a single theme dominated the governor's correspondence with the home government, the need "to prevent the French taking Possession of the lands on the Ohio." No mention was made of the dangers French occupation would pose for the Ohio Company; the French threat was described solely in strategic terms. Indeed, according to Dinwiddie's extravagant estimate, French activity at the back of Virginia was merely the opening phase of a full-scale assault on English America.[7]

During the final months preceding the outbreak of hostilities, Dinwiddie directed almost all of his official correspondence to the Board of Trade, then presided over by the ambitious and chauvinistic earl of Halifax. As the governor was well aware, no other agency in the British government was as likely to give credence to his dispatches. Taking Dinwiddie's reports at face value, Halifax promptly warned the king and council of the growing French threat in North America. In doing so, Halifax described the Ohio as "a large and important River arising within the Province of Pennsylvania and . . . flowing through part of that Province and Your Majesty's Colony of Virginia." Dinwiddie's consternation over the French fort-building program was clearly echoed in Halifax's claim that France had invaded the area drained by the Ohio, a development that had caused some of "Your Majesty's subjects . . . [to abandon] their Settlements in a great Panick."[8] Halifax's initial memorandum was quickly followed by a second describing the Ohio country as an area "indisputably belonging to Great Britain" and warning that French activities there threatened the security of England's established colonies.[9]

Prompted by the Halifax memoranda, the Newcastle ministry dispatched a series of royal instructions to Virginia in the summer of 1753. (Among other things, these instructions directed Dinwiddie to query the French directly about their intentions in the Ohio Valley, a charge that resulted in Washington's midwinter journey to fort Le Boeuf.) The most important thing to be said at this point about the instructions is that they were equivocal and reflected the cabinet's uncertainty about the significance of the reported French moves on the Ohio. Thus Dinwiddie was enjoined to remain on the defensive and "not to make use of the armed Force under your Direction *excepting* within the undoubted limits of His Majesty's Dominion's." (Italics mine.) The governor was also informed of a decision to equip the Ohio Company's as yet unbuilt stockade at the Forks with thirty artillery pieces drawn from the royal arsenal. The arms transfer was justified on the grounds that the company's fort would promote "the security and protection of our subjects, and of the Indians in alliance with us." At the same time, however, the Crown refused to help finance or otherwise assist in the actual construction of the outpost. In sum, London's response was ambiguous, the response of a government that did not want to get in too deep.[10]

The problem was that in granting a little, the home government had given Dinwiddie all that he needed: the forward policy he advocated had received what could be construed as official approbation. Moreover, since the Ohio Company's fort had been explicitly recognized as a place worthy of defending with the king's cannon, it was arguable that it had become something more than the property of a mere business corporation; in a sense at least it had become the king's fort.[11] Most important, in failing to specify what actually constituted "the undoubted limits of His Majesty's Dominions," the Crown had left Dinwiddie free to employ his own inflated definition of what those limits were and to support that claim by force of arms if necessary. In effect, the British government had left the basic question of whether there would be military conflict in the Ohio Valley up to the discretion of the governor of Virginia.

### ATTEMPTING TO RAISE TROOPS

Dinwiddie was disposed to place the broadest possible interpretation on his instructions from London and lost little time in planning a display of Virginia military power on the Ohio. The decision for a military demonstration was occasioned by George Washington's return from Fort Le Boeuf in January 1754 with news that the French intended to occupy the forks during the coming spring. Believing that Washington's report would spur the assembly into financing a military expedition to the Ohio, Dinwiddie promptly called for an emergency session of the legislature.

Meanwhile, the Ohio Company already had taken steps of its own to protect its interests in the Ohio Valley. Early in January the company sent out a construction party with orders to erect a stockade at the forks. The company's immediate objective was to deny the French prior occupancy of that strategic junction. Believing that the fort builders were in urgent need of protection, Dinwiddie began raising the first elements of an expeditionary force even before the Virginia lawmakers had reassembled in Williamsburg.

In a letter to Thomas Lord Fairfax, written three weeks before the assembly reconvened, Dinwiddie stated that "with advice of the Council, I think proper to send immediately out 200 men to protect those already sent by the Ohio Comp'a to build a Fort."[12] Dinwiddie's plan called for drafting half of this force from the militia of Frederick and Augusta counties. Accordingly, the governor ordered Lord Fairfax and Colonel James Patton, county lieutenants for those respective jurisdictions, to raise fifty men apiece for service on the Ohio. Dinwiddie was confident that many militiamen would eagerly volunteer for the expedition if only because the daily pay of fifteen pounds of tobacco was "so very good."[13] Should an insufficient number of volunteers come forward, drafting "by ballot" would secure the remainder. The men from Frederick and Augusta were to march by 20 February to Alexandria, where they would be trained by Washington, who had been retained on active duty as militia adjutant for the northern district of Virginia.[14]

The Virginia governor commissioned William Trent, a veteran Pennsylvania Indian trader, to raise the other one hundred men from among frontiersmen of a similar occupation. Trent was to lead his company to the forks with as little delay as possible and assume the task of protecting the construction party sent out earlier by the Ohio Company. In transmitting Trent's commission, Dinwiddie expressed hope that the assembly would provide him with sufficient funds for sending up an additional four hundred troops early in the spring.[15]

These measures, rapidly and confidently undertaken by a man who possessed neither military training nor experience, led directly to war. Apparently Dinwiddie hardly considered that possibility when he issued commissions and raised the troops. The risks of doing nothing were clear enough: the French would seize the forks and gain sway over the Ohio country. But it seemed never to have dawned on the governor that resort to force was risky also. After all, the French could decide to contest the issue by meeting force with force. Dinwiddie was the colony's nominal commander in chief, but he knew nothing of military affairs. Moreover, he presided over a colony that was almost totally unprepared for war. For one thing, Virginia lacked the organizational and administrative structures necessary for projecting an effective fighting force hundreds of miles into the wilderness. Another basic problem was that Virginia was an agricultural colony and produced little or none of the basic hardware that an army required: weapons, ammunition, clothing, tents, and tools. Large and frequent imports would be necessary, especially in case of a military emergency. Seemingly ignored were such crucial issues as the feeble state of the militia, the colony's limited sources of revenue, the average Virginian's lack of interest in the trans-Allegheny region, and most importantly, popular suspicion that the crisis with France had been contrived by the governor and his associates in the Ohio Company.

Dinwiddie simply assumed that a quick thrust to the forks could be made without much trouble and would be sufficient to deter the French from pressing their claims to the Ohio Valley. The effrontery of believing that the French could be checked by a hastily assembled guard detail betrayed either naiveté or arrogance or, in all likelihood, a combination of both. Future events would show that the governor's call to arms rested on a grossly mistaken estimate of French resolution and capabilities, one that was exceeded only by Dinwiddie's failure to sense the unpopularity of his western policy among the people of Virginia and the other English colonies.

The first rude taste of military reality was not long in coming. Confident that a sizable interprovincial force would "make a good impression on the Ohio and be able to defeat the designs of the French," Dinwiddie initially had proposed to augment the little army he was assembling in Virginia with men and money contributed by the Old Dominion's sister provinces. In simultaneous letters to the governors of South Carolina, North Carolina, Maryland, Pennsylvania, New Jersey, New York, and Massachusetts, Dinwiddie made a strong appeal for "all the Assistance" his counterparts in the other provincial capitals could provide.[16]

Interestingly enough, there was a striking difference between the letters that Dinwiddie dispatched beyond Virginia's borders and his letter to Lord Fairfax, although all were written at the same time and each stressed the need for vigorous measures.[17] Fairfax, like Dinwiddie, was a shareholder in the Ohio Company, and in the governor's communication to him, full mention was made of the fact that the fort being constructed at the forks was a company project. Yet Dinwiddie never mentioned the company in his intercolonial correspondence. He chose instead to wrap himself in the mantle of British patriotism. Thus, French penetration of the Ohio Valley threatened the "right" of Englihsmen "to trade . . . on the Ohio," jeopardized "the Preservat[io]n of all his [Majesty's] Dom[inion]s on this Cont[inen]t," and compromised the "Hon[o]r and Dignity of the Crown."[18]

Few people in other provincial capitals were misled by Dinwiddie's obvious attempt at confusing the interests of the Ohio Company with those of British America in general. Like most Virginians, the officials in the middle and southern colonies to whom Dinwiddie addressed his most strenuous pleas for aid suspected that the alarm raised in Williamsburg merely masked a scheme for protecting the fortunes of a private corporation. South Carolina's Governor James Glen from the first made no effort to conceal his distrust of Dinwiddie's aggressive western policy. Glen viewed the Old Dominion as a potential rival for the southern Indian trade and strongly resented Dinwiddie's attempt to obtain Indian auxiliaries by means of direct communication with the Cherokees and Catawbas, tribes the South Carolinians liked to think of as "their" Indians. Under no immediate threat herself, South Carolina not only spurned Dinwiddie's call for help but even deterred the southern tribes from assisting Virginia during the first crucial months of 1754 when the French were gaining control of the Ohio Valley.[19] In the case of Pennsylvania, Quaker principles and an internal political wrangle between the governor and assembly, together with opposition to the Ohio Company from local Indian traders, effectively foreclosed Dinwiddie's chances of support. Maryland, with her fixed western boundary, had little interest in the fate of the Ohio country.[20]

Of all Virginia's immediate neighbors, only North Carolina responded to Dinwiddie's plea for assistance. After receiving the governor's appeal, the North Carolina Assembly issued forty thousand pounds in paper currency and earmarked twelve thousand pounds of that sum for forming a regiment of volunteers who would be joined with the troops being raised in Virginia.[21] Unfortunately, this measure turned out to be little more than an empty gesture. The colony recruited about four hundred men, but the money for paying these troops ran out before they could make common cause with the Virginians. Refusing further service unless they were paid, the North Carolinians mutinied in the vicinity of Winchester and dispersed without seeing any action.[22]

In sum, with the exception of the symbolic but practically useless gesture of North Carolina, the middle and southern colonies chose not to support Dinwiddie's call to check the French advance. Their unwillingness to become involved may be attributed generally to their own relative security, their reluctance to sacrifice for a cause that promised to promote Virginia's interests far more than it did their own, and their feeling that Dinwiddie's proposals smacked too much of personal amibition and favoritism for the Ohio Company.[23]

Unaware in February 1754 that with the dubious exception of North Carolina, all of Virginia's neighboring governments would soon reject his pleas for assistance, Dinwiddie had by that time encountered serious difficulties on his own home front. His first problem involved the order he had given in January for calling up one hundred militiamen from Frederick and Augusta counties. A few weeks after issuing this directive, Dinwiddie learned that Lord Fairfax had been unable to enforce its provisions in Frederick. Some historians have suggested that Fairfax was unwilling or at least reluctant to implement Dinwiddie's instructions, but the governor himself suggested that popular defiance simply had made the task impossible. "I . . . am sorry the first Orders I gave in respect to the Militia sh[oul]d meet with such disrespect," Dinwiddie complained to Fairfax. The governor was particularly shocked when he learned that Frederick militiamen had been "spirited Up and encourag'd in this Breach of Duty by some of their Officers."[24] Efforts to raise men from the Augusta militia met with similar "ill success."[25] Virginia's first attempt at raising troops to fight the French was a clear-cut failure.

Although Dinwiddie angrily referred to the refractory members of the frontier militia as "Delinquents," the truth was that Virginia's citizen-soldiers were well within their rights in refusing to serve on the Ohio. In his haste to raise an expeditionary force, Dinwiddie had neglected to note that Virginia law made militiamen liable for service only within the borders of the Old Dominion.[26]

## THE MILITIA MENTALITY

The significance of the recalcitrant militiamen transcended the nature of the legal prohibitions that shielded Viriginia's citizen-sol-diers from executive caprice. The basic difficulty was that while Gov-ernor Dinwiddie had sold the authorities in London on the idea of a French threat at the back of Virginia, the colonists themselves were largely unpersuaded that any significant danger existed. As a result, at the very moment when the British government had given him the authority to proceed, Dinwiddie's plans were nearly sabotaged by the militia's refusal to collaborate in carrying them out. This episode is instructive for two reasons: first, it sheds light on a range of nonmi-litary factors that influenced the formulation of colonial military pol-icy; second, it reveals something about the relationship between rulers and the ruled in mid-eighteenth-century Virginia.

In addition to strictly military considerations, a variety of social, political, and economic circumstances determined the way Virginians waged war in the 1750s and 1760s. Especially crucial—particularly at the beginning of the French and Indian War—were some charac-teristically American notions about the proper uses of organized vio-lence, notions that were at odds with Dinwiddie's initial plan for securing his western design with men drawn from the militia. The problem in this instance was that Virginians conceived of warfare in defensive terms. In that sense, their thinking about war was shaped by the pervasive localism that characterized the outlook of colonial Americans in general. The world beyond his own country, or perhaps even his own farm, has little meaning to the average Virginia land-owner. Although prepared to fight for his own property, he believed it made scant sense to play soldier once the immediate threat was past: his military inclinations did not extend beyond a grudging will-ingness to serve for short periods of time within an area near his home. Thus, to most Virginians, warfare involving the general run of citizens consisted of musket-bearing friends and neighbors warding off a common threat to hearth and home. Accordingly, Virginians traditionally put their faith in an armed populace organized for defense rather than in a professional army that could wage either offensive or defensive war with relative ease.[27] To be sure, the military competence of the Virginia militia had declined as life in the colony became more settled and secure; nevertheless, the militia ideal of universal military obligation survived as a theory and as a sturdy element in colonial folklore. Governor Dinwiddie spoke for most Virginians when in 1753 he described the militia as "our chief Dependence, for the protection of our Lives and Fortunes."[28] Because a "militia mentality" continued to influence their thinking about war and military organization, Virginians in 1754 remained psychologically disposed to view war as an activity in which members of the community rallied in defense of their homes and families.

This popular conception of warfare diverged considerably from the mobilization strategy proposed by Governor Dinwiddie in January 1754. The governor had not called out the militia for the purpose of safeguarding farms, plantations, or even frontier settlements. On the contrary, he had attempted to force militiamen from their homes and families so that he might assert the pretensions of a minority over a far-distant wilderness. It was the kind of approach that would find little favor among the citizen-soldiers of the Old Dominion. Fortunately for them, Virginia militiamen had more than the force of law and custom to sustain their rejection of Dinwiddie's call to arms. As a group, they also possessed a significant measure of political influence, which they could exert on their own behalf.

Scholars usually depict mid-eighteenth-century Viriginia as a homogeneous agrarian society ordered around a generally placid politics of noblesse oblige. Virginians of middle and lower rank have been seen as freely acquiescing or "deferring" to government by a small, homegrown elite. Indeed, the readiness of lesser men to defer to a dominant squirearchy becomes for most historians the central feature of the political system of colonial Virginia, the key factor that made for a harmonious society.[29] While generally accurate, this traditional characterization should not obscure the fact that a degree of tension also governed relations between the "better sort" and those who made up the "common herd."

Most historians agree that the political system of eighteenth-century Virgina was dominated by the "gentry," a rather broad category of people possessing sufficient wealth to be classified as "gentlemen." It is also generally agreed that the members of this group did not constitute more than 5 percent of the population.[30] At the nether end of the social scale were the "inferior sort": tenant farmers, poor artisans, laborers, and drifters. Lacking land, skills, and voting rights, about 20 percent of the whites belonged to this submerged group.[31] The largest number of white Virginians were men of the "middling sort," another broad social category composed of yeoman farmers, small planters, tradesmen, and successful artisans. Men of middle rank comprised a majority of the population in every Virginia county and formed the largest single social element in the colonial militia. More importantly, most of them owned enough property to vote.[32]

The fact that a relatively large number of men were enfranchised does not, of course, mean that all members of the electorate possessed an equal measure of political influence. In reality there existed no simple one-to-one relationship between voting rights and political power in eighteenth-century Virginia. The role of the average voter was limited in the first place because there were few elective offices to fill. Down to the Revolution, the House of Burgesses was the only political body in the colony whose members were selected by popular poll. In addition, the average voter had little voice in the nomination of candidates for the lower house; his role was confined to deciding which of several politically ambitious members of the gentry would represent him in that legislative body.[33] The equanimity with which most freeholders accepted their exclusion from the inner workings of colonial politics turned on the general consensus among Virginia voters that political leadership was the natural duty, indeed, the virtual obligation, of the "better sort." Therein lay the basis for a deferential political order.[34]

Deferential politics in late colonial Virginia ultimately hinged on the shared awareness of great and "middling" men that a harmony of interests existed between them. Most men from both groups were bound together in the first place by a common interest in the tobacco culture upon which the colonial economy was based. They were linked as well by their common whiteness in a society in which black slaves comprised about 40 percent of the population. Both groups also perceived that their political interests were harmonious, at least to the extent of agreeing that government was the privilege and responsibility of wealthy and successful men. Precisely because they were wealthy and successful, so the theory ran, such men were more likely to be wise, just, and disinterested, and therefore most qualified for public office. Also at hand was a compelling practical reason for upper-class control of politics: freeholders of middling estate could ill afford the expenses of campaigning and residing in Williamsburg for extended periods while the assembly was in session. On the contrary, the needs of their farms and families argued for their presence at home.[35]

But in spite of general acquiescence in upper-class control of public affairs, political power in Virginia did not wholly reside with a privileged few. It rather was divided between the members of a small upper crust who wielded most political authority and those belonging to the "middling" majority who exercised a little. But however trifling the influence of men of "middling" fortune as individuals, in the aggregate they constituted a political mass to be reckoned with. As many as three-quarters of the voters owned less than three hundred acres of land, and about 25 percent owned only one hundred acres.[36] This meant that the gentry could not remain wholly insensitive to the concerns of the electorate at large. Men of modest means who could vote simply were too numerous to be ignored. Potent social credentials notwithstanding, members of the upper crust risked repudiation at the polls if they or the policies they espoused were generally unpopular with the voters.

The candidates themselves were well aware that the "middling sort" acted as the final arbiters of political success or failure. Late in life James Madison remembered that even in prerevolutionary days it had been customary for Virginia politicians "to recommend themselves to the voters . . . by personal solicitation."[37] The importance of winning popular support certainly was not lost on one John Littlepage, a candidate for the House of Burgesses in 1763. In person and by letter, Littlepage urged his candidacy on the electors of Hanover County, culminating his campaign in a painstaking canvass of the voters in order "to know their Sentiments" on the issues of the day.[38] Not all office seekers were so openly solicitous as Littlepage, but the widespread practice of "treating" the voters to food and drink as election day drew near revealed that nearly all politically astute members of the gentry saw the necessity of wooing the favor of men who were socially and economically inferior to themselves. Even members of the most distinguished families found that failure to court public opinion was politically dangerous. Reflecting on his defeat at the polls in 1768, Colonel Landon Carter acknowledged that he had been "turned out of the H. of B." because he "did not familiarize myself among the People." By way of contrast, Carter recalled his son's "going amongst them [the voters] and carrying his Election."[39]

The picture should not be overdrawn: eighteenth-century Virginia was no middle-class democracy. Nevertheless, the hold that upper-class men had on elective office was more tenuous than it first appeared. It was precarious because the willingness of lesser men to look to their betters for political leadership was not coerced but freely given. Come the next election, the political favor that previously had been bestowed on one member of the gentry could always be withdrawn and vested in another gentlemen candidate newly judged as more politically attractive by a majority of the voters. In short, it behooved incumbents and candidates alike to show a measure of concern for the interests and opinions of the electorate, a practical necessity that gave a reciprocal dimension to the workings of political deference in late colonial Virginia.

To be sure, not all issues elicited the same degree of concern among the mass of "middling" voters. There are, however, grounds for supposing that the average Virginia freeholder was intensely concerned about a policy that might result in his taking the field for an extended period of soldiering. For the freeholders of Frederick and Augusta, the yeoman farmers who formed the backbone of the militia in those counties as they did elsewhere in the Old Dominion, that unhappy prospect was a very real possibility under the terms of Governor Dinwiddie's initial mobilization order. Their reaction to that order, and the subsequent response it brought forth from men of position and influence, help reveal the close connection between politics and military policy in Virginia during the era of the French and Indian War.

As noted previously, the governor's plan for confronting the French with a force drawn willingly or unwillingly from the frontier militia was openly and unceremoniously rejected by the men of Frederick and Augusta. Several factors account for their refusal to answer the call to arms. First, there was the aforementioned difficulty of mobilizing a defensively minded population for an offensive campaign. Second, Virginians were hardly unaware that soldiering was a dangerous business, especially in the North American wilderness, where the hazards of nature, disease, and rudimentary logistics could be as threatening as the enemy. Finally, in the agrarian world of eighteenth-century Virginia, active military service not only imperiled a man's life but jeopardized his livelihood as well.

Prolonged service in distant parts was especially threatening to small-scale agriculturalists. Men whose economic well-being depended on their own self-sufficiency simply had too many tasks to perform at home. Any lengthy absence from their farms might easily result in severe hardship for their families and the precipitate decline of their modest estates. Extended military duty also endangered the personal interests of more substantial planters who were engaged in the commercial type of agriculture on which the colony's economy was based.

Direction of the "little world" of the tobacco plantation was a time-consuming business involving, as one contemporary put it, "a good deal of skill and trouble in the right management of it."[40] Rich or poor, a landowner's prospects turned on the productivity of his estate, and a productive estate required the presence, care, and close attention of its owner. Reason enough, as far as the residents of Frederick and Augusta were concerned, for spurning the governor's mobilization order.

More significant than the yeomanry's understandable lack of relish for soldiering was the fact that when, early in 1754, backcountry farmers refused to serve on the Ohio, they were upheld by men with influence in the highest councils of provincial government. The intervention of these unnamed "Persons of weight" marked an early turning point in the evolution of Virginia's military policy. Following his meeting with these individuals, Dinwiddie abandoned his plan for calling up the frontier militia in favor of organizing an expeditionary force composed entirely of volunteers. Although individual militiamen were conscripted under the provisions of a series of highly selective draft laws enacted between 1755 and 1758, no further attempts were made at mobilizing large groups of citizen-soldiers indiscriminately except during periods of genuine military emergency.[41]

There were two puzzling features about the switch from militia to volunteers. In the first place, why should representatives of the colonial elite take it upon themselves to represent a group of frontier militiamen? Put another way, why should the composition of Dinwiddie's modest expeditionary force be a matter of concern to leading Virginians? Equally curious was Dinwiddie's willingness to give way on an issue that directly touched his authority as Virginia's commander in chief. As attested by his dogged insistence on levying the universally unpopular pistole fee, the governor could be a decidedly stubborn man once he had publicly identified himself with a particular course of action. In that sense it was characteristic of Dinwiddie that when he first learned his orders for mobilizing citizen-soldiers in Frederick and Augusta counties had been flouted, he had threatened the recalcitrant militiamen with criminal prosecution.[42] Following a meeting with the concerned squires, however, all plans for compelling cooperation were quietly dropped. The "Persons of weight" apparently had made a very convincing case for leaving the militia alone.

Precisely what line of argument the governor's conferees employed remains a matter of speculation. Dinwiddie himself claimed, a few months after the meeting, that questions of geography and colonial law prompted his decision to man the Ohio expedition with volunteers. The governor explained that during the conference it had been pointed out that there was some doubt about whether the forks of the Ohio were "in this Dom[inio]n or [on lands] belonging to Pensylvania [sic]." The question of location was important, Dinwiddie noted, because under Virginia law the militia could not be forced to serve beyond the known borders of the colony. Dinwiddie claimed that he thought it best, under these circumstances, to act judiciously and rely on "Men rais'd voluntarily."[43]

In fact, there is some question about how much the indeterminate location of the forks actually influenced the governor's decision to employ volunteers. The primary reason for suspecting that other factors were at play is that over a month before Dinwiddie justified his excusal of the militia on the grounds of geography and law, the Virginia assembly publicly proclaimed that the French had "encroached" on lands that did, in fact, fall within the borders of the Old Dominion.[44] This assertion presumably cleared the way for employing militiamen at the forks, but the governor made no effort to do so, even after it had become evident that few men were interested in volunteering for duty on the Ohio. The question necessarily follows: armed with the admission that Virginia territory had, in effect, been invaded, why did Dinwiddie not return to his original plan and call out the militia, especially since building an army from scratch was bound to be slower and more difficult?

One explanation for Dinwiddie's curious handling of the mobilization issue is that he had no choice. As Dinwiddie himself put it: "300 Men rais'd voluntarily will do more Service than 800 Men of the Militia forc'd on Service."[45] What should be dismissed is his stated justification for replacing militiamen with volunteers: it was not the restrictive provisions of the militia statute but a fundamental problem of politics that determined Dinwiddie's course of action. Apparently, in his January meeting with the gentry, the governor had been put on notice that his plans for using the militia were politically infeasible and, if pressed, might even jeopardize the colony's consensual social order. In that regard it is well to remember that at a time and place where the level of military technology was low and most men were armed, resort to coercion could be a tricky business and might provoke violent resistance that the authorities would be hard pressed to subdue.

More basic was the issue of whether the governor could even consider coercion as a viable option. The essential difficulty was that at this time (early 1754) military power in Virginia resided exclusively with the militia. Accordingly, if Virginians had to be forced into guarding the forks of the Ohio, Dinwiddie would have to employ militiamen in the distasteful duty of compelling their relatives and neighbors to take up arms. Whether the militia would have obeyed an order of that kind is at least open to question. Dinwiddie was dependent on an institution that, in a crisis, he might not be able to control.

A similar situation characterized the governor's relationship with the colonial legislature. Without the cooperation of the lower house of assembly, within whose purview fell all questions of colonial finance, Dinwiddie would be unable to maintain any standing force at all, regardless of its size or composition. As for the burgesses, they had their constituents to think about, and it is doubtful whether they would have jeopardized their own political futures by threatening any sizable number of voters with military service in some distant woods. Thus the gentry's representations on behalf of the citizens of Frederick and Augusta probably were strongly influenced by political considerations. On such crucial questions of military policy as conscription, politically powerful men in mid-eighteenth-century Virginia had to exercise power carefully, knowing that it would be dangerous to irritate the largely enfranchised members of the militia. Such were the considerations that weighed on the burgesses when they arrived in Williamsburg in mid-February to take up, as Landon Carter recorded in his diary, the "disagreeable . . . Subject . . . of defence."[46]

When the general assembly reconvened on 14 February, Dinwiddie lost no time in regaling its members with a lurid description of the horrible fate that awaited frontier families at the hands of "a Crowd of [French and Indian] Miscreants."[47] Expressing confidence that the "efforts" of the legislators would be "equal to the Occasion," the governor called upon the burgesses to vote a "proper Supply" for the "common cause." With an eye on the still festering pistole fee dispute (since referred to the Board of Trade for a decision) and the widespread suspicion that his western policy was serving only the interests of a privileged few, Dinwiddie also voiced hope that the members would rise above "Prejudice or unreasonable Divisions . . . W[hi]ch at present w[oul]d be particularly fatal."[48] The governor capped his appeal by making support for his western design a test of the legislators' patriotism and willingness "to assert the Honour and Dignity of our Sovereign."[49] In a subdued response made on the following day, the burgesses tersely and unenthusiastically promised to uphold "the Duty we owe our King and Country."[50]

Privately the burgesses grumbled and dragged their feet. "[M]uch art was used to get one penny for the defence of the Country," according to Burgess Landon Carter. Carter blamed this reluctance on the feeling of many members that their constituents were "too poor" to pay the extraordinary taxes that would be required to defray the costs of an expedition against the French.[51] Complaining that "I never met with so much trouble in any thing I had Managem't of, as this [appropriations request]," Dinwiddie later reported that one member of the lower house even "pretended to ascertain the Right of the French to [the] Lands" on the Ohio.[52] At last, and only by what Landon Carter called a "side Glance," the burgesses approved a military supply bill for ten thousand pounds.[53]

After the assembly had adjourned, an angry and frustrated Governor Dinwiddie termed the ten-thousand-pound appropriation "a mere trifle." Worse yet, the governor found the bill "so clogg'd with unreasonable regulat[ion]s and Encroachm[en]ts on the Prerogative," that only the crisis over the Ohio Valley saved it from his veto.[54] The object of Dinwiddie's greatest ire was a proviso in the bill that established a military appropriations committee to decide how the ten thousand pounds should be spent. The bill required all civil and military officials spending or otherwise committing public funds for any war-related purpose to submit their accounts to the appropriations committee, which had "the sole Power of adjust[in]g and liquidat[in]g such Acc'ts."[55] As a practical matter, this meant that the actions of every officer involved in such routine military business as purchasing provisions, securing recruits, or paying troop salaries, were subject to the committee's scrutiny.[56] The members of the committee, in turn, were responsible to the general assembly for their own proceedings.[57]

The appropriations committee, popularly known as the "Country Committee," or simply, "the Committee," consisted originally of fourteen members, ten from the lower house and four from the council. They were a who's who of the colony's political power structure, men whose position in Viriginia society presumably would compel respect and discourage excessive squabbling about their decisions.[58] The size of the committee varied slightly during its four-year existence, but it continued to be distinguished by the prominence of its membership.

There was some precedent for the "Country Committee," notwithstanding the governor's charge that it represented "an Alteration of a fundamental part of the Constitution."[59] An identical measure had been enacted in 1746 during King George's War, when the lower house voted four thousand pounds for sending a force of volunteers to

Canada.[60] But, as Jack Greene has pointed out, a committee to oversee military appropriations was created in that instance largely because poor health prevented much-respected Governor William Gooch from personally supervising defense expenditures.[61] The situation with Dinwiddie was quite different. Although his health was declining by 1756 and the effects of an apparent stroke would prompt his resignation the following year, Dinwiddie was still a remarkably robust man early in 1754. What had deteriorated by that date were the harmony and good feelings that characterized relations between the governor and the lower house in the 1740s.

To be sure, the burgesses' assumption of absolute authority over military expenditures is explained in part by a proclivity, common to all colonial legislatures, for intruding into the executive sphere whenever possible. By exploiting both Dinwiddie's eagerness to forestall French occupation of the forks and their own exclusive power to tax and frame money bills, the lower house found it relatively easy to encroach on the governor's responsibility for military affairs.[62] There is, however, little direct evidence that the burgesses' action was inspired by an ideological concern for establishing legislative supremacy over the military: their creation of the "Country Committee" seems to have been motivated primarily by their personal distrust of Dinwiddie. Nevertheless, the existence of the committee had the practical effect of making Virginia's military leaders answerable to, and dependent upon, legislative authority. In that regard it is worth noting that when the committee went out of existence in March 1758, the lower house continued its domination over military policy by including in subsequent appropriations bills detailed estimates concerning the size, organization, provisioning, and employment of the colony's armed forces.[63]

## FORMING THE VIRGINIA REGIMENT

With the "Country Committee" looking over his shoulder, Dinwiddie set about raising a regiment of 6 fifty-man companies. This force comprised the nucleus of what soon became known as the Virginia Regiment, the most important element in the Old Dominion's military structure during the French and Indian War. The governor calculated that this little corps could be led by fifteen officers and was gratified by the "Numbers that...were desirous to serve" in such a capacity.[64] (Unlike militia officers who were selected by the leading men in their home counties, provincial officers received their appointments directly from the governor.) Notwithstanding the number of applicants, the selection of officers was hampered by a dearth of

qualified candidates. Men with military experience were at a pre-
mium in mid-eighteenth-century Virginia. After weeks of picking
and choosing, Dinwiddie confided to Governor James Hamilton of
Pennsylvania: "We are in great want of proper officers, but [I] have
from the best Informat'n and Recommendat's Commision'd the best
I c[ou]ld meet with."[65]

To command the Virginia Regiment, Dinwiddie picked Joshua Fry
of Albemarle County. Fry, an experienced frontier explorer and one-
time mathematics professor at the College of William and Mary, was
county lieutenant of Albemarle at the time of his appointment.[66]
George Washington was chosen as second in command with the rank
of lieutenant colonel. The post of regimental major went to George
Muse, a veteran of the Cartagena expedition and one of the few men
in the Virginia militia who had seen active service.[67]

Five of the fifteen commissions issued by Dinwiddie went to Scottish immigrants.[68] One member of this group, a thirty-year-old man
named Adam Stephen, shortly became the Virginia Regiment's senior
captain. Stephen held a medical degree from the University of Edin-
burgh and had sailed briefly as a surgeon on a British hospital ship
before coming out to Virginia in 1753. He served in the regiment
throughout the war and in 1761 was made its commander.[69] The
remaining three captains' commissions and six lieutenancies went to
young volunteers with a hankering for military adventure. There
were no representatives from Virginia's leading families among them,
but as a group they possessed respectable, if unremarkable, social
credentials. Though not members of the elite, they were the kind of
men who could be trusted by the colonial establishment.[70]

The men who served in the ranks of the Virginia Regiment were
called provincial troops, and in terms of their employment, organization, and conditions of service, they occupied a place somewhere
between that of British regulars and the part-time citizen-soldiers of
the militia. Historians have tended to slight, where they have not
passed over completely, the differences between provincial troops and
militia. In Virginia, at least, those differences were substantial.[71]

The militia law in force at the beginning of the French and Indian
War required "all free male persons, above the age of one and twenty
years" to be listed on the muster rolls of their home counties.[72] By
way of contrast, initially at least, no man was compelled to serve in
the Virginia Regiment. When first organized, the regiment was composed exclusively of volunteers, men who willingly took up arms with
the understanding that they would be paid for doing so. In addition,
unlike the militia, which was organized on a county basis and whose

members served with their neighbors in local companies drawn from an even smaller geographic area, the Virginia Regiment was composed of men drawn from across the colony and beyond. Indeed, it is quite likely that those who volunteered for duty early in 1754 were the type of men who fell outside the militia system to begin with. According to George Washington, "the generality of those" who signed up for service on the Ohio were "loose, Idle Persons. . . quite destitute of House, and Home."[73] If most of the provincial recruits were in fact men who lived on the margins of society and possessed no fixed residence, it is entirely possible that they would have escaped the notice of county muster masters whose rolls generally did not list the names of "men on the move."[74] By 1756, a significant number of men in the Virginia Regiment were not Virginians at all. In Septmber 1755 Washington had ordered several officers "into the back parts of Maryland, Pennsylvania, or such other Places as you shall think most advisable, to Expedite the Recruiting Service."[75] A muster roll of Captain Christopher Gist's company taken eight months later revealed that out of a total complement of sixty-eight, only eight men had enlisted in the Old Dominion.[76] Although the number of non-Virginians in Gist's company was unusually high, it was by no means unique. In May 1756 non-Virginians formed more than half of Captain Robert Stewart's light horse troop.[77]

Significant contrasts in conditions of service also served to differentiate Virginia's provincial soldiers from her militiamen. Thus while individual militiamen eventually were drafted for duty with the Virginia Regiment, militiamen qua militiamen were only called upon to serve during periods of emergency. As a result, militiamen measured their service in terms of days and weeks. Members of the provincial corps, whether volunteers or conscripts from the militia, were subject to a longer period of service, with enlistments generally lasting from nine months to one year.[78]

As the conflict with France wore on, the members of the Virginia Regiment also became subject to increasingly rigorous forms of military discipline. When the war began, it was uncertain just what kind of military law governed the provincials or if, indeed, they were under any law at all. Thinking back on the matter, Washington doubted whether in 1754 the disciplinary provisions of the provincial military statutes then in force extended to the men in the Virginia Regiment. To compensate for the absence of a provincial code, Washington and his officers during the first campaign took it upon themselves to instill "Notion's into the Soldiers (who at that time knew no better) that they were Govern'd by the [British] Articles of War."[79]

Washington and his fellow dissemblers apparently had little trouble in keeping their credulous troops in line until the fall of 1754 when the regiment took up garrison duty at Wills Creek; thereafter, the maintenance of discipline was a constant problem.[80]

As a remedy, the colony in 1755 strengthened its military code. In August of that year, Virginia's provincial troops were made liable to the revised provisions of a statute on invasions and insurrections. As originally written, the Invasions and Insurrections Act of 1748 contained no mention of the military crimes of mutiny and desertion, and soldiers found guilty of ignoring or disobeying orders were subject only to fines.[81] Mutiny and desertion were, however, recognized in the August 1755 revision, and soldiers found guilty of such offenses could receive corporal punishment "not extending to life or members."[82] An even more dramatic revision was enacted in October 1755 when military courts gained the option of imposing the death penalty on those convicted of mutiny, desertion, or even simple disobedience.[83] Those stern provisions were written at a time when Virginia's military fortunes were at low ebb, and the terms of the October revision applied equally to provincial troops and to militiamen whose units had been called into active service. Interestingly enough, six months later the Virginia assembly created what amounted to a dual system of military justice. "An Act for preventing Mutiny and Desertion," passed in April 1757, continued to authorize capital punishment as the ultimate sanction for mutiny, desertion, or disobedience to orders, but only for men in provincial service.[84] A separate military law code for militiamen mustered into active duty was approved the same month. This act authorized only corporal punishment "not extending to life or member" for the same offenses that could bring death to a provincial soldier. In the case of simple disobedience, a militiaman could escape punishment altogether by paying a five-pound fine.[85] The dual system of military justice that prescribed a harsh code for provincial troops and a much milder one for militiamen continued in force until the end of the war.

Finally, there were differences in the pay received by provincials and that authorized for militiamen called onto active service. Provincial officers received a higher salary than their militia counterparts. The pay differential between ensigns was about 50 percent, and a colonel in the provincials earned two-thirds more than a colonel in the militia. In the case of common soldiers, the situation was dramatically reversed. Sergeants in the provincials earned more than their militia counterparts, but privates in the militia were paid almost twice as much as enlisted men in the Virginia Regiment: 1s. 3d.

per day versus 8*d.* per day.[86] The low pay of provincial soldiers is cast into sharper perspective when it is recalled that even unskilled workers in late colonial America are estimated to have earned 2 or 3 shillings daily for their labors.[87]

From the Virginia assembly's point of view, of course, the low pay authorized for provincial soldiers was but another compelling reason for leaving militiamen at home. Aside from Dinwiddie's short-lived plan for forcing productive citizens onto guard duty at the forks, nothing was more politically unpopular in the spring of 1754 than voting increased taxes for what the governor liked to call "my Proceedings ag[ain]st the enemy."[88] But however attractive an alternative the Virginia Regiment may have appeared to cost-conscious politicians, it is clear that actual duty in its ranks promised little but hard service under harsh discipline for minimal wages.

If a private's lot in the provincials compared so unfavorably with that of his militia counterpart by such basic tests of soldiering as length of enlistments, severity of discipline, and rates of pay, it seems fair to suppose that only those with no other options would freely join the Virginia Regiment. The notion is sustained by Washington's aforementioned reference to the "loose, idle Persons" who turned up in his camp. Washington went on to claim that many volunteers lacked even shoes while "other's want Stockings, some are without Shirts, and not a few . . . have Scarce a Coat, or Waistcoat, to their Backs."[89] The unmistakable impression is that the Virginia Regiment was an army of rabble. And so it was meant to be. Since it was politically unacceptable to impose on property-owning citizens, provincial soldiers of necessity were recruited among the poor, the unemployed, and the unlucky.[90]

The composition of its provincial army illustrates an important point about how Virginians went about organizing themselves for war in the 1750s. As we have seen, Governor Dinwiddie had lost no time in acting on Whitehall's loosely worded endorsement of his forward western policy. But during the first months of 1754, leading Virginians acted with no less speed to mitigate the unpleasant consequences of that policy by shifting the military burdens that accompanied it onto the shoulders of the poor. Leading Virginians were more concerned with political consequences than military effectiveness; their basic organizing principle for the upcoming campaign was that members of the "better" and "middling" sectors of society should be spared the unpleasant tasks of fighting and dying in pursuit of a dubious cause.

# · 3 ·

# "POMPOUS UNDERTAKINGS AND INGLORIOUS RESULTS"
## The Campaigns of 1754 and 1755

*And how gloomy and ill-boding was the aspect of our affairs in the
first years of this war! ... What abortive schemes and blasted
expeditions! What sanguine hopes and mortifying disappointments!
What pompous undertakings and inglorious results.*
                                    THE REVEREND SAMUEL DAVIES, 1760

The Virginia government never really considered the possibility of
defeat when it raised a scratch force of volunteers in the spring of
1754 for the purpose of guarding a construction party at the forks of
the Ohio. But the expectation that the French and their Indian allies
would quail at the sight of a handful of ragged men with guns in
their hands soon proved illusory. Instead of deterring the enemy, the
colony's forces were overwhelmed. Surprised but not unduly alarmed
by their early reverses in the field, Governor Dinwiddie and the Virginia assembly quickly looked to Great Britain to resolve their military problems for them. When Major General Edward Braddock and
his regulars arrived early in 1755, Virginians believed that the dispute
over the Ohio country was all but resolved. Anticipation of a cheap
and easy victory was widespread. The mere presence of Braddock's
army, it was assumed, would convince the French of the futility of
further resistance.

Braddock's unexpected and spectacular defeat radically transformed the military problem facing Virginia. Instead of vanquishing
its enemies, the colony had seen both its own forces and the vaunted
British regulars soundly defeated; instead of seeking peace, the
French and their Indian surrogates were inspired by victory and carried the war home across the borders of the Old Dominion. Down to
the summer of 1755 the military initiative had lain with Virginia;
the colony had waged war largely on its own terms and beyond its
own borders. All of that now changed. By the fall of 1755, the picture
was clear: Virginia had blundered into a serious conflict.

War had not been forced upon Virginia in the spring of 1754; it was an option that provincial authorities had freely chosen. The plain truth is that the dangers of resorting to a military solution were never grasped until eighteen months later when, in the wake of Braddock's defeat, dependence upon military force became mandatory.

### RECRUITING PROBLEMS

In the spring of 1754, leading Virginians did not give much thought to the possibility of becoming involved in a large-scale war. But their governor was very much aware of the dangers of military inaction. Writing to the earl of Halifax in early March, Robert Dinwiddie expressed hope that "we shall be able to make good our ground ag[ain]st the French Incursions," and promised to "do every Thing in my Power to execute it [the Ohio expedition] with all possible Dispatch." A few weeks later Dinwiddie warned the governor of South Carolina that "no Time is to be lost in preventing . . . the further Invasion [of the French] on his M[ajest]y's Lands."[1] As he had been from the beginning, however, the Virginia governor was operating far in advance of public opinion. Within the Old Dominion itself, there existed little popular support for a military confrontation with the French. Nor did the burgesses' unenthusiastic concurrence in Dinwiddie's military schemes ease the practical problem of finding volunteers who were willing to carry them out.

As an "Encouragem't to the People to enlist with Spirit," Dinwiddie issued a proclamation in mid-February promising a share in 200,000 acres of land along the upper Ohio River "to such persons, who by their voluntary engagement and good behavior in the said service, shall deserve the same." In addition to the land bounty, recruits received an enlistment bounty of one pistole in advance of their regular salary of eight pence a day. One individual later testified that "few or none" of the volunteers were attracted by the low wages of a common soldier. According to John Shaw, an Irish sailor who served in the 1754 campaign, those who "embraced" the governor's recruiting "Proposals" were lured solely by the promise of free land (and presumably a fresh start) in the West.[2]

Shaw's appraisal of soldierly motivation was likely an accurate one, particularly since the problem of low pay was compounded by uncertainty about whether provincial troops would be paid at all. Late in 1754 ex-Private Shaw complained that he "never received one farthing [of his promised pay] tho' he was above five Months in the Service."[3] Earlier that year George Washington, then acting as the colony's chief recruiter, had written that "the objection many had against Enlisting . . . was not knowing . . . the times for payment." Like John Shaw, those who did sign up were in arrears of pay virtually from the outset of their service, a situation that caused a "general Clamour" among the "Needy" men who comprised "the first Enlisters." As he would on future occasions, Washington found it necessary to dissemble in order to hold the regiment together. Pleading for funds, Washington told the governor in early March: "I have sooth'd and quieted them as much as possible under pretence of receiving your Honor's Instructions in this particular [the matter of troop salaries]."[4]

With their prospects limited to the promise of a future land grant in the wilderness and low or no pay in the meantime, it is not surprising that few volunteers came forward as the campaign season grew near. More than three weeks after the assembly had voted funds for an expedition to the Ohio, only twenty-five individuals had volunteered for service—this at a time when the free white adult male population of Virginia exceeded forty thousand.[5] By the end of March, barely more than seventy men had been recruited, and most of those were, according to their drillmaster, "selfwill'd, ungovernable People."[6]

The early recruiting shortfalls of the Virginia Regiment illustrate a larger point: the business of war was far more complicated than either Dinwiddie or the assembly yet realized. Because even a small-scale backwoods campaign was a much more complex undertaking than it first appeared, one of the things that Virginia's leaders needed most in the spring of 1754 was some sort of coherent administrative apparatus that would, among other things, help expedite the recruiting process through the establishment of an adequate payroll system. Lacking such a mechanism, confusion, delay, and unpaid troops were all but inevitable. Serious though it was, however, the matter of troop salaries was only one of the many administrative problems that faced the Virginia Regiment on the eve of its first campaign.

## FOOD AND FODDER

During the early months of 1754, the Virginia Regiment camped at Alexandria. That Potomac River town was also the base of operations for John Carlyle, a thirty-four-year-old merchant whom Dinwiddie had named chief of supply for the provincial army. Carlyle owed his appointment principally to two things: his personal connections with leading members of the Northern Neck establishment and his membership in the Ohio Company. Carlyle was related by marriage to Colonel William Fairfax, whose "recommendation" it was that his son-in-law be named to head the military commissariat.[7] Dinwiddie was happy to oblige. Fairfax was a man well worth cultivating, and by honoring his "recommendation," the governor strengthened his personal and political ties with one of the most influential oligarchs in northern Virginia. Moreover, Carlyle's performance as commissary presumably would be inspired by his association with the Ohio Company since it gave him a vested interest in the success of Dinwiddie's plans for securing the forks.

Carlyle occupied a key position: food and fodder were as crucial to military operations in the eighteenth century as fuel and high explosives would be to those of the twentieth. Making Carlyle's post all the more sensitive was the fact that he bore almost total responsibility for the administration of the provincial supply service. Carlyle's primary responsibilities centered on obtaining provisions "of all kinds" and securing the transport needed to convey them. In a personal covering letter that accompanied his commission, Dinwiddie elaborated on Carlyle's duties and furnished his new logistics director with a bit of reassuring advice. Carlyle was ordered to "procure a sufficient Qu[anti]ty of Flower, Bread, Beef and Pork for 500 Men for six or eight Mo[nth]s." Speed was essential, and the governor emphasized that this hefty list of stores must be secured as quickly as possible. Dinwiddie ended his letter with the soothing assurance that "Provis[ion]s are very plenty in the back Co[un]t[r]y."[8]

The casualness with which Dinwiddie ordered the marshaling of tons of provisions together with his confidence about the easy availability of surplus foodstuffs in the backcountry betrayed the governor's failure to appreciate the enormous difficulties involved in supplying an army in the wilderness. In fact, the supply arrangements for the 1754 campaign soon proved woefully inadequate.

Dinwiddie later blamed the supply muddle on everyone but himself. The governor was especially critical of Commissary John Carlyle. Carlyle, who throughout the period of the campaign never bestirred himself from his place of business in Alexandria, blamed the logistics mess on unreliable frontier contractors and on an insufficiency of funds with which to make the necessary purchases.[9] Privately agreeing that Carlyle's operations were hindered by a "want of Money," Dinwiddie was exasperated nonetheless by the commissary's inability to keep the Virginia Regiment furnished with adequate provisions. "The Men must have proper supplies, I therefore desire You w[oul]d [not] trust to Promises," Dinwiddie told Carlyle on 27 June, adding that "I fear the Waggoners . . . trifle with You, and do not perform their Duties." Before the year was out, Dinwiddie had grown much more critical. By December he was writing darkly about teamsters who had "made a Property of Mr. Carlyle's Ignorance, or Ill Conduct."[10]

Perhaps because he had been groomed for business himself and was familiar with mercantile practices, Dinwiddie was suspicious of the men he appointed to head the military commissariat and often was at odds with them. This pattern was established early and clouded the governor's relations with Carlyle during much of the latter's tenure as commissary. Indeed, when Carlyle was, in effect, fired as Virginia's chief of military supply in December 1754, Dinwiddie flatly accused him of "irregular" conduct. The imputation of dishonesty involved Carlyle's apparent failure to reimburse individuals who had supplied the regiment with livestock even through the commissary had been provided with nine hundred pounds in public funds for that very purpose.[11]

Although he left office under a cloud, Carlyle continued playing a role in the colony's military supply service. Early in 1755 Dinwiddie advised Carlyle's patron, Colonel Fairfax, that "Mr. Carlyle will continue to act in any thing . . . that may be necessary at Alexa[ndri]a."[12] The governor's interest in maintaining congenial relations with the Fairfax family apparently overrode any inhibitions he had about directing some of the public's business in the way of the likes of John Carlyle. In a broader sense, this episode offers support for John Shy's view that "the commercial activity required by a colonial army took place within a highly political setting."[13] Shy reached that conclusion after studying the operations of British army contractors in East Florida in the 1760s, but the nexus between politics and military contracting seems no less close in Virginia during the preceding decade.

Individual malfeasance notwithstanding, Virginia's most basic logistical problem in 1754 and, indeed, in every succeeding campaign was one of organizing the supply and getting the material to the army. In the first place, a sizable quantity of horses, wagons, teamsters, and forage had to be collected if the regiment was to be adequately supplied. The movement of provisions was further complicated by the primitive state of land communications in the Old Dominion. The heaviest military activity took place on the frontier, where the roads, if they existed at all, were primitive and often impassable during Virginia's rainy seasons of spring and fall. Inadequate roads and the difficulty of gathering horses and wagons in the numbers necessary for supplying the needs of even a few hundred men resulted in severe and persistent shortages of food and equipment.

As in the case of the chaotic military pay situation, however, the feeble state of the provincial supply service was mostly the result of deficiencies in organization and administration. To begin with, a military logistics system had to be created out of nothing in 1754. Colonial leaders had few precedents to draw on in building a logistical organization, and there were few men on hand with the requisite experience necessary to effectively oversee such an organization once it had been created. In that sense, John Carlyle's mercantile background, his attendant familiarity with contracting, and his contacts with British suppliers gave a certain legitimacy to what otherwise could be dismissed as a purely "political" appointment. In spite of his admittedly valuable experience and business connections, however, there was nothing in Carlyle's background that adequately prepared him for the complexities of supplying an army operating in a far-distant wilderness. More than anything else, administrative inexperience and inadequate organization—augmented by periodic infusions of simple incompetence—created the grevious material shortages that plagued the Virginia Regiment throughout its existence.[14]

### FIRST DEFEATS

Several weeks before the arrival of spring came word that the French would descend on the Ohio sooner than had been anticipated. The news caught Dinwiddie by surprise, and the governor hurriedly directed Washington "to march what Soldiers you have enlisted, imediately [sic] to the Ohio." Colonel Joshua Fry and the remainder of the regiment would be sent up to reinforce Washington's vanguard as soon as possible. Washington's orders were "to act on the Defensive, but in Case any Attempts are made to obstruct the Works [the Ohio Company's fort then under construction at the forks] . . . to restrain all such Offenders, and in Case of resistance to make Prisoners of or kill and destroy them."[15]

Two weeks were spent in gathering additional recruits and in contracting for supplies. Washington at last broke camp on 2 April and marched west at the head of 120 troops formed into two companies. Accompanying him were a handful of commissioned and noncommissioned officers, a surgeon, a drummer, and one "Swedish Gentleman" volunteer.[16] Trundling along behind the column were two farm wagons carrying meager stocks of food and ammunition. The abbreviated supply train and ramshackle scratch force of men who lacked even the basic "Conveniencies [sic]. . . to make the Service tolerably agreeable," aptly symbolized the amateurish nature of the 1754 campaign.[17]

Washington's advance corps made its first important stop at Winchester, the seat of Frederick County and the future headquarters site of the Virginia Regiment. Here Washington had expected to obtain additional wagons for transporting provisions and forage. What he met instead was the first of several major disappointments that marked the course of his expedition. In this case the desperately needed wagons had not been collected. All that awaited Washington was Captain Adam Stephen and a welcome reinforcement of thirty-nine men Stephen had recruited in the local area. On the other hand, this additional company also increased the need for supply wagons. Washington knew that once beyond the cluster of farms on the south branch of the Potomac, provisions were not to be had for any price.[18] This, in turn, meant that the men of the Virginia Regiment had to carry their supplies with them or go without.

To remedy his transport problems, Washington delayed his stay in Winchester, intending to impress the wagons he required, even though authority to seize items of personal property for military use was vested legally only in county lieutenants and the field-grade officers under their command. Washington felt such high-handed proceedings were justified because Thomas Lord Fairfax, county lieutenant of Frederick, had neglected to marshal the necessary wagons and teams. Seventy-four wagons eventually were commandeered for the fifty-five-mile march up to Wills Creek, where the Ohio Company had erected a small storehouse. But much to Washington's chagrin, no more than ten of the seventy-four wagons were surrendered by their owners. Some that did arrive were drawn by horses so feeble that soldiers had to be employed in "assisting them up the Hills." Shortly after he left Winchester, Washington noted in disgust that he expected fewer problems from the French than he had received at the hands of the residents of Frederick County.[19] The French very shortly proved him wrong.

As Washington's column was slowly edging its way up to Wills Creek, a one thousand-man force of French and Indians descended the Allegheny River and on 17 April captured the hastily constructed Virginia fort at the forks of the Ohio. The much more formidable Fort Duquesne soon was erected at the same site. Undeterred by news of the French stroke, Washington marched his troops toward Redstone Creek, a stream that entered the Monongahela about thirty-seven miles south of the forks.[20] There he planned to post his three companies until joined by the remainder of the Virginia Regiment and the other forces Dinwiddie had promised to send up. The first real fighting occurred late in May when Washington and forty Virginians, supported by a few pro-British Mingo Indians, attacked and defeated a French patrol led by Ensign Joseph Coulon de Jumonville.[21] (Shortly after the encounter with Jumonville, word arrived that Colonel Fry had died after a fall from his horse and that command of the Virginia Regiment had passed to Washington.) Intent on avenging their comrades, the French advanced on the two hundred Virginians with five hundred of their own troops and a war party of Indians. News of the French movement resulted in Washington's retreat to Fort Necessity, a small palisade he previously had erected at a place called the Great Meadows (about forty miles northwest of Wills Creek). After a nine-hour battle on 3 July 1754, Washington surrendered his hopelessly outnumbered forces with the understanding that the Virginians could return unmolested to the Old Dominion. The surrender document was written in French, and in signing it Washington was unaware that he also was admitting that Jumonville had been "assassinated" and that the Ohio Valley belonged to France.[22] So ended the Virginia Regiment's first campaign.

By almost any standard, Virginia's initial thrust into the Ohio Valley was a disaster. Virginians had fired the first shot, but the campaign of 1754 revealed a serious misunderstanding, not only in the West but also at home, of military realities: what would be necessary to mobilize, deploy, and use military power in an unpopular war. The problems associated with eighteenth-century Virginia's first significant foray into military affairs were many, but those associated with logistics, manpower, and public indifference topped the list.[23]

Plagued by supply and transportation problems from the outset, the expedition's meager store of provisions was exhausted weeks before the climactic engagement at the Great Meadows early in July. Washington's supply of flour ran out by 6 June, and his subsequent appeals for provisions went unanswered.[24] As a result, the officers and men of the Virginia Regiment lived on nothing but lean beef and "parch'd Corn" during their exhausting retreat through the Allegheny wilderness to Fort Necessity.[25] Indeed, according to one provincial soldier, the name "Necessity" was bestowed on that isolated palisade in the first place because of the "great difficulty of procuring necessaries for subsistence when our soldiers were there employed."[26]

In the final analysis, however, the defeat at Fort Necessity was due more to a lack of men than to a shortage of supplies.[27] The number of men under Washington's command had never exceeded 300 during the entire campaign. During the Battle of the Great Meadows, he faced approximately 700 French and Indians with only 284 effectives. The French, on the other hand, enjoyed a two to one advantage in

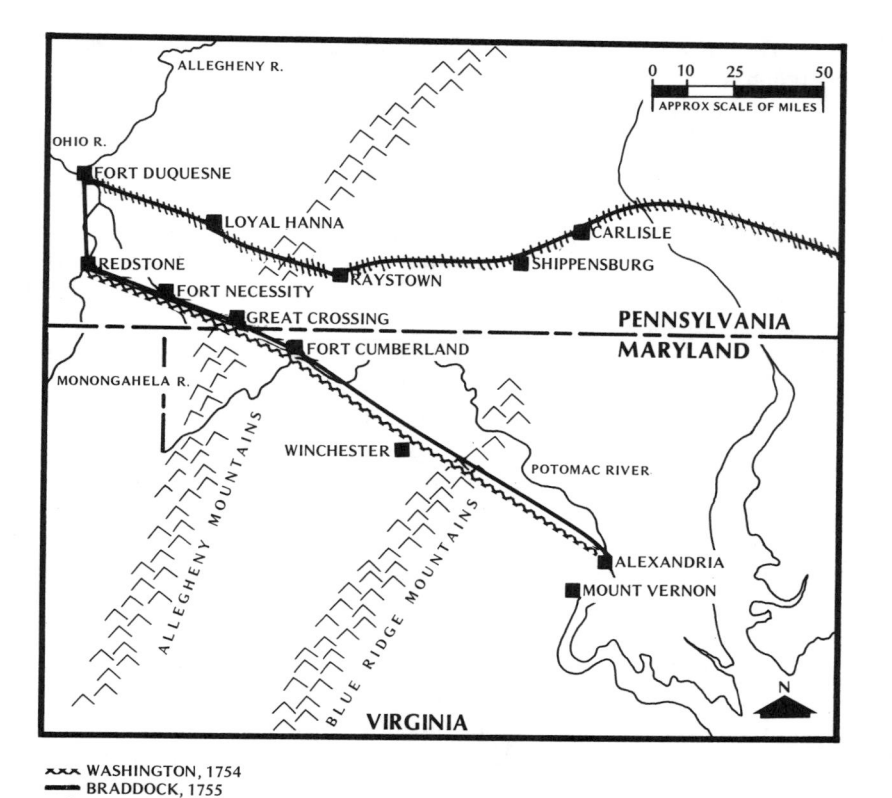

xxx WASHINGTON, 1754
━━ BRADDOCK, 1755
ꬳꬳꬳ FORBES, 1758

Lines of march of the three campaigns against Fort Duquense.

troop strength even after the Virginians were joined by a 100-man
independent company of British regulars from South Carolina.[28]
Washington's puny army—so small that its only practical choice at
Fort Necessity was surrender or annihilation—was the product of two
factors: overconfidence on the part of Governor Dinwiddie and widespread indifference on the part of almost everyone else in the Old
Dominion.

Dinwiddie had been exhausted by his struggle in mid-February to
wrest a modicum of financial support from the House of Burgesses
and never involved himself in any serious way in recruiting men for
the 1754 campaign. Disregarding Washington's warnings about the
scarcity of volunteers, the governor beguiled himself with the notion
that because they were volunteers, the provincials' esprit would compensate for whatever they lacked in numbers.[29] As for the burgesses,

after offering token financial support for the expedition, the members adjourned, returned to their private pursuits, and all but ignored military developments on the Ohio. Dinwiddie later complained that the legislators were far less concerned about the French than they were about charges from their constituents labeling them "Dupes . . . [for] loading y's Dom'n with all expence" of making war.[30] Within the broader circle of Virginia society, the popular apathy, if not simple disbelief, that greeted the governor's alarms concerning the French "threat," was evidenced most clearly by the fact that less than 1 percent of the eligible males volunteered for military service in 1754.[31]

The decision made by thousands of Virginians of military age not to jeopardize their own safety and comfort by joining the provincials foreshadowed a problem that would become much more serious in the future. The essence of the problem involved the mobilization of public opinion; that is, the arousal of support for raising and maintaining a provincial army worthy of the name. Because the military difficulties facing Virginia in 1754 were still limited, so were the colony's attempts to mobilize. The problem of motivating the populace for violence on a significant scale was only a small cloud on the horizon. But what if the conflict with the French assumed more serious proportions? In that case Governor Dinwiddie would be confronted by the need for scraping up a considerably larger number of men for extended service, a situation that then would raise the politically intricate problem of mobilizing both armed force and public opinion.

### THE PLIGHT OF THE REGIMENT

The French victories at the forks and the Great Meadows evoked scant concern on the Virginia home front. These isolated skirmishes in the western wilderness simply had little impact on the lives of most Virginians. Even the more educated citizens were only dimly aware in 1754 of locations that soon would become well known and well watered with British and American blood. Writing to an English relative two months after the French had secured control of the Ohio River, the Reverend James Maury, a leading Anglican parson with an active interest in public affairs, referred vaguely to the forks as a "place in dispute . . . about two hundred miles back of our nearest mountains."[32]

The importance of the forks was equally remote as far as the House of Burgesses was concerned. Only a handful of land speculators had any real economic stake in opposing the French in the West, and like most of their constituents, the members of the lower house did not feel that the presence of Frenchmen in that far-distant region menaced Virginia's security. Accordingly, the burgesses received news of the colony's military reverses with equanimity and had no compunction about exploiting what Governor Dinwiddie called "these dangerous Times" for partisan political purposes.[33] Seeking funds for another attack on the French before the year was out, Dinwiddie reconvened the legislature on 22 August and requested a supplemental military appropriation. All went well until the final reading of the military supply bill, at which point "a litigious Spirit prevailed," and the lower house added a rider awarding twenty-five hundred pounds to Attorney General Peyton Randolph for serving as their agent in London during the pistole fee controversy. Dinwiddie and the council protested in vain that attaching a private measure to a public bill was unconstitutional. Neither side would compromise, and the bill was ultimately vetoed by the upper house.[34] In a speech that "carryed all the Venom and all the Falsehood of an Angry Passionate man," the governor prorogued the assembly until October and gave up hope of renewing offensive operations in 1754.[35]

Dinwiddie's empty military chest did more than frustrate his plans for a counterattack; it also made difficult the retention of even a handful of men in garrison. The ten thousand pounds voted by the assembly in February was nearly exhausted by July. The resulting stringent fiscal situation further exacerbated morale problems among the men of the already ill-paid, ill-fed, and ill-equipped Virginia Regiment. In a letter dispatched to Washington early in August, the governor noted that he was "sorry Y[ou]r Regim't have behav'd so very refactory, tho' they have a right to their Pay."[36] But there was no alleviation of the soldiers' physical and financial distress during the weeks that followed. The plight of those wounded during the Fort Necessity campaign was especially wretched. Over two months after the Battle of the Great Meadows, Dinwiddie sadly acknowledged that he had "not yet been able to procure a proper Allowance for the poor Sick & Wounded."[37] In spite of their pathetic situation, or more likely because of it, Washington's troops could not "get credit even for a Hatt." Their miserable condition was further underscored by Washington's request that an assistant surgeon be sent up to the regimental camp at Wills Creek. The single physician then working in the camp, Washington explained, "has more business than he can well manage." The sorry state of the Virginia Regiment reflected not only disregard for the assorted miseries of hungry, broken, and "Naked" men; it also pointed up how lightly most Virginians viewed their colony's recent military misadventures in the West.[38]

Under the circumstances it surprised no one that the Virginia Regiment was fast melting away. As of 1 June the regiment had totaled 293 officers and men; by 14 August that figure had declined to 186. One former soldier estimated that by the beginning of September, "full two-thirds" of the enlisted men had deserted.[39] Aware by summer's end that he could do little more than try to "keep the few People we have," Dinwiddie posted one company of provincials on guard duty along the frontiers of Augusta County. The remainder of the regiment was employed in building a fort at Wills Creek (soon to be named Fort Cumberland), which would serve as a supply depot and base of operations for future expeditions.[40] To sustain the troops in their winter labors "at a Time, W[he]n our Finances are so low," Dinwiddie recommended a diet based on "Ind[ia]n Meal, w[hi]ch is a hearty Food and comes much cheaper than Flour." The governor's suggestion had a significance that transcended economics: as the ragged and neglected veterans of Fort Necessity were no doubt aware, in eighteenth-century Virginia, Indian meal was the humble fare customarily reserved for slaves.[41]

The dwindling size of the Virginia Regiment and the burgesses' inclination for playing politics at a time when, in Dinwiddie's opinion, "the enemy is so near our Frontiers," led the governor to intensify the requests for aid he had been sending to London since the previous spring. Citing the burgesses' latest instance of noncooperation, he warned that without British assistance "our whole dependence will be on our militia, w[hi]ch at pres't are in bad Order, and have been with[ou]t proper discipline." In words calculated to arouse the home government, Dinwiddie further claimed that once they had secured their hold on the Ohio country, the French planned "to invade some of our Colonies." Virginia was in real danger of falling "a Sacrifice to their rapacious designs" unless Great Britain intervened.[42] Unbeknownst to Dinwiddie, decisions had already been reached in London that favored the course he was urging. News of Washington's defeat may have left the people of Virginia unmoved, but it markedly increased British fears that a serious threat lurked at the back of the Old Dominion.

## BRITISH INTERVENTION

The government of the duke of Newcastle did not share the Ohio Company's enthusiasm for promoting English settlement in the trans-Allegheny west. The ministry's chronic Francophobia and mercantilist predilections did, however, inspire its view that destruction of the company's fort plainly challenged the "Commerce of Our Subjects" and, potentially, "the Safety of Our [existing] Colonies."[43] Alarmed by the passivity of the Virginia assembly, Newcastle himself contended that "All North America will be lost, if these Practices are tolerated, And no War can be worse to this Country, than Suffering Such Insults, as These."[44]

In September the ministry formally advised M. de Rouille, Louis XV's minister of marine, of its belief that France was pursuing a "premeditated Plan" for disrupting England's Indian trade and for committing "the most glaring Encroachments and Usurpations" upon British territorial claims in the Ohio Valley. The same dispatch warned that unless France withdrew her forces from the area south of Lake Erie, George II would authorize "such Measures there [in the Ohio country], as He shall think proper."[45] A diplomatic exchange dragged on through the winter of 1754–55, but it was clear by fall that both sides were prepared to defend their respective claims in the trans-Allegheny west by force of arms if necessary. In fact, the British decided upon a military solution within weeks of lodging their initial protest over the French advance into the Ohio Valley. On 3 October the British ambassador to Paris was advised that two regiments on the Irish establishment would shortly sail for Virginia.[46]

Overall command of the regulars, and of all other British forces in North America, fell to Major General Edward Braddock, a veteran of forty-five years' service and a favorite of George II's younger son, the duke of Cumberland, then captain general of the British army.[47] Acting on Cumberland's advice, the Newcastle ministry devised plans for 1755 calling for attacks on Fort Duquesne and the French posts at Niagara and Crown Point. Braddock himself was assigned the task of reducing Fort Duquesne.[48]

Virginians received their first indication of growing British involvement in the Ohio Valley dispute when word arrived in October that the ministry was contributing twenty thousand pounds to the colony's war chest and two thousand small arms to its depleted arsenal. "These distinguished Marks of His Majesty's paternal Care" were much stressed by Dinwiddie when the assembly reconvened later that same month.[49] Also influential in making this what Landon Carter called "the Harmonious Session" was the fact that the year-long controversy over the pistole fee at last had been resolved. The Privy Council's final judgment favored the governor but not in every respect. As a result, both sides felt vindicated and "having got Something, both seemed to hugg themselves with a Victory." The upshot was that there was "no Contest" among the burgesses regarding the governor's request for a military appropriation. The members matched the Crown's grant by voting twenty thousand pounds for defense.[50]

## SELECTIVE SERVICE

The lower house was less forthcoming on the crucial question of military manpower. Because he could not legally "oblige [militiamen] to march out of the Countries [sic] of Virginia," Dinwiddie asked the assembly for a law authorizing either the impressment of vagrants or the conscription of every tenth man in the militia.[51] The governor personally favored the latter alternative, but the burgesses opted for a more selective approach and agreed that compulsory service should be limited to men between the ages of twenty-one and fifty "who have no visible Way of getting an honest Livelihood."[52]

The draft act of October 1754 was closely patterned after an earlier "Vagrant Act" passed at the time of the Cartagena expedition almost fifteen years before.[53] The resemblance between the two laws reflected the similarity between the conditions leading to their enactment. As far as the average Virginian was concerned, the Ohio country was hardly less distant than far-off Cartagena—neither was a spot over which large numbers of men would willingly risk their lives. In each case, however, peculiar circumstances gave both places a political significance that overshadowed popular estimates of their relative military value.

Cartagena assumed political importance for Virginia authorities in 1741 by virtue of a British demand for colonial participation in Admiral Edward Vernon's descent on the Spanish Main. By way of contrast, the importance of the forks in 1754 turned largely on the question of appearances. The burgesses at first had shown little inclination to redeem the affront to Anglo-American arms and prestige suffered at Fort Necessity. But the successful resolution of the pistole fee controversy and, more importantly, the aforementioned infusion of British money and weapons caused the lower house to reconsider its position. In the end, narrow calculations of provincial self-interest suggested that colonial leaders adopt a more belligerent pose toward the French. The importance of projecting an aggressive image was explained by Burgess Landon Carter. As Carter described it, the collective wisdom of the lower house was that by approving a military supply bill rivaling the Crown's bequest, "we might shew our mother Country our own Sensibility of danger *and excite their Care.*"[54] (Italics mine.)

There was only one difficulty with the burgesses' plan for inducing support from abroad by striking a more militant posture at home: some Virginians would have to bear the hardships and dangers of actual service in the colony's provincial forces. The politicians' way out of this difficulty was to fall back on the same system for raising men they had employed in 1741: soldiering was made the duty of the poor and unemployed, those for whom society had no other use. In such an answer, colonial leaders believed, lay the means for avoiding a number of political and economic problems that a broader and more inclusive approach to mobilization could have created. In the first place, by forcing their scruff and scum into the provincials, Virginians could have an army without disrupting the lives of productive citizens and therefore the colonial economy. The "act for raising levies and recruits" drawn up in October 1754 demanded twelve months' service of provincial soldiers. That was a lengthy requirement in an agricultural society whose staple kept its cultivators busy for nine months of the year.[55] Few members of the gentry would willingly entrust their fortunes to an overseer for so extended a period. On the other hand, any absence from the necessary round of sowing, transplanting, weeding, topping, worming, striking, and curing tobacco could spell ruin for the independent yeoman. A military draft that imposed only on the unemployed and thus avoided the ominous economic implications of a less selective policy had obvious attractions.

Purely political considerations were no less important than those of the economic variety. In a social order that was deferential but fragile, impressing men from the mudsill neatly defused the potentially explosive question of who should serve. By specifically exempting "any person to serve as a soldier, who hath any vote in the election of a Burgess," the assembly foisted an unpleasant, often arduous, and sometimes dangerous task on politically powerless men while leaving undisturbed those who possessed even a minimal voice in government.[56] It was an appealing solution to the delicate problems of fighting an unpopular war without endangering the congenial relationship between the "better" and "middling" sorts, the groups that really counted in Virginia society. The attractiveness of a draft system that preyed exclusively on those without influence or importance was enhanced by the fact that the governing elite lacked European-style institutions for suppressing a defiant populace. The gentry had no real police force at their disposal, and whether militiamen could be expected to ride down their white friends and neighbors was at best an open question. In short, in a situation where the political costs of imposing an unwanted military burden on the greater part of the white male population could be high, impressing only the disadvantaged and disfranchised was socially and politically the most prudent course of action.

## PREPARING FOR ANOTHER THRUST

Dinwiddie had not gotten his entire way with the assembly, but on the whole the governor was gratified by the outcome of the October session. Equipped with twenty thousand pounds and the authority to impress vagrants, he again considered the possibility of renewing operations on the Ohio. However, plans for what Washington termed a "suicidal mission" in midwinter soon were abandoned because of a lack of interest on the part of Virginia's neighboring colonies and the slow rate with which men and supplies were raised within the Old Dominion itself.[57]

One measure that the governor did carry through involved the reorganization of the Virginia Regiment into ten independent companies. The restructuring was intended to serve as a means of avoiding disputes over rank between provincial and regular officers. Wrangling over "punctillos about command" between Washington and regular Captain James Mackay of the South Carolina Independent Company had bedeviled the waning days of the 1754 campaign. The "unhappy Dispute" later was renewed at Wills Creek, where the regulars from South Carolina, since joined by two additional independent companies from New York, were encamped with the Virginia Regiment. By reducing the regiment to independent companies, Dinwiddie could recall the field-grade commissions he had issued in the spring and offer nothing but captaincies in their stead. Since provincial captains were unquestionably subordinate to regular captains, the rank dispute would be eliminated quite nicely. Among the senior officers of the Virginia Regiment, Washington alone resigned rather than accept reduction in grade.[58]

Organizing a coherent logistics system proved a much more difficult chore than reorganizing the Virginia Regiment, and to it Dinwiddie devoted considerable time and energy during the winter of 1754–55. The governor's early optimism about the ease of obtaining provisions in the Virginia backcountry had long since evaporated. It had been replaced by awareness that no reliance could be placed on the kind of jury-rigged supply arrangements that had been employed in the 1754 campaign. In order to expedite operations in 1755, Dinwiddie saw that his principal logistical task involved the stockpiling of provisions as far up on the line of march to the Ohio as possible. It was for that purpose that the surviving members of the Virginia

Regiment had been ordered in September to begin constructing "a Magazine for Stores" at Wills Creek.[59]

In December Dinwiddie named Dr. Thomas Walker and Charles Dick as commissaries of stores and provisions in place of John Carlyle.[60] Walker, who mixed the activities of a physician with those of an explorer, land speculator, and politician, played a leading role in the colony's military logistics system throughout the remainder of the war.[61] Like his predecessor Carlyle, Dick was an Alexandria merchant whose career as a logistician was similarly short lived. In announcing their appointment, the governor described both individuals as persons of "great Activity," while acclaiming Dick for being "well-known in the back Counties."[62]

The dual appointment of Walker and Dick made possible a division of labor that helped rationalize the operations of the provincial supply service. It was a step Dinwiddie hoped would "for the Future, keep the Forces properly Supplied." Under the new arrangement, Dick ranged the backcountry to "make Purchases and order the Prov[ision]s." Walker was based at Wills Creek, where he received and paid for the supplies sent up by Dick and saw that they were "próperly issued to the Men." To expedite deliveries, Dinwiddie authorized Walker and Dick to appoint an assistant in Winchester with responsibility for "forw[ar]d[ing] Things to the [regimental] Camp."[63]

Dinwiddie initially had promised his new commissaries that he would "leave every Thing to Y[ou]r Prudent and good Managem't," but with characteristic assertiveness he soon was showering Walker and Dick with advice, instructions, and occasional reprimands.[64] His letters also lay bare the complexities of provisioning an eighteenth-century army operating in the North American wilderness. Even in the case of the basic foodstuffs, timing and coordination were essential if such staples as flour and beef were to be furnished on a regular and dependable basis and in the volume necessary for sustaining hundreds of men living beyond the limits of settlement. For example, the availability of fresh meat meant nothing unless there was sufficient salt on hand for curing it and, once salted, casks in which to store it. Purchases of salt and casks, in turn, were controlled by the availability of wagons for hauling them, for forage for the horses providing the motive power, and of the horses themselves.[65]

The accumulation of provisions gained new urgency after word was received in mid-December that two regiments of British regulars had been dispatched to drive the French from the Ohio Valley. Governor Dinwiddie promptly ordered his agents to scour the Virginia backcountry for pork and to let contracts in Pennsylvania and Massachusetts for tons of flour and fish. By the early spring of 1755, after weeks of "great Care and infinite Trouble," Dinwiddie felt reasonably sure that he had massed sufficient provisions at Wills Creek to sustain a force of nearly three thousand men for eight months.[66] By that time also the governor had learned that even the complex business of provisioning an army was less wearisome a problem than that of mobilizing manpower.

## ANTIDRAFT SENTIMENT

Dinwiddie initially had planned to raise two thousand men for the 1755 campaign. In less than a month, that recruiting goal was reduced by 50 percent. A few weeks later in mid-December 1754, the governor established a new and even lower target of eight hundred men. By the first of the year, no more than five hundred men had been enlisted, and Dinwiddie could only "hope" that an additional three hundred recruits might somehow be secured by spring.[67]

Several factors account for these unimpressive returns. Many Virginians of military age were put off by the assembly's failure to authorize enlistment bounties, by the low pay of common soldiers, and by the general unpopularity of the war. In a way that its authors had not anticipated, the "vagrant act," passed in October, also contributed to the slow rate of enlistment. By imposing mandatory service only on members of a socially disreputable group, the assembly stigmatized enlisted duty in the provincials as a disgraceful form of employment. The resulting odium cast upon those in the ranks doubtlessly deterred men of higher quality from volunteering. Most discouraging of all were the tales of adversity and neglect spread "over the country" by veterans of the 1754 campaign. According to George Washington, the former soldiers "fix'd in the Populace such horrid Impressions of the hardships they had Encountered, that no Arguments could remove these prejudices, or Facilitate the Recruiting Service."[68]

Governor Dinwiddie's analysis of the recruiting situation was much less precise and betrayed a marked insensitivity to the plight of a small but militarily significant portion of the population. In Dinwiddie's view, the colony's recruiting shortfalls resulted from a "Lethargick Supineness" of such proportions that he doubted "if any Thing can be done to bring the wrong-headed People in this Part of the World to a proper Understand'g of their pres't Danger."[69] The governor's evaluation was not wholly inaccurate: most Virginians during the winter of 1754–55 believed that the French "threat" was no threat at all. What Dinwiddie failed to realize, however, was that although poor Virginians did not feel themselves endangered by the French, they did fear and resent the draft law that authorized their impressment into the provincials. Even less did the governor anticipate their defiance of that law. Like many powerful men, Dinwiddie often was unmindful of the anxieties of those beneath him. Rather than seeking to "sell" the war by mobilizing emotions and public opinion, the governor merely assumed that the riffraff would meekly do their "duty"; that is, that they would do whatever their "betters" told them to do. He was all the more surprised, then, when those who had been made the recruiters' lawful prey refused to cooperate in their own victimization. Indeed, enforcement of the assembly's "vagrant act" produced full-fledged draft riots in at least two important Virginia towns.

The first disturbance occurred in Petersburg in November. On that occasion "the Com[mo]n People" forcibly "prev[en]t[ed] . . . [the] enlisting," and in the process "some of the Mobb" assaulted a regimental recruiting officer. This violent outburst of antidraft sentiment caught Dinwiddie by surprise, the more so because local authorities did not restrain the "Rioters . . . [that] so much abused Mr. McNeill and the others." Fredericksburg was the scene of a similar commotion a few weeks later. During that row the town fathers not only countenanced the "Mobish" behavior of the people but even "encourage[d] their Insolence in the breach of the Peace and Prejudice to his M[ajest]y's Service." Believing that anti-impressment attitudes along with the Rappahannock would make it "impossible to keep them [the conscripts] in good Order," the governor in December ordered that the new levies be marched "immediately" for the backcountry.[70]

Historians have passed over these dramatic instances of crowd activity with little or no comment.[71] It is a curious omission, particularly when similar confrontations between Amercian colonists and British press gangs have been accorded so much attention. One recent study asserts that conflict between the British army and American civilians over such issues as impressment was an important source of revolutionary attitudes traditionally associated with the years after 1763.[72] Whatever the merits of that argument, the draft riots in Petersburg and Fredericksburg at least remind us that there was more than one dimension to civil-military conflict during the 1750s. Civil-military discord pitted Americans against each other as well as against the representatives of the Crown.

The Petersburg and Fredericksburg riots also suggest that civil-military conflict did not always spring from a developing American concern for individual rights. The defense of liberty against arbitrary power is a favorite theme for those who study the often strained relations between Americans and British military commanders. By way of contrast, however, the disturbances in Virginia turned less on a solicitude for liberty than on a careful regard for personal interest. Dinwiddie touched on the real cause of the riots in a letter written to provincial recruiting officers in mid-January 1755. "I have sent £30 to C[ap]t[ain] Mercer, to pay their [the drafted vagrants] trifling Debts," the governor advised, taking care to add, "but w[he]n You come into a Town You sh[oul]d send the Drum with a Serjeant to desire . . . that no Body trust them, or they will not be paid."[73] When it is recalled that local magistrates had connived in the violent proceedings at Petersburg and Fredericksburg, the real meaning of those words becomes clear: the riots had been inspired by angry creditors whose only interest in the drafted vagabonds was that they were being dragged off to a distant frontier before paying their debts. As prosperous members of the community and quite possibly creditors themselves, the magistrates also took a dim view of a draft law that enabled debtors to avoid their legal obligations.

## FIRST ENCOUNTER WITH BRITISH REGULARS

By spring the internal dissension produced by the colony's mobilization program had given way to angry squabbling between Virginians, and the British army sent out to salvage the defeats of 1754. Accompanied by one thousand of the king's troops and a sizable train of artillery, General Braddock had reached Virginia in mid-February 1755 and established his headquarters in Alexandria soon after. Preparations were promptly begun for a march to the Ohio, a march that Virginians believed could end only in British victory.

Braddock initially had praised Dinwiddie for "the zeal which he has shown . . . for the good of the service."[74] His esteem proved fleeting. A variety of supply and manpower problems soon arose, which delayed the start of the campaign and caused Braddock to revise his opinion of the governor. By May the general was complaining about "the folly of Mr. Dinwiddie and the roguery of the [Virginia] assembly."[75] From Braddock's point of view, there was reason enough for complaint. Dinwiddie had amassed sufficient provisions for the 1755 campaign, but a number of other crucial needs remained unsatisfied. Wagons, horses, forage, Indian auxiliaries, and acceptable recruits were especially difficult to obtain. After lingering in Alexandria for nearly two months, Braddock got his army in motion only after Benjamin Franklin wheedled a contribution of 150 wagons from Pennsylvania farmers. The general later described Franklin's assistance as "almost the only instance of capacity and honesty that I have seen in all these provinces."[76] Although Braddock reserved most of his contempt for civilian politicians, Virginians in uniform were also the objects of his scorn.

The approximatley 800 men Dinwiddie had gathered by February initially were divided among the colony's ten independent provincial companies.[77] The following month Braddock reorganized about 450 of the Virginians into one light horse troop, two companies of carpenters, and six companies of "foot rangers."[78] The remaining Virginia troops were integrated with Braddock's two regiments of regulars. Only "picked men" who represented the "best" of Dinwiddie's recruits were selected for duty with the regulars, but old-soldier Braddock was decidedly unimpressed with the "best" that Virginia had to offer. Shortly after disembarking at Hampton, Braddock characterized the provincials as "very indifferent Men" and described their officers as "very little better."[79] These sentiments were echoed by Robert Orme, the general's principal aide-de-camp. In Orme's opinion the Virginia companies were "languid, spiritless, and unsoldierlike in appearance, which considered with the lowness and ignorance of most of their officers, gave little hope of their future good behavior."[80]

The disparagement of provincial officers by Braddock and members of his staff had been foreshadowed the previous November by a royal order subordinating provincial officers to men of equivalent rank who possessed regular commissions.[81] At that time it was further decreed that all provincial field-grade officers "were reduced to the status of junior captains" on those occasions when provincials were joined with regular forces.[82] Since it already had been established that they possessed second-class commissions, the provincial officers in Braddock's camp needed no further reminder of their inferior status. The general's obvious disdain for their soldierly qualities was, therefore, all the more strongly resented. Years later the contemptuous attitude of Braddock and his entourage still rankled in the memories of Virginia officers. In August 1757, while serving with a detachment of regulars under more congenial circumstances, Captian George Mercer noted, "We are looked upon in quite another Light by all the British Officers than we were by Gen[eral] Braddock and Mr. Orme."[83]

However much provincial officers may have felt themselves abused by their redcoated colleagues, service with the regulars was, quite literally, a much more painful experience for many enlisted men. Late in 1754, Parliament extended the provisions of the British Mutiny Act to the king's troops on duty in North America. At that time it also decreed that provincial troops would be subject to British military law whenever they served alongside regular forces.[84] Under such circumstances provincial soldiers were liable to the same harsh punishments that were routinely meted out to British enlisted men in the eighteenth century.

Braddock's reputation as a brutal martinet has been exaggerated, but he and his officers did enforce a stern discipline over those in the ranks.[85] Sentences of one thousand lashes were imposed even for such commonplace offenses as drunkenness, theft, and gambling. On 30 March 1755, a general court-martial sentenced Private James Anderson of the 48th Regiment to one thousand lashes with "a Cat of Nine Tails."[86] Another general court ordered that Private John Nugent of the 44th Regiment, found guilty of theft, was "to receive One Thousand Lashes and be drum'd out of the Regt. with a halter about his Neck." The standard punishment for drunkenness was "Two Hundred Lashes without a Court Martial." Gamblers received similar treatment: three hundred lashes were summarily imposed on both the gamesters and on "all Standers by or lookers on." In the case of the more serious crime of desertion, Braddock announced that "any Soldier who shall Desert tho he Return Again shall be Hanged without Mercy."[87]

As products of a society in which almost half the inhabitants were slaves and the lash a familiar means of social control, Virginians were hardly shocked by the sight of one set of men inflicting harsh physical punishment on other men. Nevertheless, the pain and humiliation that were routinely inflicted on soldiers in the British army contrasted sharply with the mild punishments prescribed by the provincial military codes then in force. The Militia Act of 1738 and the Invasions and Insurrections Act of 1748 provided the basis for military justice in the Old Dominion at the time of Braddock's march. The only physical penalty mentioned in either law was the punishment known as "tying neck and heels." Although an extremely painful and potentially fatal punishment if applied for a long period, men subjected to this torment for behaving "refractorily or mutinously" during militia musters could be so trussed for only five minutes. The resulting discomfort was considered so mild that this chastisement was reserved exclusively for first offenders. Repeated acts of defiance were punished by fining and short jail sentences.[88]

The brutal treatment of British enlisted men made a significant impression on provincial officers who were unaccustomed to the workings of such a ferocious system of military justice. More importantly, exposure to British practices during the campaign of 1755 informed the way order and discipline were later maintained in the Virginia Regiment. By 1756 provinical officers were reasoning that since their own troops, like those in the king's regular regiments, consisted largely of "worthless vagrants" (as one Virginia clergyman styled them in June of that year), fierce punishments were an equally appropriate means for intimidating both. There was also a kind of psychological imperative at work. Treating enlisted men with the nonchalant cruelty displayed by their British counterparts would make provincial officers appear more like regulars, a guise that would help bolster the shaky self-image that had been fostered by their service under Braddock. Perhaps that explains the apparent gusto with which Lieutenant Colonel Adam Stephen reported on the fate of two would-be deserters in July 1756: "We . . . have wheal'd them," Washington's second-in-command recorded, "till the Spectators shed tears for them."[89]

Imposition of a sterner discipline among the provincials found favor with colonial politicians during the panicky days that followed Braddock's defeat. In October 1755 the Virginia assembly made provincial soldiers subject to penalties that differed in no significant way from those exacted of enlisted men in the British army. The following month Washington informed Lieutenant Colonel Stephen that "We now have it in our Power to enforce obedience; . . . the Men being subject to death, as in [British] Military Laws." Executions and "whipping stoutly" thereafter became regular features of provincial camp life.

The resemblance between the punishments meted out in the Virginia Regiment and those employed in regular British regiments is dramatically evident in the penalties imposed on wayward provincials during a two-month period in 1757. Between May and July, fourteen provincial soldiers received the death penalty for desertion. (How many of those convicted of a capital offense were actually executed is unknown.) Almost 7000 lashes were allocated among a dozen others who had been found guilty of less serious offenses. The mildest lash conviction consisted of 250 stripes awarded to a corporal who had broken into a woman's home in Winchester and demanded a "part of her bed." Assuming that the remaining lash sentences were actually imposed and evenly distributed among the remaining eleven transgressors, the lash average for mid-1757 in the Virginia Regiment (approximately 613) was not much below the 1757 lash average in the British Army (731).[90]

In fact, Braddock's defeat performed a double service as far as the bruised egos of provincial officers were concerned. On the one hand, by fostering the imposition of harsh discipline it enabled amateurs like George Washington to pattern themselves more fully after men whose behavior, as far as Americans were concerned, set the standard of professional officership. On the other hand, by revealing the British army at its worst, the debacle on the Monongahela had the simultaneous effect of making the provincials look like reasonably good soldiers when compared with the discredited regulars in whom so much confidence had been placed.[91]

Ironically, expectations of victory were never higher than on the very day of Braddock's "Unhappy Action." Before adjourning the assembly on 9 July, Governor Dinwiddie expressed his "great Hopes, before this, that General Braddock is in Possession of the Fort on the Ohio, that the French took from us last Summer."[92] Even while the governor was speaking, French and Indian marksmen were cutting Braddock's army to pieces.

### IGNOMINIOUS RETREAT

Early morning, 9 July 1755: led by Lieutenant Colonel Thomas Gage, the advance guard of about four hundred men had splashed across the Monongahela at dawn. There, just a few miles from Fort Duquesne, it had been feared that the French might have laid an ambush. But the crossing was unopposed, and by early afternoon the last of Braddock's men had scaled the steep bank on the far side of the river. At that moment, according to one officer, the troops "hugg'd themselves with joy at our Good Luck in having surmounted our greatest Difficultys, & too hastily Concluded the Enemy never wou'd dare to Oppose us."[93]

By most accounts Braddock had taken pains to protect his army from surprise attack from the moment it had left Fort Cumberland some six weeks earlier. Then, at the very end of their 110-mile march through a rugged wilderness, the British made a fatal mistake. Overly confident, they lost that sense of alertness that soldiers need in an enemy's country and failed to secure a ravine that paralleled their left flank and a nearby hilltop that dominated their right. At that very moment they collided with a French and Indian force sent out from Fort Duquesne to intercept them. The men in Gage's vanguard formed a skirmish line, fired a volley, and gave ground. After a moment's hesitation, the enemy, who themselves were surprised by this sudden encounter, took shelter in the trees and rushed along both flanks of the British column. The French secured the hill on Braddock's right and the ravine on his left. In the meantime, as Gage withdrew, he fell back upon a large detachment that Braddock had ordered up at the first sounds of battle. Confusion turned into panic as the hidden enemy poured heavy and effective fire into the packed and milling British ranks. When the slaughter ended more than three hours later, two-thirds of Braddock's 1,459-man force were either dead, wounded, or missing. Finally, about sundown, the remnants of Braddock's army fled back across the Monongahela, taking with them their mortally wounded leader.[94]

The survivors of the battle continued their headlong retreat until they reached Christopher Gist's plantation, forty-three miles east of the battlefield. Braddock died of his wounds two days later, and the command passed to Colonel Thomas Dunbar. "[N]otwithstanding their was not one Indian or french man in persute," Dunbar foolishly complied with the dying general's final instructions, destroyed his provisions and military stores, and withdrew in indecorous haste to Fort Cumberland. One witness to these panicky proceedings later claimed that the "confusion, hurry, and conflagration attending all this cannot be described, but . . . it affected every body who had the least sense of . . . honour."[95]

Dunbar's ignominious retreat did more to dishonor British arms in the eyes of the people of Virginia than had the calamitous Battle of the Monongahela.[96] Dinwiddie argued frantically but to no avail that with twelve hundred regulars, an ample stockpile of supplies at Fort Cumberland, and several months of good weather remaining, Dunbar should at least establish an advanced post astride the road that Braddock had opened between Fort Cumberland and Fort Duquesne.[97] Dunbar chose instead to quit Virginia entirely and marched for Philadelphia, where he put his army into winter quarters in the middle of August.

The task of guarding the long and thoroughly exposed Virginia frontier became the responsibililty of the surviving handful of Virginia provincials, a single independent company of regulars from South Carolina, and several hundred wounded and diseased British soldiers whom Dunbar had left behind.[98] Large-scale desertion further thinned the ranks of Virginia's defenders as many among that motley band, "thinking the Colo[nel] had left them [behind] to be destroy'd by the Enemy," abandoned their frontier posts for safer places of residence in the more settled regions of the colony. Stunned and angered that Dunbar had left the Old Dominion open to her enemies, Dinwiddie personally condemned the British colonel for his "monstrous" conduct and declared that words could not describe the "Dissatisfact[io]n, Discontent and Clamours of all ranks of People here on . . . [being left] so much expos'd."[99]

The consequences of Braddock's defeat and Dunbar's precipitate flight were felt almost immediately on the Virginia frontier. Before July was out, Indian raiding parties had killed at least thirty-five people in the backcountry, a foretaste of the slaughter that occurred with dreadful regularity during the late summer and fall of 1755. By August the Virginia frontier was being "daily ravaged by savages, . . . who . . . captivate and butcher our out-settlers, and have drove great numbers of them into the thicker inhabited parts." A few weeeks later an officer in the Virginia Regiment on his way up to Winchester claimed that "it was with difficulty he passd [sic] the [Blue] Ridge for the Crowds of People who were flying, as if every moment was death."[100]

## UNANTICIPATED DIFFICULTIES

So ended the campaign of 1755. When it began, the people of Virginia were arrogantly confident of success. Braddock's expedition was looked upon as a kind of parade through the enemy's country, a grand march toward assured victory. Better yet, Virginians believed that for them the victory would come cheap. The conclusion was not unreasonable. The march on Fort Duquesne would, after all, disrupt only the lives of men the colony was well rid of, the less than a thousand ne'er-do-wells who had been drafted into the provincials. And although a war tax had been imposed on the more respectable citizens, the levy was a light one because the spring session of the assembly had voted only ten thousand pounds for defense.[101] Further mollifying the taxpayers was expectation that, since Virginia was "possessed of every [military] advantage," there would be no further requirement for funds "for the protection of his majesty's subjects, against the insults and encroachments of the French." Indeed, as Virginians viewed the situation between the fall of 1754 and Braddock's defeat the following summer, their fundamental military problem was not posed by the French at all. It rather consisted of getting the British to intervene in an obscure and still limited conflict.[102]

In the end, British intervention made Virginia's military difficulties much worse. The surprise defeat of Braddock's "well appointed army" emboldened the colony's enemies and left the Old Dominion facing its first significant military crisis in generations. "An hundred years of peace and liberty in such a world as this, is a very unusual thing," declared the Reverend Samuel Davies in August 1755, "and yet our country [that is, Virginia] has been the happy spot that has been distinguished with such . . . blessings with little or no interruption." Davies then offered the needless reminder that "now the scene is changed."[103]

The change in Virginia's military situation was all the more alarming because it had been so rapid. What had begun as a rather offhand land grab suddenly and without warning had become a full-scale war to defend and hold territory well within the colony's established borders. The feelings of vulnerability and fear that swept through the province during the summer of 1755 were further magnified by the fact that Virginians had to grapple with the problem of defense by themselves. After Braddock's defeat, the main tide of battle shifted northward, and there it remained until the end of the war. Except for an occasional recruiting party, the regulars never returned to the Old Dominion. This development, generally unnoticed by historians, meant that Virginians were left in almost total control of their military fortunes, free by necessity to work out the problems of providing for their own defense. The methods that they chose determined the fate of the colony for the next seven years.

## · 4 ·

# "BAD NEWS FROM EVERY QUARTER"
## *The Colony Besieged*

*There is nothing here but bad news from every quarter.*
WILLIAM ALLASON, 1757

For Virginians the nature of the French and Indian War changed dramatically in 1755–56. The most obvious changes were of the military variety. The main theater of the war moved northward and remained there until the fall of Canada in 1760. After 1755 the Old Dominion was no longer the scene of dramatic preparations for large-scale offensives. During the remainder of the Great War for Empire, with the exception of the Forbes campaign against Fort Duquesne in 1758, Virginia played no part in the major battles that determined the political future of North America. Instead of an offensive war, a war of movement conducted beyond her borders, Virginia's war became a savage and frustrating struggle characterized by a defensive strategy and small-unit actions, generally initiated by the enemy and fought on the enemy's terms. It was, for the most part, a war of petty but bloody ambushes and unconnected skirmishes—war at its most basic level: man hunting man.

Although the Old Dominion became a strategic backwater as far as the mother country was concerned, the Virginians themselves never saw it that way. They did not because in the wake of Braddock's defeat and Dunbar's withdrawal, the war for them had become an exclusively Virginian affair. Down to 1758 the British provided the colony with neither manpower nor money; indeed, they provided precious little even in the way of advice. When it came to formulating military policy and to the much more difficult business of actually raising, supplying, and employing an army, Virginians were left largely on their own. The colony's military problems were compounded still further by the fact that the Old Dominion was no longer waging a war to gain territory; rather, it was fighting to defend the settled portions of Virginia itself. The events of 1755 also had dashed initial expectations that the war would be a short one. By the late summer of that year, Virginians found themselves faced by the necessity of planning for a war of longer duration. This, in turn, meant that the Old Dominion's military policy had to be more systematic; the ad hoc approaches of 1754 and 1755 would no longer suffice. As raiding parties of hostile Indians descended on isolated frontier settlements, the war became not only protracted but increasingly expensive in terms of human life as well. Down to the capture of Fort Duquesne in 1758, the horrors of war visited the Virginia backcountry in ways that the military planners of 1754 had never imagined.

## A SERIOUS MILITARY PROBLEM

During the last half of 1755 and well into the following year, provincial authorities in Williamsburg were subjected to a continual stream of pleas for protection from the embattled residents of the Virginia frontier. A few weeks after Braddock's defeat, a resident of Louisa County reported, "Our frontiers are daily ravaged by savages, and worse than savages, papists, who . . . captivate and butcher our out-settlers and have drove great numbers of them into the thicker inhabited parts." Two months later in the vicinity of Winchester, a contingent of recruits for the Virginia Regiment spent one night "encamped . . . at a poor man's house . . . the people driven off by the Indians." The former residents had fled their farm so quickly that the soldiers "found plenty of corn, oats, & stock of all kinds left behind." Such scenes of desolation were a common sight during the autumn of 1755. Midway through that season, it was estimated that "above 100" frontier residents had been killed or "carried off" by "flying Parties of Fr[ench] and Ind[ian]s." Terror and death continued to stalk the western settlements for months thereafter. Writing almost a year after the annihilation of Braddock's army, the Reverend James Maury noted that "ever since the tragical event last July, on the banks of the Monongahela, our frontiers have been ravaged and dispeopled, great quantities of the stock of the back inhabitants driven off by the French and their Indians to Duquesne." Maury estimated that Virginia's "frontiers have been contracted in many places 150 miles, and still are drawing nearer to the centre." The "horrid devastations" of the French and their Indian allies forced Virginia leaders to recognize their colony's military predicament.[1] For provincial politicans it was no longer a question of organizing a scratch force of volunteers to guard a construction detail or of forming a few companies of auxiliaries to tag along with the regulars. By the midsummer of 1755, there was need for an armed force that could constantly patrol the frontier and serve as a nucleus for provincial defense.

Ironically enough, for all of her military difficulties, between 1755 and 1758 Virginia's existence was never really in jeopardy. There was mayhem aplenty, but aside from an occasional scare that penetrated the more settled regions, it was confined to the frontier. In short, during this period Virginia was confronted by a serious military problem but not by a true military emergency. The distinction is significant. Because Virginia's existence was never seriously threatened in an ultimate sense, the military effectiveness of her armed forces became less important than developing a military system that was politically appealing. Indeed, for the first time since Bacon's Rebellion eighty years before, the question of military policy became the most significant issue in Virginia's political life. Stated most simply, that question was this: How was Virginia to fight an unpopular war without disturbing the established political and social order?

Virginia political leaders responded to this question by opting for continued reliance on the Virginia Regiment as the mainstay of provincial defense; that is, despite the colony's recent and unexpected military reverses, the leadership in Williamsburg pursued a military policy based only on a partial and selective mobilization of the colony's manpower. They did so because they sensed that the dangers of wholesale mobilization exceeded the benefit of greater security such mobilization could bring to the troubled backcountry.

## THE PERILS OF MOBILIZATION

As far as Virginia's leading men were concerned, there were several hazards involved with full-scale mobilization. Chief among them was the fear that calling up the militia en masse for any protracted period would weaken the colony's internal security. One of the militia's primary functions was to guard against slave insurrections. Accordingly, it was feared that posting large numbers of militiamen on the distant frontier would leave the more populated areas relatively defenseless. It is true, of course, that Virginia's slave population has been relatively docile throughout the first half of the eighteenth century. As late as 1751 it was asserted that Virginians felt no particular "uneasiness" from the growing number of blacks among them.[2] But that kind of confidence did not survive Braddock's defeat. For at least a year thereafter, white Virginians expressed fears that their slaves would take advantage of the military crisis and rise in revolt.

"The Villany of the Negroes on any Emergency of Gov't is w't I always fear'd," Governor Dinwiddie recorded after receiving news in mid-July 1755 that a slave conspiracy was brewing in Lancaster County. Nothing came of it, but white Virginians remained uneasy about the possibility of future "combinations of the Negro Slaves, who have been very audacious on the Defeat on the Ohio." Lingering apprehensions were evident months later when Dinwiddie advised the War Office, "We dare not venture to part with any of our White Men any distance, as we must have a watchful eye over our Negro Slaves, who are upwards of 100,000." The following August Dinwiddie claimed that the colony's sizable slave population "alarms our People much and [they] are aff'd of bad consequences if the Militia are order'd to any great Distance from the pres't Settlem'ts."[3] In a word, the ever-present possibility of insurrection compounded Virginia's military problems and reduced the number of men available for duty on the frontier.

In addition to bolstering Virginia's internal security, keeping the militia at home also made sound economic sense. Shuffling large numbers of militiamen between their farms and the frontier would seriously disrupt the colony's agricultural cycle. By the late spring of 1756, the same period during which much of the colony's future military policy was being determined, Virginians had acquired just enough experience with such disruptions to appreciate the potentially ruinous consequences. Earlier that year, after receiving reports that a large French and Indian invasion force was descending on the backcountry, Governor Dinwiddie had called out the militia of ten Piedmont counties. The reports proved false, but not before scores of yeomen farmers had lost weeks of planting time while marching from their fields to the colony's western rim. One observer pointed out that since this episode had come "at a season of the year when men could least be spared from home, . . . [their] long continuence on duty must have blasted all expectations of a crop in those who had no slaves to labor for them."[4] The plight of small farmers called onto active service in 1756 was exacerbated by the skimpy harvest of 1755. That year's grain crop had been ruined by an early drought so serious that for a time it "threatened famine." Late arriving rains allayed fears about "the sustenance of our people," but "vast numbers" of livestock perished for want of food.[5] Like fears of a slave insurrection, the realities of an agricultural economy provided a strong argument for leaving the militia alone. But in a real sense both economics and worries about internal security were merely parts of a larger political problem, a problem that lay at the heart of the political and social order of eighteenth-century Virginia.

The basic problem of government in eighteenth-century Virginia turned on the relationship between the upper and "middling" classes. The "better sort" led the political nation; men of the "middling sort" made up the largest portion of that nation and of the militia that was its armed expression. Thus, anything that seriously menaced the political consensus between the elite and the "middling sort" also threatened the most important bond in colonial society. Full-scale mobilization, which would of necessity require a wholesale call-up of the militia, carried with it precisely that threat.

"Our Militia consists of at least 36,000 Men," Governor Dinwiddie wrote early in 1756, adding, "but [they are] chiefly Free-holders, who insist on y'r Privileges not to enlist or serve but on imminent danger."[6] There was the rub: imminent danger. Even during the darkest days of 1755–56, the Indians marauding along her rimlands never seriously jeopardized Virginia's actual existence, and only rarely did they as much as threaten the colony's more populated parts. Even on the frontier where lives were very much imperiled by the Indians' hit-and-run attacks, enemy raids were more episodic than continuous. In short, by any politically acceptable definition, the danger confronting Virginia was not sufficiently "imminent" to justify calling out the militia for protracted service, even in the frontier counties. Repudiation at the polls was the most likely fate for colonial politicians who disrupted the lives of large numbers of property-owning (and thereby enfranchised) militiamen. And there were other possibilities. Because the militia was chiefly composed of politically conscious men with guns in their hands, those possibilities included the almost unthinkable prospect of violent opposition, the chance that a call for a general mobilization would be met by widespread and violent resistance. That kind of defiance, in turn, would have ominous implications for the political consensus between the "better sort" and the "middling" majority. Nor was the prospect of armed defiance altogether inconceivable. Time had softened its edges, but the shadow of Nathaniel Bacon still loomed in the memory of the provincial elite.

## FORMULATING A MILITARY POLICY

Of Bacon's Rebellion the historian Thomas J. Wertenbaker has written that "the fury and horror of that outburst were not forgotten, and never again did governors or aristocracy drive to despair the commons of the colony."[7]

When it comes to collective remembrance of great public catastrophes, eighty years is not a long time, and leading Virginians seemed conscious of Bacon's Rebellion as they went about the business of formulating a military policy in the fall of 1755 and spring of 1756. A few generations earlier the ill-considered policies of a largely autonomous colonial elite had brought about civil war in Virginia. Or-

der was soon restored, but the power of local oligarchs was not.
Authority passed instead into the hands of a succession of English
soldier-administrators who dominated provincial affairs for the next
fifty years.[8] After the 1720s the provincial elite recovered much of its
accustomed sway, but it had done so with the knowledge that its
position could be compromised, perhaps permanently, if another uprising resulted in the reimposition of direct imperial control. Fearing
popular turbulence even more than they feared the incursions of hostile Indians, leading Virginians in 1755–56 were determined not to
let a military problem become a political crisis.

Unfortunately, simply leaving the militia alone was no guarantee
that a political crisis could be avoided. The experience of Bacon's
Rebellion once again was instructive, for it showed that a feeble military policy could produce political consequences every bit as unset-
tling as the domestic uproar that full-scale mobilization might create.
After all, it was the inability or unwillingness of the Berkeley regime
to protect Virginia frontiersmen from Indian raiders that had pro-
voked the followers of Nathaniel Bacon in the first place. Thus, provincial leaders also placed their political futures at risk if they
embraced a military policy so flabby that it drove another generation
of frontiersmen to desperate measures.

The situation was complex and called for a military policy that,
while not unduly ruffling the lives of militiamen, would demonstrate
that provincial authorities were serious about protecting the backcountry. Apparently with little argument, Virginia leaders agreed
that the way out of this dilemma was continued reliance on the
Virginia Regiment as the backbone of colonial defense. In broad out-
line it was the approach the Old Dominion had followed since 1754,
a politically sensitive—even politically timid—policy that placed the
colony's military burdens on provincial troops who were outside of
the regular militia system. But with this difference: the provincial
army planned by colonial leaders during the late summer and fall of
1755 was to be larger, better trained, and more disciplined than either
the expeditionary force of 1754 or the independent companies of provincials that had marched with Braddock. As envisaged by its design-
ers, the reconstituted Virginia Regiment would be an almost wholly
remodeled armed force capable of fighting a protracted war. Between
August 1755 and June 1756, provincial authorities turned to the task
of creating such an establishment.

## SOCIAL COMPOSITION OF THE REGIMENT

On 5 August 1755 the Virginia assembly met in emergency session
and began fashioning plans for preserving their "Fellow Subjects from

the base and horrid Butcheries" of the French and Indians.[9] In their August meeting and in subsequent sessions held late in October and during the following spring, colonial politicians laid the groundwork for the military policy Virginia would pursue down to 1758. That policy was composed of three major elements: a defensive strategy anchored around a line of forts running the length of the colony's western border; employment of the Virginia Regiment as a frontier constabulary with the mission of manning those outposts and policing the backcountry; and wooing such Indians as might side with Virginia in the war against the French. Unfortunately, this tripartite strategy soon proved unequal to the military challenges at hand.

In his opening address to the hastily assembled lawmakers, Governor Dinwiddie minced no words in discussing the Old Dominion's military plight: he told members of the assembly that only their "most vigorous and speedy Efforts" could save the colony from "the most fatal Consequences." The governor then appealed for men, money, a new militia act, and a law patterned after "the Measures taken by our Brethren of New-England . . . by giving a Reward for the taking or scalping [of] our Indian Enemies."[10] The assembly quickly approved Dinwiddie's requests. It allocated forty thousand pounds for the protection of the frontiers, authorized a provincial army of twelve hundred men, enacted a measure subjecting provincial soldiers to more stringent discipline, and replaced the militia act of 1738 with a new statute that established more demanding training standards. Colonial lawmakers also supported the governor's call for a scalp bounty. Citing the "shocking inhumanities" committed by their "malicious and detestable enemies" as justification, the legislators approved a law whose not very discriminating terms promised a reward of ten pounds for the scalp of "every male Indian enemy, above the age of twenty years."[11] By way of contrast, Virginia lawmakers acted with much more circumspection when it came to the politically charged question of raising men for provincial military service.

At the time of the assembly's August meeting, the Old Dominion's active duty forces consisted of three ranger companies and the remnants of the independent companies of provincials that had accompanied Braddock to the Monongahela. The lawmakers hoped that voluntary enlistments would increase the number of provincial troops to their newly authorized strength of twelve hundred men. If, however, a sufficient number of volunteers had not come forward within ninety days, the assembly authorized a draft of unmarried men for provincial service.[12] Members of the militia thus were confronted by the possibility of involuntary military service for the first time since the struggle for the Ohio country had begun. But even as they allowed that possibility, colonial leaders simultaneously affirmed the socially selective military policy that had characterized Virginia's approach to war making since 1754.

The operation of a socially selective military policy was most evident in the fact that drafted militiamen could avoid active service by providing a substitute or by paying a ten-pound fine. These alternatives were clearly discriminatory. In a day when ten pounds might represent a poor man's entire annual income, the assembly's price for escaping conscription was impossibly high for most Virginians of humble estate. The legal alternative for someone unwilling to fight and too poor to buy his way out of serving was steeper still: an indefinite sojourn in jail, "there to remain until he shall agree to enter into said service."[13]

Evidence from a variety of sources makes clear that, as a group, those who fell afoul of the draft law of August 1755—and of subsequent draft acts passed in 1756 and 1757—were men who also fell outside the mainstream of Virginia society. In June 1756, for example, the Reverend James Maury claimed that during the preceding twelve months, "no person of any property, family or worth" had enlisted in the Virginia Regiment. A few months later the lieutenant of Fairfax County conducted a draft lottery at which the "single Men present" who could not afford the ten-pound exemption fee were "drawn up in a Line" for the balloting. County Lieutenant William Fairfax bluntly characterized "most" members of that unhappy remnant as "almost naked and in a poor condition." Data contained in regimental "size rolls," one of the few sets of official records that have survived from the Virginia Regiment itself, tend to corroborate the observations made by "respectable" men like Parson Maury and Colonel Fairfax.[14]

Twenty-two size rolls, so-called because they recorded the height—or "size"—of individual soldiers, have been preserved in the unpublished papers of George Washington. Fifteen rolls were compiled during the summer of 1756; the remaining seven were drawn up during the latter half of 1757. Although no size rolls were found for earlier or later periods in the Virginia Regiment's eight-year history, those that were located cover most of the two-and-one-half-year period when provincial authorities relied on a manpower policy of compulsion. Insofar as their contents reveal the character of Virginia's provincial army during 1756 and 1757, information contained in the rolls indicates the regiment's social composition during the last half of 1755 as well.

The size rolls contained four additional categories of information about provincial soldiers: their age, place of birth, place of residence, and occupation. All told, these data are suggestive of the kinds of men who fought for the Old Dominion during the most difficult days of the French and Indian War.

About two-thirds of the Virginia Regiment's troop strength in 1756 and 1757 consisted of men in their twenties. Teenagers accounted for about 11 percent of the provincial forces in 1756 and approximately 8 percent in 1757. (The youngest member of the regiment in 1756 was a thirteen-year-old drummer; two fifteen-year-olds shared that distinction in 1757). Men in their thirties constituted the second largest age grouping: 14 percent of the soldiers fell into that bracket in 1756 and about 18 percent in 1757. In 1756 the percentage of soldiers who were upwards of forty years of age was less than 10 percent. (In 1756 the oldest soldier was a man of sixty; in 1757 two 58-year-old privates qualified for that designation.) The size of the two older age groups increased in 1757 when men in their forties and fifties constituted 12 percent of the colony's long-term soldiers. The trend for this two-year period shows a steady increase in the percentage of older men serving in the provincial forces. In 1757 almost one-third of Virginia's provincial soldiers were men above the age of thirty, and close to one-half of that group were in their forties. By military standards historically, a sizable minority of the provincials were old men (see table 1).

The size rolls also show that whatever their age, most of Virginia's long-term soldiers were not natives of the Old Dominion. Well over 50 percent of the men serving in 1756–1757 had been born elsewhere; most (over 47 percent in each year) were European immigrants (see table 2).

Although the tidewater region was the section that was threatened least, the size rolls indicate that most of Virginia's provincial troops were drawn from that area. The percentage of frontier residents serving in the provincials more than doubled in 1757, but between them, the tidewater and piedmont counties still provided almost 75 percent of the old Dominion's long-term soldiers. Relative population densities help account for the large number of men from the eastern counties. So does the fact that the colony's landless poor were concentrated in the older and more settled areas—men who could not seek exemption from extended military service on the basis of being freeholders. According to one estimate, almost 40 percent of the white men living in the tidewater region between 1763 and 1788 owned no land, and

Table 1

Age Distribution of Virginia Provincial Troops

1756–1757

| Age Group | 1756[a] | 1757[b] |
|---|---|---|
| 15–19 | 69 | 50 |
| 20–29 | 406 | 360 |
| 30–39 | 83 | 108 |
| 40–49 | 47 | 57 |
| 50–60 | 4 | 11 |
| No Age Given | 10 | 8 |
| Total | 619 | 594 |

[a] Calculated from: Size Rolls for the Virginia Regiment in George Washington Papers (MSS, Library of Congress, Washington, D.C.), ser. 4, 4: items 424–35, 452, 461, 463.

[b] Calculated from: Size Rolls for the Virginia Regiment in Washington Papers MSS, ser. 4, 4: items 103–4, 710, 731, 756, 759, 778.

perhaps a third of the white males in the piedmont fell into the same category (see table 3).[15]

Most of Virginia's landless, and hence militarily available, men were artisans and poor farmers, the "Tradesmen and inferior Planters" that Governor Dinwiddie described as constituting the "lowest Class of our People."[16] The Virginia Regiment contained a high proportion of men drawn from both occupational groupings. In 1756 approximately 35 percent of the provincial troops described themselves as "farmers" or "planters."[17] A far larger number, almost 60 percent, claimed they had pursued non-farming occupations in civilian life. Close to 70 percent of the latter group identified themselves as artisans of one kind or another, but there was a sprinkling of men drawn from other occupations; among them were seamen, laborers, barbers, hunters, and schoolmasters. Over 5 percent listed no occupation at all. The distribution of occupations was substantially the same in 1757, although the proportion of provincial soldiers who claimed no civilian occupation increased to almost 9 percent (see table 4).

Among other things, the size rolls reveal that the Old Dominion's long-term soldiers were not ordinary Virginians. In a colony where the great majority of freemen were yeoman farmers, most provincial soldiers had followed some other form of employment. Moreover, in

Table 2
Place of Birth of Virginia Provincial Troops
1756–1757

| Place of Birth[a] | 1756[b] | 1757[c] |
|---|---|---|
| Virginia | 244 | 260 |
| Other British Colonies | | |
|   Maryland | 50 | 22 |
|   Pennsylvania | 12 | 8 |
|   New York | | 3 |
|   New Jersey | 2 | 6 |
|   North Carolina | 1 | 1 |
|   "New England" | 2 | 3 |
| British Isles | | |
|   England | 125 | 125 |
|   Ireland | 97 | 104 |
|   Scotland | 55 | 40 |
|   Wales | 3 | 3 |
| Continental States | | |
|   Germany | 7 | 6 |
|   Holland | 6 | 3 |
|   France | 1 | 1 |
|   Switzerland | 1 | |
|   Sweden | 1 | |
| None Given | 12 | 9 |
| | 619 | 594 |

[a] In 1756 the approximate percentage of enlisted men born in Virginia was 39.4%; outside Virginia 58.6% (10.8% in other colonies and 47.8% in Europe). In 1757 the approximate percentage of enlisted men born in Virginia was 43.7%; outside Virginia 54.7% (7.2% in other colonies and 47.5% in Europe).

[b] Calculated from: Size Rolls for the Virginia Regiment in Washington Papers MSS, ser. 4, 4: items 424–35, 452, 461, 463.

[c] Calculated from: Size Rolls for the Virginia Regiment in Washington Papers MSS, ser. 4, 4: items 103–4, 710, 731, 756, 759, 778.

Table 3
Place of Residence of Virginia Provincial Troops
1756–1757

| Place of Residence | 1756[a] | | 1757[b] | |
|---|---|---|---|---|
| | Number of Men | Approximate Percentage of the Regt. | Number of Men | Approximate Percentage of the Regt. |
| Tidewater Counties of Virginia[c] | 232 | 38% | 234 | 40% |
| Piedmont Counties of Virginia[d] | 182 | 30% | 186 | 31% |
| Frontier Counties of Virginia[e] | 58 | 9% | 139 | 23% |
| Other Colonies | 98 | 17% | 29 | 5% |
| Not Given | 39 | 6% | 6 | 1% |
| Total | 619 | 100% | 594 | 100% |

[a] Calculated from: Size Rolls for the Virginia Regiment in Washington Papers MSS, ser. 4, 4: items 424–35, 452, 461, 463.
[b] Calculated from: Size Rolls for the Virginia Regiment in Washington Papers MSS, ser. 4, 4: items 103–4, 710, 731, 756, 759, 778.
[c] The Virginia tidewater region (the region east of the Fall Line) includes the following counties: Henrico, Charles City, James City, York, Warwick, Isle of Wright, Elizabeth City, Northampton, Nansemond, Norfolk, Northumberland, Gloucester, Lancaster, Surry, Westmoreland, New Kent, Richmond, Accomack, Middlesex, King and Queen, Princess Anne, Essex, King William, Prince George, King George, Caroline, Southampton, and Sussex.
[d] In the 1750s the Virginia piedmont region (the region generally running west of the Fall Line and east of the crest of the Blue Ridge Mountains) included the following counties: Stafford, Hanover, Spotsylvania, Goochland, Prince William, Brunswick, Orange, Amelia, Fairfax, Louisa, Albemarle, Lunenburg, Culpeper, Cumberland, Chesterfield, Dinwiddie, Prince Edward, Loudoun, Fauquier, Amherst, Buckingham.
[e] The counties of Hampshire, Frederick, Augusta, Bedford, and Halifax comprised the Virginia frontier during the period of the French and Indian War. (Bedford and Halifax fall within the piedmont region geographically, but in the 1750s they constituted the edge of white settlement in Virginia's southwestern corner.)

Table 4
Civilian Occupations of Virginia Provincial Troops
1756–1757

| Occupation | 1756[a] | | 1757[b] | |
|---|---|---|---|---|
| | Number | Approximate Percentage of Enlisted Men | Number | Approximate Percentage of Enlisted Men |
| *Planters* (including men listed as "farmers") | 219 | 35% | 253 | 42% |
| *Artisans* | | | | |
| Armorer | | | 1 | |
| Baker | 6 | | 3 | |
| Blacksmith | 8 | | 8 | |
| Bookbinder | 1 | | 2 | |
| Brazier | 3 | | | |
| Brewer | | | 2 | |
| Bricklayer | 12 | | 7 | |
| Butcher | 2 | | 9 | |
| Carpenter | 56 | | 49 | |
| Carver | 1 | | | |
| Chandler | | | 1 | |
| Clothier | 3 | | 1 | |
| Coachmaker | | | 1 | |
| Collier | 2 | | 1 | |
| Cooper | 3 | | 6 | |
| Coppersmith | 1 | | | |
| Cordwainer | 1 | | 1 | |
| Distiller | 6 | | | |
| Ditcher | 1 | | 1 | |
| Dyer | | | 1 | |
| Fuller | | | 1 | |
| Furrier | 2 | | | |
| Glassmaker | | | 2 | |
| Glover | | | 1 | |
| Hatter | 5 | | 1 | |

Table 4 (continued)

| Occupation | 1756[a] | | 1757[b] | |
| --- | --- | --- | --- | --- |
| | Number | Approximate Percentage of Enlisted Men | Number | Approximate Percentage of Enlisted Men |
| Joiner | 7 | | 7 | |
| Malster | 1 | | | |
| Mason | 3 | | 2 | |
| Miller | 1 | | | |
| Miner | 5 | | 2 | |
| Peuterer | | | 1 | |
| Plasterer | | | 1 | |
| Saddler | 2 | | 7 | |
| Sailmaker | 1 | | | |
| Sawyer | 16 | | 13 | |
| Shearman | 1 | | | |
| Shoemaker | 33 | | 42 | |
| Silktwister | | | 1 | |
| Silversmith | | | 1 | |
| Skinner | | | 1 | |
| Staymaker | | | 1 | |
| Stone Raiser | | | 1 | |
| Tailor | 36 | | 27 | |
| Tanner | 1 | | 2 | |
| Tinker | 1 | | 1 | |
| Tobacco Spinner | | | 1 | |
| Turner | 1 | | 3 | |
| Upholsterer | | | 1 | |
| Vintner | | | 1 | |
| Weaver | 19 | | 11 | |
| | 241 | 39% | 234 | 40% |
| *Personal Services* | | | | |
| Barber | 6 | | 3 | |
| Coachman | 1 | | 1 | |
| Doctor | | | 1 | |

Table 4 (continued)

| Occupation | 1756[a] | | 1757[b] | |
|---|---|---|---|---|
| | Number | Approximate Percentage of Enlisted Men | Number | Approximate Percentage of Enlisted Men |
| Gardener | 7 | | 3 | |
| Surgeon | 2 | | | |
| Valet | 1 | | | |
| Waiting Man | 1 | | | |
| | 18 | 3.0% | 8 | 1.3% |
| *Mercantile Activities* | | | | |
| Clerk | 1 | | | |
| Indian Trader | | | 2 | |
| Ironmonger | | | 1 | |
| Jobber | | | 1 | |
| Merchant | 4 | | 1 | |
| | 5 | .08% | 5 | .08% |
| *Laborer* | 17 | 2.7% | 15 | 2.5% |
| *Seaman* | 33 | 5.3% | 19 | 3.1% |
| *Soldier* | 17 | 2.7% | | |
| *Other* | | | | |
| Drummer | 4 | | | |
| Gentleman | 4 | | | |
| Hunter | 16 | | | |
| Piper | | | 2 | |
| Schoolmaster | 6 | | 5 | |
| Wagoner | 1 | | | |
| Waterman | 1 | | 2 | |
| | 32 | 5.2% | 9 | 1.5% |
| *No Occupation Given* | 35 | 5.6% | 52 | 8.7% |

[a] Calculated from: Size Rolls for the Virginia Regiment in Washington Papers MSS, ser. 4, 4: items 424–35, 452, 461, 463.

[b] Calculated from: Size Rolls for the Virginia Regiment in Washington Papers MSS, ser. 4, 4: items 103–4, 710, 731, 756,. 759, 778.

their peacetime occupations as carpenters, sawyers, shoemakers, tailors, coachmen, watermen, and day laborers, they generally had ranked below farmers in the colony's social and economic order.[18] Whether some of them had any history of employment at all is an open question. In addition, close to a quarter of Virginia's provincial troops had been recruited directly from other colonies—they were men who did not actually "live" in Virginia. About 7 percent of the provincials claimed no place of residence whatsoever.

A few other scattered references in the size rolls also are suggestive of the kinds of men who served in the Virginia Regiment. Thus one recruit, a twenty-three-year-old "planter" from Surry County, was identified as a "Negro." A size roll drawn up in July 1756 listed a soldier of mixed Negro-Indian ancestry, and two mulattoes were mentioned in another size roll recorded eighteen months later. Since blacks customarily were employed as soldiers only as a last resort, their presence in the provincials suggests true desperation on the part of recruiting officers. And given the racial attitudes of the day, it seems likely that an army that included blacks would have scant appeal to any but the most hopeless whites. The pattern that emerges is this: Virginia's provincial army was heavily seeded with men from the lower end of the socioeconomic scale, a large number of them were immigrants, some had never lived in Virginia, and a few were Negro-Indian half bloods, mulattoes, or blacks[19]

The size rolls—and more conventional literary materials—contain additional bits of evidence about the social character of Virginia's provincial troops. Consider, for example, what these various sources disclose about recruits and recruiting during the years immediately following Braddock's defeat.

### SCRAPING UP RECRUITS

George Washington's major responsibility during the fall of 1755 was to furnish a measure of security along the Virginia frontier, an arduous task made harder still by the difficulties he faced in recruiting men for his army. During the late summer Washington had established recruit depots at Winchester, Alexandria, and Fredericksburg. Recruiting teams, which had been scouring the countryside since August, were ordered "to repair to [those] Place[s] of Rendezvouz [sic]" by the first of October with the men they had collected. Washington accompanied that directive with a set of "General Instructions for Recruiting Officers of the Virginia Regiment," which established specific recruiting quotas and standards. "[B]y beat of Drum or otherwise," each captain, lieutenant, and ensign was expected to raise, respectively, thirty, eighteen or twelve men. Field-grade officers were given the task of receiving the recruits as they arrived in camp. According to Washington's "Instructions," all white men between the ages of sixteen and fifty were deemed eligible for provincial service providing they stood at least five feet four inches tall. Shorter men were acceptable if they were "well made, strong, and active." The only men categorically disqualified for provincial service were those with "old Sores upon their legs, or [those] who are subject to Fits."[20]

Although field-grade officers could discharge recruits who failed to meet these not very imposing standards, surviving evidence suggests that, whatever their physical condition, few volunteers were turned away. A report submitted by Captain Peter Hog in the spring of 1756 is instructive. Five weeks of recruiting had netted exactly two men. Hog remarked that one was subject to daily "Convulsive Fitts" and described the other as "a Soft sort of Fellow & dull of hearing." Such decrepit specimens were not untypical. "Lame in his Left leg... one Eye out... bushy Head with a most horrid aspect." So runs the litany of physical disabilities afflicting individual soldiers as recorded in various size rolls from the summer of 1756 and fall of 1757. Sprinkled among the provincials—quite literally—were the lame, the halt, and the near blind.[21]

There was also at least a sprinkling of men on the wrong side of the law. For example, after being condemned for horse stealing in 1756, one John Catlet was promised a reprieve if he would enlist in the provincials. Significantly, while the death sentence was stayed, Catlet did not receive a formal pardon—a procedure presumably intended to insure his good behavior and continued presence in the ranks.[22]

At this time Virginia law made no mention of enlistment bounties, although some officers apparently used the two pistole bonus (about £1 17s. in the English money of the day) as a de facto bounty for luring volunteers. The only official inducement for volunteering in the fall of 1755 was a grant of certain immunities from civil action. Thus, soldiers in the Virginia Regiment were exempted from the payment of all public, county, and parish levies, and from all civil processes for debts of less than ten pounds. The assembly further decreed that no man in provincial service could be jailed for debts of less than ten pounds.[23]

The hopes of colonial lawmakers that these immunities would inspire enlistments among men of little means were quickly confounded. Reports from various sources during the late fall and early winter of 1755 made it clear that volunteers were in extremely short supply. Washington complained in late November that "several" officers had "been out 6 weeks, and two months without getting a man." The following month Captain Robert Stewart, one of the Virginia Regiment's most energetic young officers, acknowledged that efforts to complete his light horse troop were "in a great measure ineffectual." A despairing Stewart noted that "with all my Industry, . . . [I] have only been able to produce five Recruits in near two weeks." So disappointing was the response in Virginia that before year's end Stewart and other provincial officers extended their search of recruits into the backcountry of Maryland and Pennsylvania.[24]

The misguided zeal of one volunteer recruiter exacerbated the problems experienced by Stewart and his fellow officers. During the closing months of 1755 an aspiring provinical ensign named Denis McCarty was busily obtaining recruits "by forcibly taking, confining, and torturing those, who would not voluntarily enlist." Needless to say, such practices placed other recruiters and the regiment itself in ill repute. In ordering McCarty to abandon his high-pressure methods, Washington observed that "it is next to an impossibility to get a man where you have been." Captain Christopher Gist was another energetic recruiter. Gist's glib (and deceitful) promises to Marylanders prompted strong complaints during the summer of 1757 from Governor Horatio Sharpe. In reply, Washington excused Gist's artful techniques as "nothing more than one of those little subterfuges which, from the disagreeable nature of the Recruiting service, has, at some junctures been considered necessary." Provinical officers also resorted to the traditional gambit of plying potential recruits with strong drink. In October 1755 Captain Charles Lewis reported marching from Fredericksburg with eighty newly enlisted men, "most of them drunk."[25]

Drunk or sober, a sizable number of the men scraped up between 1755 and 1758 were less than choice specimens. In the spring of 1757 Washington asserted that "many" of those who had served in 1756 "were unfit for any sort of Duty." Recruiting problems continued the following year. At the height of the 1757 campaign season the provincial rank and file numbered 699 men (meaning the regiment stood at about 55 percent of its authorized strength), and a large proportion of those troops were, in Washington's phrase, "dastardly draughts." All considered, perhaps the best explanation for the persistently dismal recruiting situation had been offered in the fall of 1755 by a resident of Richmond County. In a letter to Washington written in late September of that year, William Brokenbrough explained that his son had been unable to meet the quota of eighteen recruits expected of lieutenants because "the People. . . are deaf to reason[,] persuasion & Even intrest [sic]. . . in short they are determined not to go till they are force'd."[26]

### Harsh Discipline and a Defensive Posture

The inequities of the military program devised by Virginia politicians in the late summer of 1755 did not end with a conscription policy directed at the poor. In addition, and unlike their more affluent neighbors who remained at home in the militia, the penurious farmers and artisans in the provincials also lived under a stringent code of military discipline based upon the rope and the lash. As revised by the August session of the assembly, "an Act for making provision against Invasions and Insurrections" authorized corporal punishment "not extending to life or members" for provincial soldiers found guilty of mutiny, desertion, or sedition. The penalty for lesser offenses such as simple disobedience, drunkenness, and "prophane swearing" was either twenty lashes or a five-pound fine. For cases of treason, a crime that went unmentioned in the original (1748) statute on invasions and insurrections, the death penalty was specified. Interestingly enough, while the military pressures of the moment caused a doubling of the fines that could be imposed on militiamen for disobedience and failure to muster, the assembly made no attempt to back up these comparatively mild sanctions with the threat of sterner punishment. Indeed, in the same August session that approved lashing and hanging for delinquent provincials, the assembly eliminated all vestiges of corporal punishment from the militia statute.[27]

The question of military discipline arose anew when the assembly reconvened in October. In his opening remarks, Governor Dinwiddie claimed that the disciplinary provisions of both the newly revised statute on invasions and insurrections and the new militia act were "very deficient." The governor did not detail his complaints about the militia law, nor did he offer recommendations for its improvement. In the case of the Virginia Regiment, Dinwiddie was more specific and urged that the provincials be placed under "the Military Law, as the Troops in His Majesty's immediate Pay are subjected to." In short, the governor called for imposing the harsh provisions of the British Mutiny Act on the colony's provincial army. Dinwiddie warned that lacking such a stern instrument, provincial commanders would be unable to keep their men "under strict Discipline, and in a proper Submission to their Officers." In making that request, Dinwiddie was echoing the demands of George Washington for a more stringent code of military discipline. Washington, who had been recommissioned as commander of the Virginia Regiment in mid-August, was threatening to resign that post by early October "unless the Assembly will Enact a Law, to enforce the Military Law in all its Parts." Washington insisted that the "confined...punishments" authorized by the assembly in August were the direct cause of "growing Insolence" among the enlisted men and "Indolence and Inactivity" among the provincial officers.[28]

Colonial lawmakers ignored the governor's call for imposing more rigid standards on the militia. But the provincials were another matter. Perhaps fearing that Washington—at twenty-three the colony's most seasoned military leader—would carry out his threatened resignation, the assembly passed a sweeping revision of the invasions and insurrections statute enacted only three months before. The list of crimes that could cost a provincial soldier his life was quadrupled. In addition to treason, the death penalty was authorized for mutiny, desertion, insubordination, and striking a superior officer. These amendments erased any real difference between Virginia's martial law and the British Mutiny Act in terms of the penalties that could be exacted under each. For example, simply refusing an order could cost a man one thousand lashes—or even his life—in either the regulars or the Virginia provincials. Aside from a few procedural limitations, after October 1755 provincial commmanders enjoyed the same generous discretion in matters of discipline that custom and law bestowed on their counterparts in the regular British army.[29]

Turning to another piece of legislation enacted during the August session, Dinwiddie requested that the rewards promised for enemy scalps be extended to "our friendly Indians." The members obliged the governor by agreeing that the bounty system would be of even greater value if it was thus "enlarged." The only other war-related matter considered during the short October session concerned the appointment of representatives to an intercolonial congress that had been called by Governor William Shirley of Massachusetts, at that time serving simultaneously as commander in chief of British forces in North America. The assembly voted against participating on the grounds that Virginia had "already raised as many Men as this Country is able to support."[30]

Virginia's defense needs again dominated the proceedings when the assembly of 1756–1758 convened for the first time on 25 March 1756. The members' fixation on that issue, coupled with the difficulty of raising men for service within the colony (less than six hundred recruits had been collected by late February), caused them to reject

Governor Dinwiddie's call for reinforcing a planned Anglo-American expedition against the French stronghold at Crown Point, New York. "[T]he very Extensive Frontiers we have to protect." the burgesses concluded, made any commitment of Virginia's slender military resources against so distant a target "very imprudent."[31]

The preoccupation of Virginians with the threat along their own borders was matched by a growing concern about the level of security within them. As noted earlier, the military reverses of 1755 had heightened fears of a possible slave uprising. With their frontiers besieged by hostile Frenchmen and Indians, the anxieties of white Virginians over the presence of potential enemies within their own midst were further inflamed by the unexpected arrival of some eleven hundred Acadian refugees early in 1756. In Virginia no less than in Nova Scotia, these unhappy people were viewed as a public menace. So intense was popular concern about the "Neutral French Roman Catholics" that the newly seated assembly, as its first order of business, "chearfully" [sic] approved a proposal for shipping the Acadians off to England at public expense. The governor signed a deportation bill a few days later, well aware, as he later informed the War Office, the he "c'd not shun consent'g thereto from the gen'l Clamour of the whole Co'try."[32]

Legislation aimed at safeguarding the home front did not stop with the expulsion of the Acadians. Virginia's military reverses evidently had aroused suspicion about the loyalty of Roman Catholics in general. At the same time it called for banishing the Acadians, the assembly passed a law disarming all resident "Papists and reputed Papists" who refused to take the oaths of allegiance and supremacy prescribed by Parliament."[33]

Although quick to impose sanctions on suspect minorities, Virginia lawmakers moved slowly on the much more politically sensitive matter of military preparedness. For weeks during the early spring of 1756, Washington had been calling for a near doubling of the Virginia Regiment's authorized strength of twelve hundred men. His requests were accompanied by warnings that "unless a stop is put to the depredations of the Indians, the Blue Ridge will soon become our frontier." Contrasting Washington's alarms with the burgesses' measured approach, Willaim Fairfax, a member of the governor's council, chided the lower house for moving so "slowly notwithstanding on hearing of the many and repeated Invasions of our Enemies."[34]

Fairfax's criticism was overdrawn. A few days earlier the burgesses had, in fact, supported Washington's call for more troops by voting a 25-percent increase in the size of the colony's provincial army. That a new defense bill had been almost a month in preparation was less the result of the members' lethargy than it was of their concern about meeting Virginia's military needs on a more carefully reasoned basis. The military legislation approved by the burgesses had two main features: the aforementioned increase in the Virginia Regiment's authorized troop strength and, reflecting the colony's new defensive stance, a grant of two thousand pounds for constructing a network of forts along the western frontier. The puny blockhouses, stockades, and fortified cabins that were hastily thrown up in the backcountry symbolized, as did nothing else, Virginia's transformation from aggressor to besieged victim during the years between 1756 and 1758.[35]

"An Act . . . for the better protection of the Frontiers" directed that the "chain of forts" should stretch from Great Cape Capon in Hampshire County to the south fork of the Mayo River in Halifax County. Determination of the number and location of the forts was left up to Dinwiddie, who in turn delegated that task to Washington together with the responsibility for designing and constructing the outposts. A total of eighty-one forts—some described as mere "log pens"—eventually were built along a line that zigzagged almost four hundred miles from north to south.[36]

Virginia's motley cordon of frontier forts soon proved a most uncertain barrier; nevertheless, these outposts played an important part in the Old Dominion's military policy down to the capture of Fort Duquesne in December 1758. Isolated and unimposing, the forts at least furnished a neighborhood refuge where frontier families might gather with some greater hope of survival than would have been the case had they remained in their own lonely cabins. In September 1757 Washington calculated that during the Indian raids of the preceeding spring, about half the residents of Frederick County had "sought refuge" in the few forts that were locally available. What this suggests is that the real significance of the forts was psychological rather than military and lay in their importance as symbols of the provincial government's concern for the welfare and security of frontier residents. In that sense they served a vital function, for to the extent that the scattered backcountry outposts prevented wholesale depopulation of the frontier, they shielded the Virginia Regiment from a logistical predicament of potentially disastrous proportions. That was the problem Washington had in mind when in October 1757 he wrote of the "incredible number of Inhabitants that has fled" from the fertile bottomlands along the Shenandoah River. Weighing the consequences of a continuing large-scale exodus, Washington warned, "where are we to get the supplies of provisions for our armies, when this valley which is the only support of them, is entirely

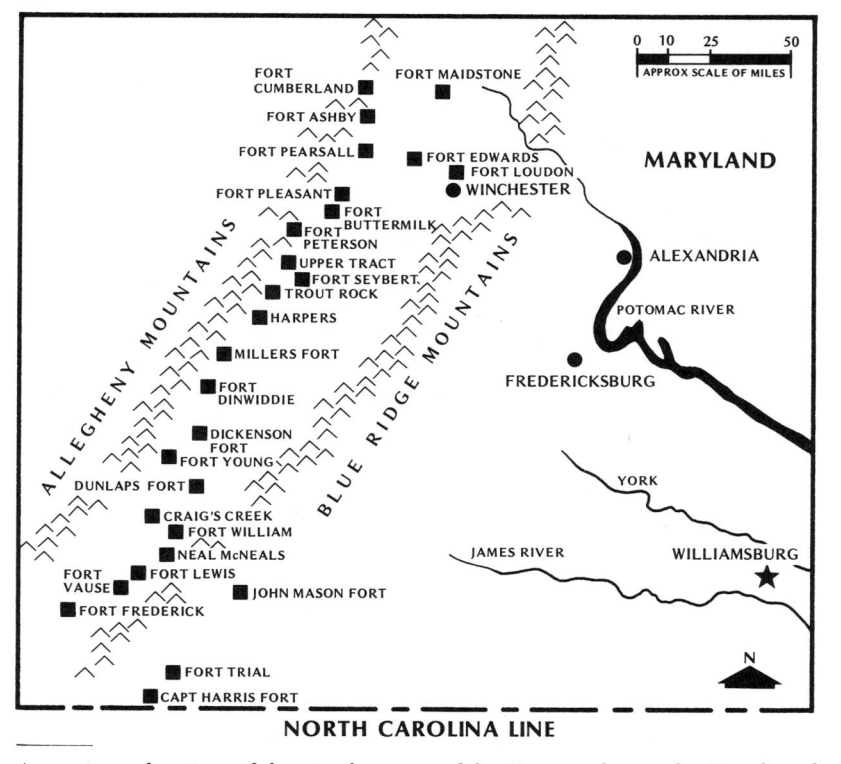

Approximate locations of frontier forts erected by Virginia during the French and Indian War; based on a sketch in F. B. Kegley's *Virginia Frontier* (Southwest Virginia Historical Society, 1938).

abandoned to an Enemy, which by that means will be entirely possessed of every thing necessary to pursue their conquest."[37] In addition to footing the bill for a line of outposts on Virginian soil, the assembly also funded construction of a fort in the Cherokee country adjoining the colony's southwestern border. This project had its origins during the winter of 1755–56 when Dinwiddie dispatched two of his councilors, Peter Randolph and William Byrd III, on a diplomatic mission to the Cherokee and Catawba Indians. The Cherokee in particular had long enjoyed generally cordial commercial relations with their English neighbors in Virginia and the Carolinas, relations Dinwiddie hoped would serve as the basis for an anti-French military alliance between that powerful tribe and the Old Dominion.[38]

Randolph and Byrd took with them six hundred fifty pounds worth of gifts as a sign of Virginia's "sincere F'dship." Encouraged by this "Present," during the winter of 1756 some 130 Cherokee warriors joined an expedition led by Major Andrew Lewis of the Virginia Regiment against the Shawnee towns on the Ohio River. Known as the Sandy Creek Expedition, this foray against the Old Dominion's major Indian adversary confirmed both the importance of Indian allies and the apparent wisdom of pursuing a defensive strategy. The month-long (February-March 1756) campaign was a total disaster. Undertaken at Dinwiddie's insistence, the late winter march through the wild country at the back of Virginia was fatally flawed by hurried planning and slipshod organization. The most serious error lay in issuing only fifteen days' worth of rations for a three hundred-mile trek that might easily require a month or more to complete. These provisions soon ran short, and the mixed force of 340 provincials, frontiersmen, and Cherokee auxiliaries went on half-rations while still miles from its objective. A few days thereafter one soldier made the following entry in his journal: "We were now in a pitiable condition, our men looking on [one] another with Tears in the Eyes and lamenting that they had ever Enter'd in to a Soldier's life." The expedition was abandoned less than a month after it had begun when all but a handful of the starving and near frozen troops refused to continue.[39]

So ended the last significant offensive operation that Virginia would attempt down to its participation in the Forbes expedition of 1758. In the aftermath of this misadventure, even the customarily aggressive Washington acknowledged that "a defensive plan" had become Virginia's only alternative since another fiasco such as Sandy Creek "would entirely lose us the interest of every Indian." And in the wake of the Sandy Creek debacle, the value of Indian allies seemed more obvious than ever. Indeed, the only group who emerged from the expedition with credit were the Cherokees, whose "conduct" put "to shame [their] cursing, swearing. . .and complaining" white comrades in arms. Washington was so impressed by reports of the Cherokees' performance that he advised Governor Dinwiddie of "their [the Cherokees'] power to be of infinite use to us; and without Indians, we shall never be able to cope with those cruel foes to our country." Dinwiddie agreed and, hoping that as many as a thousand Cherokee and Catawba warriors might participate in the spring campaign, shortly wrote of his "great Dependence on these Indians for the Protection of our Frontiers." For their own part, before placing a larger number of men at Virginia's disposal, the Cherokees insisted that Dinwiddie build them a fort where their braves might secure their dependents before taking the warpath. With the assembly's support, the governor sent a sixty-man construction party into the Cherokee country in April for the purpose of erecting a stronghold at the junction of the Tellico and Little Tennessee rivers.[40]

The initiatives taken in the winter of 1755 and the following spring marked the beginning of a rocky three-year alliance between Virginia and the tribes on her southern flank, an alliance in which each side exploited the other for its own calculated purposes. By the middle of the eighteenth century, both the Catawbas and the Cherokees had grown increasingly dependent on English trade. Their reluctance to jeopardize its continuance inclined them toward accepting employment as allies. Their proxim‸ y to Virginia also made it politically dangerous for the tribes to spurn Williamsburg's diplomatic overtures. In short, as far as the Cherokees and Catawbas were concerned, political realities—as well as a desire for English trade goods—argued on behalf of aiding their white neighbors. But if the Indians realized that they could not refuse their services entirely, neither did they seek wholesale involvement in Virginia's military embroilments. In that important regard, their wishes diverged considerably from the desires of provincial authorities in the Old Dominion.

Imbued with the idea that "Indians are the best match for Indians," in the spring of 1756 and for several springs thereafter, Virginians simultaneously cheered and deluded themselves with exaggerated hopes about the willingness of the Cherokees and Catawbas to do their fighting for them. Accordingly, the cost of a fort was deemed a small price for the services of people who were considered "no less subtle than the enemy, as bold, and equally well versed in all the barbarian arts and stratagems of war." Besides their value as formidable fighters, it was further assumed that the services of the Cherokees and Catawbas would come cheap since, as one Virginian put it, they would "certainly require less costly clothing, and perhaps be satisfied with lower wages than soldiers are commonly allowed."[41] The clear expectation was that the Southern tribes would be amiable and inexpensive pawns that the Old Dominion could manipulate for its own strategic purposes.

In the spring of 1756, few Virginians would have admitted the possibility that the Cherokees and Catawbas might be equally adept at manipulating them. Yet by summer's end there were already indications that the Indians were skillful practitioners of the politics of self-interest. An early instance of such opportunism occurred when the Cherokees contributed only 150 warriors to the spring campaign. When compared with Dinwiddie's anticipation of a war party almost ten times as large, and especially with the one thousand pounds Virginia spent on building the Cherokees a fort, the modest contingent furnished by them was almost insultingly small. Nor was this paltry number generally much exceeded during subsequent campaigns, a situation that made Dinwiddie's successor, Francis Fauquier, "very apt to believe [that] the service they [the Southern tribes] do is very inadequate to the expense they occasion." The real problem, as Washington noted in the summer of 1758, was that the Cherokees and Catawbas were "too sensible of their high Importance to us, to render us any very acceptable Service." At the same time, the few warriors that these tribes did send forth moved among white clients who, in spite of their dependence upon them, never overcame a tendency to, as one English visitor put it, "esteem and use the Indians as dogs." It was an old story that reached a predictable conclusion in 1759 when Virginia's alliance with the Cherokees dissolved in mutual recrimination, bloodshed, and war.[42]

Virginia's overture to its Indian neighbors had important long-run consequences for both sides that neither foresaw. The same may be said of that portion of the military bill enacted in April 1756 that dealt with raising men for the newly expanded Virginia Regiment. Following the precedents laid down in the military bills of May and August 1755, the April act authorized conscription if an insufficient number of volunteers came forward. But in several other important respects, the new law differed considerably from previous legislation on military manpower. For example, unlike the earlier measures, which merely had made conscription a gubernatorial option, the April act mandated a draft in every county (excepting frontier Hampshire) that could not meet a standard enlistment quota equivalent to 5 percent of the men enrolled in the county militia. In frank recognition that recourse to conscription was likely and the "many persons" would wish "to avoid being drafted as soldiers," the members of the assembly also worked at closing loopholes that had existed in the earlier statutes. One favorite ploy of draft evaders was to declare themselves overseers of slaves, an occupational group traditionally exempt from militia duty and hence free also from the workings of the draft law. The assembly attacked this practice by excusing from the draft only men who had been "bona fide an overseer" on or before 25 March 1755.[43]

The actual process by which men were conscripted also became more elaborate and more stern in the spring of 1756. Heretofore, the selection of conscripts had been made directly by county militia officers, the law requiring only that those they impressed be men "who have not wives or children." On its face, the selective service system introduced in 1756 seemed a more equitable alternative: rather than relying on the personal caprice of local militia officials, drafting henceforth would be conducted by means of a public lottery.[44]

Under the provisions of the April act, county lieutenants were given twenty days to compile a list of "all the able-bodied single men" resident within their respective jurisdictions. Ten days later, all those deemed eligible for military service were required to gather at county court houses throughout the colony, whereupon they would be given the opportunity of volunteering for the provincials. If fewer than 5 percent of those eligible volunteered, a draft lottery would be held on the spot to make up the difference. Conducted by the county lieutenant and senior militia officers, the workings of the lottery were impartial enough down to the time ballots actually were drawn. At that point a special provision in the law made it possible for those who had picked a marked ballot to escape service if they could "immediately pay down...the sum of ten pounds." Thus, while it established a more tightly organized draft system, a system from which men were less likely to escape because of administrative sloppiness or oversight, the statute enacted in April 1756 resembled the earlier laws in one important respect: it worked to the disadvantage of the poorest members of the community. Indeed, in that regard the new act was even more oppressive, as it insisted that the ten-pound exemption fee be paid "immediately." In the past draftees had been allowed a grace period of nine months for paying that fine.[45]

The coercive pattern established in 1755 and refined in 1756 was continued and made even more strenuous in 1757. In April of that year, "an Act for the better protection of this colony" ordered justices of the peace and senior militia officers in each county (and officials holding comparable positions in the city of Williamsburg and borough of Norfolk) "to meet...and examine and enquire into the occupation and employment of the several inhabitants of the said counties, city and borough between the age of eighteen and fifty years." After studying county muster rolls and conducting such "other methods of inquiry" as they thought "expedient," these draft boards compiled rosters listing able-bodied men who were unemployed, husbands who had abandoned their wives and children, former conscripts who had deserted from the Virginia Regiment before their term of service had expired, and "all other idle, vagrant or dissolute Persons" who were living within a board's area of jurisdiction. In case this winnowing process turned up an insufficient number of candidates, draft boards could supplement this list with the names of such other propertyless and voteless men "as they shall think proper." County sheriffs and militia officers were allowed ten days for round-ing up the ne'er-do-wells and misfits. After these unfortunates had been collected, the board convened a second time and selected for the provincials a group of men whose number equalled one-fortieth of the local county militia force.[46]

The most striking feature of the act of 1757 was its authors' reliance on naked force as a means of tightening the provincial draft net. The act required those identified by the authorities as likely candidates for the Virginia Regiment to post a fifty-pound bond guaranteeing their appearance before their draft board on conscription day. Men who could not meet that stiff requirement, and few potential conscripts could have commanded such resources, were thrown into jail until the draft board passed on their fate. In addition, as they scoured the countryside for undesirables, county sheriffs were empowered "to raise any number of men sufficient to apprehend" a likely recruit. Fines of five pounds could be summarily imposed on anyone who refused a sheriff's request for help. Moreover, the new law prescribed the death penalty for any prospective soldier who resisted conscription by force of arms. Execution also awaited those who made common cause with violent resisters. On the other hand, anyone apprehending a draft evader was promised a ten-pound reward.[47] These stringent provisions did more than distinguish the statute of 1757 from earlier draft legislation; their punitive nature and severity suggest that colonial authorities had encountered substantial opposition to coerced military service.

## COOPERATION IN WILLIAMSBURG

During the two years following Braddock's defeat, Virginia leaders had wrestled almost continuously with the problem of defense and the challenges of fielding a sizable provincial army. This task was the major item of business before the colonial legislature in all save one of its five meetings between the summers of 1755 and 1757. In the main, the assembly had supported Governor Dinwiddie's proposals for strengthening Virginia's military posture. Unenthusiastic at best about the war in 1754 and early 1755, the burgesses came to recognize the need for defensive measures and gave them the kind of support they had been unwilling to extend the offensive designs of Dinwiddie and Braddock. In the spring of 1755, for example, the lower house had insisted that a military appropriation in excess of £10,000 would bankrupt the colony; three months later, inspired by the threat of large-scale Indian raids, the burgesses voted £40,000 for military purposes in a single session. By the middle of 1757, the assembly had approved a total of £158,000 for the colony's defense, most of it for defraying the expenses of recruiting, equipping, paying, and otherwise maintaining the Virginia Regiment.[48] The ironies of the situation were rich: a colonial legislature that formerly had refused anything more than minimal financial assistance had become willing to pass comparatively massive defense bills and support an upward spiraling military budget; a colonial governor who for over two years had sustained an unpopular military policy against the French only with great difficulty, suddenly enjoyed the support of a majority of provincial lawmakers because that policy had collapsed.

While colonial leaders were cooperating on matters of policy in Williamsburg, in distant Winchester George Washington had been doing his best to create a provincial army worthy of the name. Month after month he had pushed his recruiting officers, wrestled with intractable logistics problems, and fussed over the host of administrative matters that plague military commanders in all times and places.[49] More than anything else, Washington's labors had been directed at remodeling the Virginia Regiment into an effective fighting force. In person and by letter, he had conferred frequently with Governor Dinwiddie about the proper deployment of provincial units and the best locations for frontier forts.[50] Training and disciplining his army concerned him endlessly. The caliber of the provincial officer corps was a matter of special interest. As a commander, Washington believed it was his duty "when occasion requires, [to] condemn as well as applaud." He minced no words with poor performers or with those who "acted inconsistently with the character of a Gentleman, and . . . Officer." Even old friends were censured if their conduct violated Washington's concept of officership. "Remember," Washington counseled his subordinates, "that it is the actions, and not the Commission, that make the Officer and that there is more expected from him than the Title."[51] Whether they legislated in Williamsburg or commanded at Winchester, Virginia's political and military leadership had grappled long and hard with the problem of defense. Unfortunately, their exertions had not eased the plight of the western frontier.

## DESERTION AND DISARRAY ON THE FRONTIER

The Old Dominion's military situation in the fall of 1757 was desperate. Looking ahead to 1758, William Allason, the Virginia agent for a Scottish mercantile house, noted that "in the spring tiss thought there will be much blood shed." Another Virginia merchant writing at about the same time predicted that "they [the French] will in a few years be masters of this great continent." Edmund Pendleton, a member of the House of Burgesses, surveyed the colony's military affairs late in 1757 and concluded that only "God...knows when it will be better." A few months later, the Reverend James Maury, after informing a fellow parson then residing in the tidewater of a vacant pastorate on the frontier, guessed that his colleague would "think his Scalp in such Danger, that he'll deem it more eligible to run the Risque of starving here, than of being scalped there."[52] Virginia's military fortunes were indeed at low ebb.

Several factors accounted for the Old Dominion's lackluster military performance between 1755 and 1758. First, due primarily to a combination of white mismanagement and the Indians' own well-founded suspicion that when it came to bleeding and dying, the people of Virginia would have been perfectly happy to fight to the last Cherokee or Catawba, the vaunted alliance with the Southern tribes—once an important element in the Old Dominion's strategy—never fulfilled its sponsors' original expectations.

Second, and more basic still, by the middle of 1757, it was clear that the defensive strategy the colony had been following for two years was a failure. In a letter to British Colonel John Stanwix written in September of that year, Washington stated his conviction that if Virginia continued "to pursue a defensive plan, the country must be inevitably lost." The following month he warned Governor Dinwiddie and Speaker of the House of Burgesses John Robinson that "if we still adhere to our destructive, defensive schemes, there will not...be one soul living on this [west] side [of] the Blue Ridge the ensuing autumn." In Washington's opinion, "nothing but vigorous offensive measures...can save the country...from inevitable desolation."[53]

Washington's analysis was sound: Virginians had, in fact, been following a military strategy that was ill suited to the realities of their situation. Their province guarded the longest and most exposed frontier of all of Britain's North American colonies. In retrospect, it seemed a forlorn hope that a perimeter three hundred to four hundred miles long that arched across a wild and mountainous country could have been defended successfully from about eighty unimposing forts. Built on the average some twenty miles apart, the Old Dominion's "chain" of forts was more like a sieve through which Indian raiding parties passed before reforming themselves to the eastward. Moreover, effectively policing an area of that size would have required a large number of troops. By Washington's estimate, no fewer than 2,000 men could perform that mission adequately.[54] And that factor was the third major defect in the colony's military policy: the inability of Virginia leaders to find and retain a sufficient number of recruits for their provincial army. While volunteers for the Virginia Regiment were always in short supply, conscription proved no answer to the colony's manpower needs either. Between 1755 and 1757, years when provincial leaders were enacting increasingly rigorous draft laws, the regiment seldom was at more than half of its authorized strength. During the first six months of 1756, there were fewer than 600 men in provincial service. That number inched upward until by July the regimental rolls carried the names of 619 enlisted men. At that time the regiment's authorized troop strength was 1,500 men. Officers included, a regimental return for 1 January 1757 put the total number of men in provincial service at 655. In April of that year the assembly voted to raise 1,270 men for the provincials. As noted above, by mid-summer the rank and file totaled about 700, a figure that remained more or less stable through the end of the campaign season.[55]

A number of factors explain the disappointing results of the three conscription statutes enacted between the summer of 1755 and the spring of 1757. To begin with, the laws themselves were seriously flawed by the ten-pound exemption provision. The exemption fee simply proved too easy and too attractive an escape hatch for too many people. In May 1756 Governor Dinwiddie observed that "the Draughts in most of the Counties paid Fines rather than go to Winch[es]t[er] [where the headquarters of the Virginia Regiment was located]." During the first two months of its operation, the draft law of April 1756 netted only 246 men. Their number did not much increase as the summer wore on. In mid-August Dinwiddie acknowledged that "the Draughts. . .[are] much short of my expectation" and blamed the exemption fee for having "entirely defeated" the purposes of the draft statute.[56]

Loopholes in the law were only part of the problem. Some men evaded the draft by avoiding the draft lotteries—they simply went into hiding. In the spring of 1756, Colonel Landon Carter expected that he would have "to hunt the swamps" for Richmond County's eligible young men. In some other cases the failure of the draft laws was blamed on their sloppy administration by local officials.[57]

Many drafted men who lacked the means "to pay down the sum of ten pounds" chose the classic alternative of unwilling soldiers: they deserted. Some ran off almost immediately. In October 1755, refusing to let anything stand in their way, a group of eighteen newly drafted men in Fredericksburg made good their bid for freedom by breaking down the walls of the jail in which they had been placed for safe-keeping. Some drafted substitutes waited only to collect their bounty money before disappearing; other men bided their time. In the end, the result was the same: a staggering desertion rate.[58]

Although the Virginia Regiment had been plagued by desertion since its formation in 1754, the number of men fleeing the provincials skyrocketed during the period between Braddock's defeat and the winter of 1757—58. Desperately seeking some means of stemming desertion during the chaotic weeks following Braddock's defeat, the Virginia assembly at the end of August 1755 had promised pardons for all those who "return[ed] to their duty, on or before the 20th of September next." The assembly's offer was ignored for the most part. Shortly after the 20 September deadline passed, the *Virginia Gazette* announced that since "few of the Deserters have taken Advantage of the Offer made of Indemnity," the authorities had ordered a county-by-county search for the many runaway soldiers "lurking about in different Parts of the Colony."[59]

The exodus continued as the war dragged on into 1756 and 1757. So many soldiers took flight that Governor Dinwiddie eventually made mere suspicion of desertion grounds for imprisonment. In mid-July 1757, it was estimated that 25 percent of the men drafted during the preceding three months had deserted even before reaching Washington's headquarters in Winchester. By that fall men were deserting so quickly that provincial authorities had difficulty calculating the regiment's supply needs for military contractors who "naturally desire to know the Numbers they're to provide for." Indeed, things had come to such a pass by then that Dinwiddie concluded, "We must suspend recruiting for Some Time till a Method is found out to reclaim the Deserters, w'ch at present appears to me very difficult."[60]

The governor's pessimism reflected the frustration and perplexity felt by Virginia leaders generally over their inability to stem the rising tide of desertion. Since the summer of 1755, provincial authorities had relied on both the carrot and the stick as they groped for some means of controlling their restive soldiers. Emphasizing the importance of first impressions, Dinwiddie directed Washington in the spring of 1756 "to send some of the best and *most sedate* of Y'r Officers" to collect a group of conscripts at the recruit depot at Fredericksburg. (Italics mine.) A year later Washington lectured his subordinates on the need for "treating them [the conscripts] with kindness and humanity" so that they might acquire "a favorable opinion of the way of life they are entered upon." Whatever provincial officers may have felt about such strictures, these lofty sentiments made little impression on the common soldiers who still "embraced every opportunity to effect their escape."[61]

As a remedy for desertion, harsh punishment proved no more effective than had cajolery. Captured deserters customarily were flogged, sometimes severely. In the spring of 1757, for example, a provincial court-martial decreed sentences of a thousand lashes apiece for six convicted deserters and fifteen hundred lashes for four others. Five hundred lashes were ordered for one unfortunate who was merely suspected of harboring an intention to desert. Liberal use of the whipping post was accompanied by recourse to the gallows.[62]

As employed in desertion cases, the death penalty was used as much as a means of intimidating the innocent as for punishing the guilty. For example, in May 1756 a provincial court-martial condemned two men for the same crime of desertion. One soldier, an old veteran who had "behav'd formerly well," was given another chance, but his accomplice was hanged in the belief that his "suffer'g [would]. . . deter others from that growing fault [that is, desertion]." In August 1757 Washington reported hanging two deserters at his Winchester headquarters "just before the companies marched for their respective posts." He added that their execution "conveyed much terror to others; and it was for example sake, we did it."[63]

The "terror" produced by such spectacles apparently was short lived. Only a few weeks after extolling the value of exemplary punishment, Washington wrote that upon considering whether "to punish or pardon the criminals [two condemned provincial soldiers], I have resolved on the latter; since I find example of so little weight." But leniency proved no answer either. In September 1757 Washington disclosed that one runaway soldier who had been captured and "condemned to be hanged, deserted immediately upon receiving his pardon." As mentioned earlier, by that time Governor Dinwiddie was despairing of any solution to the desertion problem. "I'm sorry so many have deserted," he wrote to Washington as the fall of 1757 approached, "[n]or do I know w't to do [about it]."[64] Indeed, provincial soldiers deserted in droves regardless of what the authorities did.

Provincial soldiers deserted for a variety of reasons. Some fled because of the dangers of soldiering. The hazards of military duty on the frontier were touched on by Washington when he reported losing "near an hundred Men killed and Wounded" during 1756. That figure constituted a significant percentage (over 16 percent) of the Virginia Regiment's total strength. Washington was hardly overstating the matter when he claimed that such a casualty rate was not "inconsiderable" in "a small Regiment, dispersed over the Country. . . acting upon the Defensive."[65]

In the Virginia Regiment the conventional risks of soldiering were accompanied by other hardships that also help explain why so many provincial troops fled their posts at the earliest opportunity. The deprivation produced by an unreliable supply system doubtless contributed to the exodus. The problems of sustaining even a small eighteenth-century army operating in the wilderness began as early as 1754 and were always substantial, and, in fact, an adequate logistics system never developed during the years that followed. Shortly after reassuming command of the provincial forces in the fall of 1755, Washington complained that incompetent commissaries and slipshod administration had left "this place [Washington's headquarters at Winchester] with[ou]t Flour, and [the reception center at] Fredericksburg with[ou]t any Provisions for ye rec[rui]ts." Shortages of arms, tools, clothes, and shoes constituted additional major grievances. Thomas Lloyd, an Englishman who served as a regimental surgeon in 1756, once complained of going without food for "3 or 4 Days together[.] [A]s for Beding & Cloathing [sic]," Lloyd wrote, "I am so used to it [that is, going without such articles] now if I get a Blanket I am satisfy'd."[66] The sufferings of Lloyd and his comrades were recorded in 1756 by a Virginia satirist who depicted the typical provincial soldier as a ragamuffin

> with tattered blanket round his loins,
> Vermin spawning O'ere his skin,
> No friendly shirt to lodge them in,[67]

The uncertainties of military pay intensified the woes of provincial soldiers—and their inclination to desert. In April 1757 treasurer and Speaker of the House of Burgesses John Robinson noted that the men of the Virginia Regiment were owed six thousand pounds in back pay. Dinwiddie greeted this news by warning that the provincials "w'd not march with't their Arrears." The assembly approved the necessary pay bill, but by the end of the year, two Virginia companies on detached service in South Carolina "were So distress'd for troop money that the governor had to send down for their use his own personal bill of exchange for five hundred pounds. Morale also suffered because of the shabby treatment the colony accorded its disabled veterans. "No regular provision is established for the maimed and wounded." Washington informed a British officer in 1757, adding that the lack of guaranteed pensions for disabled soldiers was "grievously complained of" by the men in the ranks.[68]

## A FAILED POLICY

For many deserters, danger, privation, and arrears of pay constituted more than sufficient grounds for absconding. But it also seems likely that the penchant for skipping out was intensified by the alienation of individual soldiers from a system that favored men with money or connections and ensnared those who lacked such advantages. In that sense their disaffection was the very human and predictable response of unwilling soldiers who had fallen afoul of inequitable draft laws. Moreover, as men whose poverty largely excluded them from the political process in Virginia, most conscripts probably felt little social obligation toward the colony to begin with, much less an inclination to fight on its behalf. On such grounds the Virginia Regiment's high desertion rate seems quite understandable and even unremarkable.[69]

Looked at another way, however, desertion can also represent a significant act of political defiance. Seen in that light, desertion is a form of insurgency in which the deserter rejects the force of laws that, regardless of their instrinsic merit of equity, have been imposed by duly constituted authority. This is not to suggest that Virginia stood at the edge of a political revolution in the mid-1750s. At no point between 1755 and 1758 did mobs of howling deserters run amok through the streets of Williamsburg. When provincial soldiers did their running, it generally was in the direction of the nearest neighboring colony.[70] Nevertheless, if one understands desertion as an act of political, as well as military, insubordination and contrasts it with the kind of behavior customarily expected of the "inferior sort" in a traditional, deferential political order, the flight of so many provincial troops constituted an implicit challenge to the gentry-dominated government and social order of the Old Dominion. More immediately, large-scale desertion also eliminated any chance the Virginia Regiment had of fulfilling its constabulary mission along Virginia's vast frontier.

As we have seen, during the period between Braddock's defeat and the winter of 1757–58, Virginia's military policy was fixed on three objectives: the establishment of a defensive perimeter along the colony's western rim; the creation of a larger and better-trained army to secure that perimeter; and the cultivation of friendly Indian tribes in the hope that they would furnish warriors to fight the Old Dominion's battles. By the close of 1757, it was clear that this policy had failed in all respects. The Cherokees and Catawbas behaved less like pawns and more like coequal partners who, well aware of their own importance, insisted on deciding for themselves when to give or withhold their support. Meanwhile, the realities of geography, the fluid nature of Indian warfare, and a persistent shortage of military manpower had undercut Virginia's frontier-fort-based defensive strategy. Most glaring of all was the Virginia Regiment's failure to carry out

Governor Dinwiddie's assigned mission of "repell'g...the Fr. and their Ind'n Allies." Unable to attract or retain anywhere near the number of men it was authorized and vexed by "mutiny, desertion, and all other irregularities," the regiment was a travesty of what its organizers had envisaged. Instead of a legion that could "guard and defend the Co'try," Virginia's provincial army was a poorly equipped scratch force, "wrechedly [sic] helpless" in the face of its enemies.[71]

More than anything else, the failure of Virginia's military policy turned on the faulty assumption that underlay the province's selective approach to mobilization: the belief that a sufficient number of men could be forced into bearing a disproportionate share of the colony's military burdens. The governing gentry elite had take it for granted that the "inferior sort" were vulnerable and submissive men, easy marks who would do as they were told. They were wrong. The "inferior sort" stubbornly, even defiantly, resisted coerced service by a variety of means: draft evasion, desertion, and, more subtly, by half-hearted, resentful, and uncaring performance of their duty. Put another way, the most serious weakness of provincial war policy was that the "inferior sort" upon whom that policy depended refused it their support. In doing so, men who for the most part were outside the political nation of Virginia caused considerable consternation among the "better sort" who sat in the councils of colonial government. The "inferior sort" were ridiculed and despised after 1757 as they had been before, but when it came to military affairs, their "betters" also had learned to take them more seriously.

# · 5 ·

# "OUR PEOPLE ARE MUCH UNEASY"
## *Dissension and Victory*

*Our People are much uneasy at the great Charge they are at in support'g our Regim't.*

GOVERNOR ROBERT DINWIDDIE, 1757

When they devised a military policy designed to hold their enemies at bay and simultaneously preserve harmony between the "better" and "middling" sectors of provincial society, Virginia's ruling elite never seriously considered that the "lesser sort," upon whom that policy depended, might deny it their cooperation. As a result, colonial leaders were all the more shocked and confused when the "lesser sort" did precisely that. Nor did the problems of colonial leaders stop there. The inability of the gentry government to raise an army worth the name also produced strong criticism of the provincial authorities and considerable internal political turmoil.

Nobody cared much for the way things were going, but unity of opinion stopped there. During 1756 and 1757, the Virginia home front echoed to a cacophony of complaints and expressions of despair and disillusionment. Even among the gentry, few could agree on solutions to the military difficulties confronting the Old Dominion. By the beginning of 1758, a political and military crisis was at hand.

Important for its own sake, the crisis, its eventual resolution, and the subsequent course of Virginia's participation in the French and Indian War also help illuminate our understanding of the less than ordinary people who did most of the fighting—understanding not only of how they behaved, but of why they behaved in the particular ways that they did.

## INTERNAL DISSENSION

There is considerable evidence to show that Virginia's lackluster military record between 1755 and 1758 sparked substantial internal criticism and conflict. In June 1756, the Reverend James Maury, Rector of Fredericksville Parish in Louisa County, attributed the "shocking outrages perpetrated on the western settlements" to the "egregious blunders" of the provincial government. Maury's criticism was echoed by his relative planter Peter Fontaine. Writing in mid-1757, Fontaine placed the blame for Virginia's "disgraceful" military performance squarely on the colony's "managers." Although Maury and Fontaine expressed their views privately in personal letters, before the close of 1756, disharmony and dissent had become prevailing themes in public discourse as well. In a sermon preached in October of that year, the Reverend Samuel Davies, Virginia's leading Nonconformist minister, traced the Old Dominion's military misfortunes to "treachery or cowardice, or at least bad conduct" on the part of "some in high places." In a subsequent public statement, Davies observed, "Every one can complain of the bad management of our public undertakings."[1]

Dissension within the ranks of the governing elite was evident when the powerful and popular John Robinson, Speaker of the House of Burgesses, blamed Governor Robert Dinwiddie for the "heavy cloud...hanging over this distressed and unhappy Country." Commenting late in 1757 on Dinwiddie's preparations for relinquishing his office, Robinson noted, "We have not yet heard who is to succeed him, God send it may be some Body better acquainted with the unhappy Business we have in hand." Dinwiddie himself railed at a variety of targets: the men he appointed to manage Virginia's chronically chaotic supply service, the provincial army, the colony's Indian allies, and craven frontiersmen whose cowardice, in the governor's opinion, was exceeded only by their avarice. Adopting the patois of the "Com'n people," the anonymous author of the *Virginia Satirist* laid the blame almost exclusively on the gentry who sat in the colonial assembly and met only "to Conshidder of ways & means to raise moneys to deir own Shweet shelves, for having thus Brot our affairs into a Confusion."[2]

The assembly's handling of military affairs was even condemned by one of its own. Writing sometime in 1756 as "Philo Patria," Richard Bland, a burgess from Prince George County and a member of one of Virginia's leading families, argued that the colony's unimpressive military record resulted from the "trifling" appropriations voted by the lower house. As Bland saw it, the members' parsimony underwrote the maintenance of little more than a scratch force whose puny numbers "could not restrain the Ravages of the Enemy." Bland further contended that continued reliance on a defensive strategy based on the "ineffectual Barrier" of frontier forts threatened Virginia with "Oblivion." A more aggressive course was urged instead. "Let us leave the Government to act as it will," Bland counseled. More specifically, Bland called upon the burgesses to be less meddlesome in their dealings with the Virginia Regiment: "Generals and Commanders of Armies must be left to act as they find it most expedient for their Country's Interest." Bland believed it was long past time to "shake off all Restrictions." In short, Bland's public letter made a case for unleashing the provincial army and placing greater power in the hands of the colony's military leaders.[3] Others were not so sure.

Most eighteenth-century Virginians had inherited an uneasiness about standing armies as part of their political and cultural heritage as Englishmen. From their knowledge of seventeenth-century English history and their reading of radical Whig theoreticians, Virginians understood that standing armies endangered the political, social, and moral order of the nations that maintained them. Although not a standing army in the classical sense, the Virginia Regiment came close enough to arouse fears that at least bore echoes of traditional English anti-army ideology. Such fears had been overcome in the immediate aftermath of Braddock's defeat by the urgent problem of frontier defense. But as the months dragged on, the colony's continuing military problems and the uneven performance of its provincial army produced an outburst of antimilitary sentiment, which added considerably to the rancorous atmosphere on the home front.[4]

## CIVIL-MILITARY FRICTION

Civil-military friction took a number of different forms during the three-year period between Braddock's defeat in July 1755 and the beginning of Brigadier General John Forbes' successful march against Fort Duquesne in the summer of 1758. Some conflicts sprang from petty disputes between individuals or arose from the kind of bickering that almost always intrudes on the relationships between soldiers and civilians living in close proximity. Squabbles of that kind occurred frequently in the vicinity of the Virginia Regiment's headquarters at Winchester. "In all things, I meet with the greatest opposition," George Washington wrote from that post in October 1755. During the tumultuous autumn following Braddock's defeat, Washington's relations with the civilian community became so strained that, by his own admission, some local residents had threatened "to blow out my brains." Civilian ill will was reciprocated by those in uniform. Writing in November 1755, Lieutenant Colonel Adam Stephen described the citizens of Winchester as "dastardly."[5]

Relations between the provincial army and the residents of Winchester remained uneasy during the years that followed. In the fall of

1757, Washington complained that local "tippling house keepers (with which Winchester abounds)" were serving as receivers of stolen "arms & [et]c. belonging to the Regiment." Washington noted further that this illicit trafficking had gone on in spite of the fact that he had "taken every precaution...to prevent the Soldiers of this Garrison from having any dealings whatever with the inhabitants of the town." Civil-military relations became even more strained after Washington charged that town magistrates had "trifled" with "the laws made for the punishment of such gross offences."[6]

On other occasions members of the provincial army were the objects of indignant complaints. A few months after reporting on the illegal arms trade in Winchester, Washington received a bill for damages from Joseph Wolgamote, a Maryland farmer whose hay meadow had been ruined by Virginia Regiment wagon horses. Wolgamote claimed that when he protested the damage, a provincial officer had threatened that "if I Was Displeased With What he had Done he Would Turn them [the horses] into my Grain AND Confine me A prisoner." Concluded farmer Wolgamote: "This Treatment from Such as Ought to be our Protectors is unjust and What We Could Only Expect from The Enemy." An especially nasty confrontation occurred in the spring of 1756 when the Virginia Regiment's Ensign George Gordon was killed in an otherwise undescribed "Fray" with a civilian.[7] Distressing enough in themselves, individual incidents such as these also helped tighten the lines of political tension in the Old Dominion.

Serious civil-military conflict had penetrated the highest levels of provincial government as early as 1756. In April of that year, Governor Dinwiddie advised Washington that members of the assembly were "greatly inflamed" by reports that certain provincial officers were guilty of "the greatest Immoralities & Drunkeness." These accusations came at a time when sizable numbers of hostile Indians were rampaging through the backcountry and aroused concern even among the regiment's staunchest supporters in Williamsburg. Although some legislators believed the tempest had been caused merely by "a few...youths in the service [who] have been at times imprudent and drank too Freely," other members did not treat the allegations of misbehavior so lightly. The highly influential John Robinson minced no words when he concluded that "the frequent Incursions of the French and Indians" were "in a great Measure" encouraged by "the Conduct of some of our Officers, of whom there are terrible reports."[8]

Denunciations of the provincial military establishment grew even more strident as mayhem on the frontier persisted. What was by far the strongest attack appeared in "The Virginia-Centinel No. X," an anonymous article published in the 3 September 1756 issue of the *Virginia Gazette*. The Virginia Regiment was never mentioned by name, but the "Centinel" clearly had the provincials in mind when he wrote: "When nothing brave is so much attempted, but very rarely, or by Accident, or for necessary Self defense; when Men whose Profession it is to endure Hardships, and encounter Dangers, cautiously shun them, certainly Censure cannot be silent; nor can the Public receive much Advantage from a Regiment of such dastardly Debauchees."[9]

The "Centinel's" attack was only one of a number of public assaults on the competence and character of the provincial army. In October 1756 Samuel Davies charged, "A spirit of security, sloth, and cowardice evidently prevails [in the Virginia Regiment]; nothing great is so much attempted, much less executed." Davies voiced even stronger criticism in the spring of 1758. In a sermon that no doubt expressed the accumulated frustrations of many Virginians after four costly and indecisive years of war, Davies broadly insinuated that provincial soldiers were lecherous, venal, tyrannical, lazy, cowardly, and even treasonous. Having evoked the image of a corrupt and contemptible corps, Davies closed sanctimoniously by leaving "others to judge, whether the original of this ugly picture is to be found any where in the universe." Reading these words many years later, one senses that Davies and his listeners had no doubts about where the "original of this ugly picture" could be found: it was located at Fort Loudoun in Winchester, at Fort Cumberland on the upper Potomac, or at any other encampment of the Virginia Regiment.[10]

### DISCORD AMONG THE ELITE
Unlike Virginia's draft laws, which impinged on the poorest fifth of the population, the financial costs of the war were shouldered by a much wider and more politically significant portion of provincial society. The colony's defense expenditures were considerable. The Virginia Regiment cost the taxpayers about £1,500 a month even during the days (1756–57) when it was chronically understrength. Scalp bounties, pensions to disabled soldiers, stipends for the families of men killed in action, salaries for militia units mobilized during periods of emergency, and the costly alliance with the Cherokees drove military expenditures—and tax levies—even higher. By January 1757 the assembly had granted a total of £125,000 for prosecuting the war, a sum that would more than quadruple in the following five years.[11]

Taxes increased in amount and in kind as the war progressed. "Taxes on taxes are multiplied, and, though it be a necessary, it is a heavy

burden," wrote James Maury in June 1756. Indeed, by the early 1760s
it seemed that the assembly had imposed "[p]ractically every kind of
tax ever devised by the ingenuity of law-making bodies." Military
expenditures initially were funded by poll taxes, a fundamentally
regressive levy that thrust the financial burden of the war "heavily
on the lower ranks of people." Poll taxes more than doubled during
the first years of war, rising from 4.6 pounds of tobacco (equivalent
to about four pence) per tithable in the early 1750s to one shilling per
tithable by the middle of 1755. (After 1757 the poll tax per tithable
rose to four shillings per annum, a rate that continued in force
throughout the remainder of the war.) In spite of increased assessments, the income produced by poll taxes alone soon proved insufficient, and in 1755 the assembly reluctantly enacted a land tax. An
acreage tax had been unknown in Virginia for a century and, for
obvious reasons, was decidedly unpopular with the larger planters.
In 1758 one of their number claimed that "the vast tax our estates
have been burdened with since the beginning of the present war" had
prevented him from meeting his obligations to English creditors.
Land taxes and poll taxes soon were joined by new levies on various
business licenses, court suits, and carriages "Contrived for ease or
Luxery [sic]." Existing rates on exported tobacco and imported slaves
also were increased. Although the relative equity of these measures
varied, war taxes nevertheless fell on rich and poor alike.[12]

Many provincial politicians were uneasy about voting for higher
taxes, and the incessant financial demands of the war eventually
produced a rather marked division on the question of military spending among members of the House of Burgesses. The outlines of this
division were noted by Burgess Landon Carter as early as 1754. Richard Bland, another insider, acknowledged the existence of strong
and conflicting sentiments within the lower house two years later in
his aforementioned "Philo Patria." Scattered references to "the other
party" and invidious comparisons pitting "the Old and Judicious"
against "the Young Members" on questions involving military appropriations further suggest there was a sizable faction of legislators who
favored cuts in military spending. The cost cutters generally lost out
when crucial military issues were being decided. But their hand was
strengthened at least momentarily in the spring of 1757 when growing concern about rising taxes was coupled with stories about drunk-
en and lustful carryings-on in the Virginia Regiment. Armed with
what amounted to political dynamite, the critics pushed through a
significant reduction of the provincial army in the very midst of the

war. They saved a little money in the process but at a great cost to civil-military goodwill.[13]

The cost cutters translated talk into action when the assembly met in April. Earlier in the year Governor Dinwiddie had advised Washington of the "Great Clamours here [in Williamsburg] ag'st the many officers in Commiss'n to command so few Men." The clamorers had a point. During the first few months following Braddock's defeat, provincial authorities had commissioned additional junior officers, hoping that the personal influence of the new subalterns would attract badly needed volunteers. That ploy worked no better than any of the other recruiting stratagems employed between 1755 and 1758. As of July 1756, the provincial army consisted of seventeen under-manned companies whose combined strength barely equaled six hundred men. Since each company was allotted three officers, the ratio between officers and enlisted men was a lopsided one to twelve. Even Washington admitted the regiment's top-heavy rank structure meant "the Officers is very near as great a Charge to the Country as the Men are."[14]

Aware that the provincial army's unbalanced rank structure was a politically charged issue, Dinwiddie had warned Washington as early as August 1756 that "there must be a reduction of Officers." That reduction was imposed by the assembly in May 1757. In midmonth the governor informed Washington that the lawmakers had voted to reduce the Virginia Regiment from seventeen companies to ten and that a proportionate reduction in the number of provincial officers had also been decreed. Although provision was made for reassigning some officers whose companies had been abolished, at least twelve men—almost 25 percent of the officer corps—were forced out of the service entirely. Those who lost their commissions during what came to be known in provincial military circles as "the Reduction" were understandably bitter. Former Captain William Peachey probably spoke for all of his cashiered colleagues when he described the lot of a provincial officer as "a service...where a man must either push himself into the jaws of death...or be subject to the calumnious tongues of a sort of base seducers."[15]

As Peachey's comments suggest, provincial officers had grievances of their own, and the reduction of the regiment and dismissal of some dozen of their comrades only deepened their feelings of resentment toward the governing gentry in Williamsburg. Significantly, by the time the reduction was ordered, long-standing complaints about pay, allowances, and conditions of service had become coupled with expressions of contempt for civilian critics who, while adept at armchair strategy, did not expose themselves to hardships and danger. In a January 1757 letter to the earl of Loudoun, Washington sneered at "Chimney Corner Politicians that are thirsting for News, & expecting by every express a circumstantial account of the Siege and reduction of Fort Duquesne." Similar disdain was evident in a petition drawn up by provincial officers a few months later following a squabble with Edmund Atkin, the newly appointed superintendent of Indian affairs in the southern colonies. Miffed because Atkin had denied them access to a French prisoner, the officers demanded that Washington "inform that Gentleman [Atkin] that as our Officers & Men risk'd their Lives in taking of the Prisoner we are entitled to speak to him when we please." Before the end of 1756, the provincial officer corps had grown angry, edgy, and resentful of civilian criticism.[16]

Although the Virginia Regiment never posed a political danger per se, its increasingly snappish officers did signal their readiness to adopt a confrontational posture and substitute threats for force as a means of influencing political behavior. The willingness of provincial officers to deal boldly with colonial politicians was particularly evident in their response to the accusations levied against them by the "Virginia Centinel" in September 1756. A few weeks after the "Centinel's" charges were published, all thirty-four officers stationed at Fort Cumberland threatened to resign en masse by 20 November unless they received "Publick Satisfaction" for being ridiculed. The officers followed up that warning with a pointed reminder that it would "be of infinite Disadvantage . . . to leave this Quart[e]r exposed to a rapacious & merciless Enemy." In a letter to Speaker Robinson, Washington also protested the "general censure" of the Virginia Regiment and warned that if the assembly gave even "a distant hint of its dissatisfaction" with his own performance, he would promptly "resign a commission which I confess to you I am no ways fond of keeping." Washington enclosed with his letter an "Address of the Officers of the Virginia Regiment to the Speaker and Gentlemen of the House of Burgess" in which the officers renewed their demand that the politicians "give us public testimony that in your esteem we have not deserved the obloquoy [sic] complained of [by the 'Virginia Centinel']."[17]

The ultimata sent down by provincial officers received a mixed reaction in Williamsburg. Some legislators were unimpressed by the substance of the officers' threats but strongly resented their temerity in making them. Landon Carter was especially nettled by the "very daring" tone of the officers' proclamations. Carter charged angrily that "these fellows write letters with the points of their Swords & Seal them with pistol bullets." Other politicians took the officers' protests more seriously. A few days before expiration of the officers' 20 November deadline for a public apology, Speaker Robinson wrote a sympathetic letter to Washington that belittled the "Virginia Centinel" as "a vile and Ignorant Scribler." Colonel William Fairfax wrote another soothing letter shortly thereafter in which he counseled that "those who unjustly and snarlingly Censure whom They can't imitate or equal are to be overlookt and contemd."[18]

In the end the officers never received their much-sought-after testimonial from the assembly. Substantial satisfaction was forthcoming, however, in the form of the public analysis of the military situation made by Burgess Richard Bland, writing as "Philo Patria." Bland made little effort to conceal his authorship of this strongly promilitary piece, and his eminent political and social status went far toward mollifying the injured feelings of the provincial officer corps. But although Bland's flattery and reassurances soothed military egos and helped abate the tempest caused by the "Virginia Centinel," civil-military relations remained clouded during the months that followed. Provincial officers prepared another "Remonstrance" about their "precarious and uncertain" situation in April 1757 when the assembly was debating the merits of the proposed "Reduction." The officers once again made threatening noises by arguing that the regiment's "serious and melancholy circumstances" promoted "langer and indifference" among its members.[19]

## POPULAR DISAFFECTION

While provincial politicians and officers wrangled over the blame for Virginia's woeful war record, the ordinary—and less than ordinary—people of the Old Dominion registered their own form of dramatic protest against colonial military policy. The sources of popular opposition were not rooted in the larger questions of strategy, leadership, and war finance that had so convulsed the "better sort" by 1758. More than anything else, popular opposition turned on a pronounced distaste for conscription, for the gentry's efforts to raise an army by force and coercion.

The level of literacy in Virginia had improved significantly by 1750, but during the second half of the eighteenth century, the common people of the Old Dominion still existed mainly in an oral culture. Nevertheless, the written sources do contain some hints about popular feelings concerning the draft. In the fall of 1755, one self-appointed spokesman for the "poor onnesht peoples" of Virginia had Governor Dinwiddie boasting:

> Yet I will do what I am able
> to [s]eize & terrifye the Rabble.

Three hundred Squires, at my Command,
shall when I nod, dragoon the Land.

Bitterness and resentment were even more apparent in a comment on the draft made two years later by "Timothy McOates." "McOates," the creation of a contemporary political satirist, was a literary composite of the "lesser sort" of men who comprised the Old Dominion's draft pool. Shortly after the assembly had agreed upon an even more hard-boiled conscription policy in the spring of 1757, "McOates" sardonically reported the "good peesh [piece of?] news—dat all the buld fellows above fifty is to be shent to faight because day dus taake up too much Room." These words convey more than the writer's talent for black humor; they also suggest the deep resentment of humble and normally submissive folk who understood that as the targets of the draft laws, they had been deemed useless and expendable by those above them in the social hierarchy, that they were people who did not count. In one sense, of course, that realization and the indignation it aroused were nothing new. The poor had always been despised in Virginia, a fact of which they were no doubt reminded daily in a hundred ways. But the workings of Virginia's socially selective draft laws exposed the "lesser sort" to a new and intensified level of contempt: they were made aware that the community was ready to throw their lives away.[20]

However suggestive, the caustic commentaries of "Timothy McOates" said less about antidraft attitudes than did the actions of the common people themselves. One particularly prevalent form of protest involved aiding deserters from the Virginia Regiment, an illegal act that encouraged further desertion. As early as the summer of 1756, Washington had complained of "the country-people who deem it a merit to assist Deserters." Within a year this practice had become so widespread that Washington doubted whether anything could "stop its scandalous progress, but the severest punishments." Dinwiddie's admission soon after that "All I can do can't prevent the People entertain'g & protect'g Deserters" underscores the extent of popular disaffection.[21]

The determination with which some civilians aided deserters was pointed up by Captain Peter Hog in December 1755. In a letter to Washington, Hog reported that two deserters from his company had been hidden by "some Lawless fellows" who lived nearby the provincial camp. When confronted by a small patrol Hog had sent out in pursuit of his missing soldiers, the civilians put up a fight and severely assaulted a sergeant. (In this case the civilians apparently came off second best since Hog stated that the sergeant "was Amply revenged by Cutting off the Arm of one!") Perhaps even more striking were reports that deserters were sometimes aided and encouraged by the "civil and military powers" in their home counties. At his court-martial in May 1757, one captured soldier offered in his own defense the explanation that the commander of his county militia unit had assured him that he and his fellow conscripts "might desert with Impunity" once they had reached the recruit depot at Fredericksburg.[22]

In the final analysis, nothing better illustrated the internal strains produced by a war gone sour than two contrasting reports, one from the frontier, the other from Richmond County in the tidewater. From the backcountry came warnings from George Washington that during the height of an enemy offensive in the spring of 1756, "numbers" of frontier residents were so "Despairing of assistance and protection from below" that they "talk[ed] of capitulating and coming upon terms with the French and Indians." A year later, one of Washington's confidants alleged that Colonel Richard Corbin, a leading resident of Richmond County and a member of the governor's council, had dismissed Washington's alarms as nothing but a "Scheme . . . to cause the Assembly to levy largely both in Money & Men, and that there was not an Indian in [that] Neighborhood." One report raised doubts about the loyalty of hard-pressed frontiersmen who questioned their government's ability to protect them from the ravages of war; the other claimed that a principal member of that government had expressed doubt about whether a war existed in the first place. The striking divergence between these reports vividly symbolized the growing discordance in Virginia's public life.[23]

## A GLOOMY SCENE

Military affairs in Virginia bore a gloomy aspect as 1757 drew to a close. The provincial army was dispirited and increasingly disaffected while backcountry residents were sunk in despair. Dismay and discord also enveloped the settled portions of the Old Dominion where civil-military conflict, factional strife among the burgesses, and growing signs of alienation on the part of ordinary Virginians had roiled the normally tranquil surface of the colony's political order. Whether they objected to conscription, resented high war taxes, or opposed the colony's flaccid defensive strategy, Virginians of every condition were distinctly unhappy with the military policy crafted by the gentlemen politicians in Williamsburg.

By 1758 there were increasingly clear signs that the war had undermined the deference and respect customarily shown the gentry by the rest of Virginia society. Draft evaders and deserters from the provincial army challenged the authority of the gentry by doggedly resisting their "betters'" efforts to put and keep them in uniform. Other displays of nondeferential behavior included the willingness of ordinary Virginians to assist runaway soldiers. War-induced social antagonism received one of its most explicit statements in the antiestablishment tirades of Presbyterian spokesman Samual Davies, who denounced the gentry for shirking their leadership responsibilities with the same gusto he employed in decrying sloth and moral turpitude among provincial military officers. Davies was at his caustic best when he assailed the gentry for having "acted as if beings of their importance and merit might certainly rest in the quiet, unmolested possession of their liberty and property... without doing anything for their own defence." In making that charge, Davies was not only indulging a Calvinistic passion for pointing out the weak and selfish ways of mankind. In fact, by implying that the gentry were more concerned with their own goods and pleasures than with the common weal, Davies indirectly called into question their fitness to govern.[24]

Given the significant internal strains it had produced, Virginia's military policy by the end of 1757 had aroused more hostility on the home front than it had eased along the frontier. In a larger sense, the internal strains produced by the war may be viewed as early tremors in the process of social disintegration and transformation that some scholars see as the key factor in Virginia history during the 1760s and 1770s. Whatever the long-range implications of the turmoil we have been discussing, at the beginning of 1758 the most pressing issues were the war, the divisiveness that it had spawned, and the urgent need to do something about them both. Early that spring the clamor for a more effective military policy was reduced at last by the arrival of a circular letter from Secretary of State William Pitt.[25]

## FUNDAMENTAL CHANGE IN POLICY

Except for a brief period in the spring of 1757, William Pitt served as the king's chief minister from late 1756 until the fall of 1761. In his official post as secretary of state, Pitt had dual responsibility for colonial affairs and for Britain's international diplomacy. By 1758—when naval and military matters had also fallen largely under his direction—Pitt's control of British war policy was complete.[26]

In strategy as in politics, William Pitt was an uncommonly aggressive man. His plan of operations for the American theater aimed at nothing less than the conquest of Canada. Although Pitt's primary target was Quebec, capital of New France and western gateway to the strategic lower St. Lawrence Valley, securing the backcountry between the Alleghenies and the Ohio was an important secondary objective. Command of the western campaign was entrusted to Brigadier General John Forbes, an able officer handpicked for the job by Pitt himself. Forbes made his principal object the capture of Fort Duquesne, the French bastion Washington once called "the fountain of all our disturbance and trouble."[27]

On 30 December 1757, Pitt forwarded circular letters to the colonial governors announcing his plans for a general offensive. Pitt's letter reached Virginia in mid-March 1758. Upon its receipt the assembly was reconvened by John Blair, president of the council and acting governor in the interim between Governor Dinwiddie's departure for England in January 1758 and Governor Francis Fauquier's arrival in June. If provincial leaders were heartened by the news of an impending expedition including "the Levying, Cloathing, & Pay" of provincial troops. As a final ingratiating stroke, Pitt also reversed the old policy of relegating provincial officers to subordinate status whenever they served with men who possessed a king's commission. In his letter of 30 December, Pitt decreed that henceforth provincial officers "as high as Colonels" would enjoy command over regular officers of lower rank.[28]

Pitt's promise of reimbursement (his so-called "subsidy policy") and the prospect of a decisive campaign dovetailed with the rising internal crisis within the Old Dominion over provincial military policy. Inspired by external inducements on the one hand and growing internal pressures on the other, the politicians who gathered in Williamsburg for the short assembly session of 30 March–12 April 1758 authorized a fundamental change in Virginia's military policy. With little apparent debate, the lawmakers voted to field two provincial regiments of one thousand men each and agreed that the entire force might "be marched [out of the colony] to annoy or attack the enemy in such manner as shall be thought proper by the commanding officer of his majesty's forces in North America." The unpretentious language of the "Act for augmenting the forces in the pay of this Colony to two thousand men" signaled the abrupt abandonment of the defensive strategy the Old Dominion had been following since the fall of 1755.[29] For the first time since the Braddock expedition, Virginia troops would march in a campaign aimed at bringing the war home to the French. The strategic shift was significant, but the real break with the past was the manner in which men were recruited for the newly enlarged provincial army.

By the spring of 1758, Virginia leaders had faced up to the fact that conscription was as unworkable as it was unpopular. That realization and, most importantly, Pitt's promise to pick up the recruiting bills, caused the assembly to abandon compulsory service and rely entirely on voluntary enlistments encouraged by a generous bounty of ten pounds. The colony never again resorted to conscription but depended instead on the bounty-volunteer system as its sole means of raising recruits down to the Virginia Regiment's final dissolution at the close of 1762.[30]

When he prorogued the assembly on 12 April, President Blair expressed hope that the bounty money would "expedite" recruiting. Shortly thereafter Washington described the ten-pound bounty as a "greater encouragement than hath been given before; and I hope [it] will be the means of procuring us the Complement we want, speedily." Given that, as noted above, ten pounds approximated half the annual cash income of many small planters and perhaps that of an entire year for those who lived in even more humble circumstances, the hopes of both men were abundantly realized. By the end of May, the troop strength of Washington's First Virginia Regiment stood at approximately 950 men. By the same time some 900 men had enlisted in the newly formed Second Virginia Regiment, commanded by William Byrd III. Both regiments were fully formed by early June, a scant six weeks since the burgesses acted. Before midmonth newly arrived Governor Francis Fauquier reported in separate letters to Secretary Pitt and the Board of Trade that the "Second Regiment of 1000 Men under the Command of Colo. Byrd, which with the other Regiment of 1000 under Colo. Washington are . . . ready to proceed . . . to . . . the General Rendezvous [at Fort Cumberland] appointed by Brigadier Genl. Forbes."[31] No contrast could be better drawn between the Virginia Regiment paid for—and conscripted—by Virginians, and the Virginia Regiment purchased—and recruited—by British sterling.

## THE FORBES CAMPAIGN

The slow but successful procession to the forks of the Ohio did not get under way until August. The methodical Forbes arrived in Philadelphia in March and spent most of the next three months there laying plans for the campaign, contracting for supplies, and organizing the approximately sixteen hundred regulars and twenty-seven hundred Pennsylvania provincials under his command. Forbes was confronted by two fundamental problems: a relatively short campaign season and a distant objective. Aware that his army could not live off a wild and mountainous country, Forbes planned his march around the establishment of a line of fortified positions that would serve as supply depots for his forces. The posts were spaced about forty miles apart, and Forbes proposed to advance from one to another until he was in easy striking distance of Fort Duquesne.[32]

Forbe's initial plan called for marching up via the old road leading out of Fort Cumberland, which had been constructed by Braddock's army in 1755. He subsequently reconsidered that route and by July had decided on a new line of march leading more or less directly west from Raystown (now Bedford), in south central Pennsylvania. The choice of a route had important economic implications, and Virginians could have counted on a number of lucrative opportunities had Forbes marched his army out of the Old Dominion along the Braddock Road. Local farmers and merchants would have reaped immediate profits if Forbes had established his base of operations in Virginia. But the real advantages would have come in the future. The reopening of Braddock's Road would have vested Virginia with control over the only improved and secure route to the west, a monopoly that would have given the Old Dominion a dominant position in the Indian trade and in the opening of the Ohio country to English settlement. Little wonder that enterprising residents of the Old Dominion were sorely disappointed when Forbes decided on the Raystown route. Still other Virginians opposed Forbes's revised plan for military reasons and worried that cutting a new road across the wooded slopes of the Alleghenies would only prolong the campaign and jeopardize its chances for success. Washington argued against the Pennsylvania route for weeks and only grudgingly marched the Virginia troops from Fort Cumberland to Forbes's new rendezvous at Raystown.[33]

There were at least as many sound reasons for advancing across Pennsylvania as for following the old road up from Fort Cumberland. Even the delays caused by road building were put to good use. The British were waging a diplomatic as well as a military offensive during the spring of 1758, and while Forbes's army inched westward, other of his emissaries succeeded in wooing the Delaware and Shawnee Indians from their alliance with the French. This diplomatic victory, formalized on 26 October 1758 by the Treaty of Easton, weakened French power in the Ohio country no less than the subsequent capture of Fort Duquesne.[34]

Notwithstanding the crucial importance of cultivating Indian goodwill, the promising negotiations at Easton made little impression on Virginia's senior military commander. Washington had been transmitting a steady stream of pessimistic reports to Williamsburg since midsummer. In September he charged: "The conduct of our Leaders [here Washington was referring to Forbes and the expedition's second-ranking officer, Lieutenant Colonel Henry Bouquet]...is temper'd with something, I don't care to give a name to, indeed I will go further, and say they are d-ps, or something worse to P-s-v-n Artifice, to whose selfish views I attribute the miscarriage of this Expedition." Washington summed up this gloomy prognosis by claiming that the "advanc'd Season" and the difficulties of cutting a road through the Pennsylvania mountains had all but eliminated any possibility of an attack on Fort Duquesne until the spring of 1759.[35]

Washington's reports added considerably to the disappointment and disgust already felt in Williamsburg over "the long delay of the march...and the partiality shewn to Pennsylvania" in the matter of the campaign route. As future events disclosed, Speaker Robinson was hardly overstating the case in observing that Virginia lawmakers "were not in a very good humor" when an empty war chest forced Governor Fauquier to reconvene the assembly on 12 September. During a brief and bumptious month-long session, the members reluctantly granted fifteen thousand pounds "for the substance and pay" of the provincial army but signaled their intention of withdrawing the Old Dominion's forces from Forbes's command at the end of 1758.[36]

When the Virginia assembly adjourned in mid-October there seemed little likelihood that Forbes could mount a decisive stroke against Fort Duquesne before the end of the year. That prospect was transformed by the fortuitous capture of a renegade Englishman and two Shawnees on 12 November. The prisoners divulged that Duquesne was defended only by a handful of French troops and that it would make easy pickings for Forbes's considerably larger force. On the basis of this intelligence, Forbes divided his army into three brigades and began a fifty-mile forced march from his camp at Loyalhannon to the Ohio.[37]

Governor Fauquier learned of these developments in an express from William Byrd warning that "our Forces will most probably be in Action before Fort DuQuesne, at the very time prescribed for their Return into the Colony." Fauquier immediately recalled the assembly for an emergency meeting and informed both houses that the long-awaited moment was at hand. In an extraordinary three-day session, the assembly amended the military bill passed just a few weeks before and authorized the governor "to continue both the regiments...on such service as he shall judge most conducive to his majesty's interest . . . till the first day of January [1759]."[38]

On the evening of 25 November 1758, the advanced columns of Forbes's army stumbled out of the woods and stared at the blackened ruins of what had been Fort Duquesne. Powerless to stop the British advance, the undermanned French garrison had burned the fort and sailed down the Ohio River just forty-eight hours before. A few days later Washington dispatched a message to Williamsburg informing Governor Fauquier "that Fort Duquesne, or the ground rather on which it stood," was possessed at last "by his Majesty's troops."[39]

## · 6 ·

## "FINE REGIMENT"
### Soldiers When They Chose To Be So

*This fine [Virginia] Regim't.*

MAJOR GENERAL JOHN STANWIX, 1760

The campaign of 1758 was important for two reasons: it heralded the end of one war and the beginning of another, and it revealed a new and aggressive spirit among the men of the Virginia Regiment. In truth, the Forbes expedition probably experienced more battles over road building than it did with the French and Indians. But violent encounters with the enemy were not entirely lacking, and the conduct of the Virginia troops during the one major battle of the campaign won them abundant praise even from the normally censorious British regulars.

The engagement itself marked the only British reverse in Forbes's slow procession to the Ohio. It was a short but bloody episode. On the morning of 14 September, British Major James Grant and a large reconnoitering party of some 800 Scottish Highlanders and contingents from various provincial units were set upon near Fort Duquesne by an even larger number of French and Indians. During the fighting that followed, the British lost upwards of 270 men, a quarter of them Virginians. Although the rout of Grant's force proved only a temporary setback, this painful affair was costly and not a little embarrassing, particularly since British casualties were multiplied by Grant's reckless posturing before the walls of the French fort.[1]

Only the Virginians emerged from the unhappy proceedings with credit. British Colonel Henry Bouquet claimed that the provincials' gallantry had prevented an even more serious defeat. In a letter to Brigadier General (later Major General) Jeffery Amherst written three days after the battle, Bouquet stated: "The Provincials appear to have done well, their good men are better in this war than the regular troops." Even the testy General Forbes, who barely a week before had described provincial soldiers as "the scum of the worst of people", joined in the applause. "[T]he General has complimented me publickly on their [the Virginia troops'] good behavior," Washington wrote proudly to George Fairfax shortly after the engagement. Common soldiers in the regular British army also were impressed by the Virginians' performance. According to Washington, "the Highlanders and them [the men of the Virginia Regiment] are become one People, shaking each other by the hand wherever they meet the perfect Stranger's."[2]

In a war that promoted far more mutual contempt than admiration between British and American fighting men, the accolades bestowed on the Virginia provincials during the fall of 1758 came as high praise indeed. Nor was this the only time during the later stages of the French and Indian War that the Virginia Regiment was singled out for acclaim by British officers. In February 1760 Major General John Stanwix, commander of British forces in the southern colonies, referred to the Virginia provincials as "this fine Regim't." Brigadier General James Murray paid similar tribute to the soldierly qualities of the Virginians in an October 1762 letter to Jeffery Amherst, by then the British commander in chief in North America. Describing the caliber of men lured into the regular British army by a fifteen-pound recruiting bounty, Murray wrote, "as those [recruits] from Carolina are as good as the Virginians[,] I can venture to assure you that the 47[th] Reg't . . . will be in as high order as any Regiments in his Majesty[']s Service." These flattering appraisals constitute a marked change from the days of Edward Braddock when British officers dismissed Virginia's provincial soldiers as "very indifferent Men" whose "Sloth and Ignorance is not to be described." They also suggest something close to a metamorphosis of military behavior. Somehow, Virginia's provincial army—undisciplined, unreliable, unspirited, and always understrength—had been transformed into an energetic, hard-hitting, and even fully manned armed force.[3]

### CHEROKEE WAR

Within a few weeks of the capture of Fort Duquesne, the Old Dominion's provincial army was halved by the scheduled dissolution of the Second Virginia Regiment. At about the same time Washington resigned his colonelcy in favor of a seat in the burgesses as a representative from Frederick County. Command of the First Virginia Regiment then passed to William Byrd III.[4]

The capture of Fort Duquesne was the high point of Virginia's involvement in the French and Indian War. But the Old Dominion's military problems by no means disappeared after British forces reoc-

cupied the forks of the Ohio. A residual French threat remained along
the northern edge of the Ohio country well into 1759, and sizable
detachments of Virginia troops were employed at Fort Pitt and its
environs until the fall of 1760.

The number of Virginia troops on duty in and around Fort Pitt in
1759 and 1760 ranged between four hundred and six hundred men.
While on that service, the Virginians helped clear the remaining
pockets of French resistance at Venango, Fort Le Boeuf, and Presque
Isle; performed garrison duty at Fort Pitt; guarded supply trains; and
carried out other less glamorous chores such as clearing and improving roads. By the end of the summer of 1760, the remaining French
posts in the Ohio country had fallen, as had their strongholds at
Niagara, Ticonderoga, Crown Point, and, most important of all,
Quebec. Montreal remained in French hands until September 1760,
but the enemy had been routed everywhere else. Meanwhile, no sooner had the Forbes campaign ended than mounting friction between
Virginia, the Carolinas, and the powerful Cherokee nation betokened
a new war, an unhappy prospect that became a full-fledged reality
in 1760. When it met in November of that year, the Virginia assembly
insisted that all provincial troops on detached service be returned to
the Old Dominion to help meet the growing Cherokee threat on the
colony's southwestern border.[5]

Cherokee animosity toward their English neighbors was rooted in
a variety of sources. The two were for years erstwhile allies against
the French and their Indian proxies, but Anglo-Cherokee relations
had been uneven at best and had left both sides nursing grievances
against the other. Also helping to unravel the alliance were centrifu-
gal tendencies within the Cherokee government structure that had
eroded the influence of pro-English tribal elders. Additionally, anti-
English intrigues hatched by the French and their Creek intermedi-
aries, the chicanery of unprincipled white traders, and growing resentment over the western drift of the line of English settlement had
pushed the two sides apart.[6]

The immediate origins of the Cherokee War dated from the spring
of 1758. Hundreds of Cherokee warriors, recruited during the previous winter, had arrived at the Virginia Regiment's headquarters in
Winchester by April, months before the provincials marched off to
rendezvous with the British. Late spring snows in the Pennsylvania
mountains discouraged raiding parties, and the Indians had little to
do but draw on Washington's military stores, shuttle back and forth
from Winchester to their own tribal lands, and get into trouble.
While moving up and down the Shenandoah Valley in May, small

groups of Cherokees stole some horses and harassed white settlers in Bedford and Augusta counties. Armed clashes with angry frontiersmen soon followed. Both sides suffered during the skirmishing, but tension and bloodshed abated by the end of the year, and there were no further threatening developments until the fall of 1759.[7]

Anglo-Cherokee relations plummeted once more in October 1759 when South Carolina Governor William Henry Lyttelton seized a number of Cherokees as hostages and demanded in exchange the warriors supposedly guilty of recent outrages in the Carolina backcountry. Shortly thereafter, Lyttelton marched into the Cherokee country with his hostages and a mixed force of fifteen hundred Carolina provincials and militiamen in hopes of relieving the isolated garrison at Fort Loudoun, located near the Overhill (or "Upper") Cherokee towns at the junction of the Tellico and Little Tennessee rivers (present-day southeastern Tennessee). At Lyttelton's request, the Virginia assembly made three hundred provincials available for duty in the Cherokee country until 1 May 1760 and posted three hundred more in defensive positions on the Old Dominion's southwestern border. Lyttelton turned back before reaching his objective but left his Cherokee hostages and a small number of reinforcements at Fort Prince George, one hundred miles east of Fort Loudoun in the Carolina piedmont.[8]

Events came to a head in February 1760 when the commander of Fort Prince George was lured into an ambush and murdered. The enraged members of the garrison promptly slaughtered their Cherokee hostages in retaliation. Full-scale war appeared imminent, and Lyttelton appealed to both Virginia and the British army for assistance. Major General Jeffery Amherst sent down by sea from New York some thirteen hundred Highlanders and Royal Scots Greys under Colonel Archibald Montgomery. Virginia dispatched William Byrd III and seven hundred provincials overland in the direction of now-besieged Fort Loudoun. By the end of June, Montgomery and his regulars had reached the Cherokee village of Etchoe, located about midway between Fort Prince George and Fort Loudoun. Montgomery ran into stiff opposition in the vicinity of Etchoe and decided that a return to Charleston was in order. After Montgomery's intentions became known, Governor Fauquier recalled the Virginia provincials, who, after a late start, had been proceeding down the interior valleys toward Fort Loudoun. Abandoned and starving, the fort's garrison surrendered to its Cherokee besiegers early in August.[9]

Notwithstanding their promise of generous terms, the Cherokees massacred many of their South Carolina captives and carried off the remainder to various Indian towns. Enraged by the Cherokee's treachery, Amherst sent down another and larger expeditionary force of 2,250 regulars under Lieutenant Colonel James Grant with orders to cut a wide swathe of destruction through the Indian country. Grant bested the Indians in a major battle and devastated fifteen of their towns during a month-long campaign in June 1761. The Cherokees sued for peace shortly thereafter, and a final treaty was ratified at the end of the year.[10]

The Virginia Regiment made an important if undramatic contribution to the victorious proceedings against the Cherokees. At General Amherst's request, six hundred provincials were massed and marched as far as the Great Island of the Holston River on the northern edge of the Overhill Cherokee towns. The provincials saw no action, but they maintained a threatening presence, and their potential intervention helped propel the Cherokees to the peace table.[11]

### THE REGIMENT DISBANDS

The Virginia Regiment's final months of existence were decidedly anticlimactic. When it met in November 1761, the assembly voted to

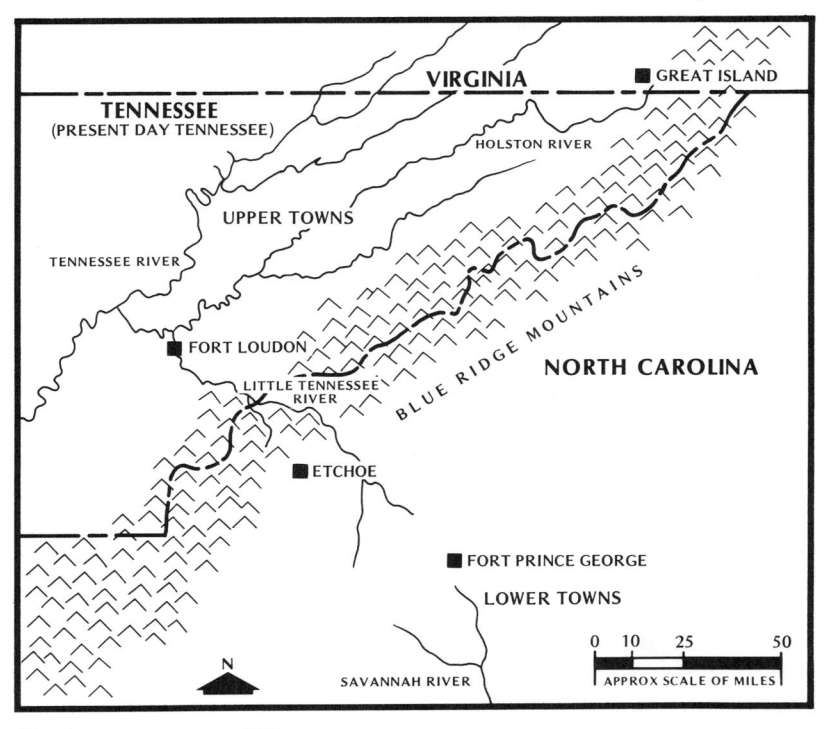

Cherokee country, circa 1760.

maintain the regiment only until May 1762, provided the Cherokee War lasted that long. The members clearly expected an early peace and, as Governor Fauquier observed, were "heartily tired of the Expence" of costly military undertakings. The lawmakers expressed that weariness in a separate proviso that ordered the governor "to disband the whole Regiment" as soon as hostilities with the Cherokees had ended. Fauquier complied with that stipulation early in February 1762 after receiving news that a formal peace treaty had been signed in Charleston.[12]

The provincial army gained a new but brief lease on life at the end of March when it was learned that Britain had declared war on Spain, lately become the ally of France. The assembly reactivated the Virginia Regiment, authorized a ten-pound enlistment bounty, and agreed that the provincials could be employed wherever the governor or British commander in chief deemed necessary. The members also agreed to raise an additional quota of 268 men "for the Regiments on the British Establishment."[13]

In keeping with Amherst's request "to Rendezvous them in the most Convenient Place, for moving Either to the North or South," Fauquier established the Virginia Regiment's main encampment at Fredericksburg. There the provincial army reassembled, trained, and made "ready to march at a moment[']s Warning." But marching orders never came, and the provincials spent the summer and fall of 1762 fighting only boredom, each other, and an outbreak of smallpox. By the end of the year, the assembly had had enough of paying for an army for which no one had any use. On 1 December 1762, the Virginia Regiment was disbanded for the second and last time. Two months later Governor Fauquier received a royal proclamation announcing the cessation of hostilities.[14]

The end of the French and Indian War was a bittersweet occasion in Virginia. To be sure, Virginians were proud of their military accomplishments and of the part they had played in the overall British victory.[15] Yet the jubilation that greeted the end of hostilities elsewhere in the colonies was largely absent in Virginia, where the announcement of peace coincided with news that British merchants had prevailed in their campaign against the colony's paper currency, the very means whereby the Old Dominion had financed its war effort.

The paper money controversy originated in a decision by the Virginia assembly to anticipate the collection of war taxes by issuing treasury notes. Significantly, the notes were not only receivable for taxes but also were made legal tender for all private monetary transactions. Between the colony's first emission of wartime paper currency in May 1755 and June 1757, Virginia's treasury notes bore a 5 percent interest rate, a feature that helped insure their value. Uneasy from the first about the practice of treating paper currency as legal tender for debts contracted in sterling, British merchants began complaining in earnest about the treasury notes in the summer of 1757 shortly after the Virginia assembly authorized the emission of non-interest-bearing notes. As far as the merchants were concerned, the Old Dominion's non-interest-bearing notes were issued against insufficient tax levies, a situation that undermined the value of the notes and spurred a sharp rise in the exchange rate between paper currency and sterling. The merchants took their complaints to the Board of Trade, which positioned itself squarely on their side. In a strongly worded letter sent to Governor Fauquier in February 1763, the board condemned the practice of treating paper currency as legal tender for sterling debts and ordered the expeditious retirement of all paper currency then in circulation. Virginia leaders greeted the board's decree with considerable resentment since they had resorted to paper money very reluctantly in the first place and then because it was the only practical alternative for funding the colony's military obligations. One contemporary spokesman, planter-historian Robert Beverley, bitterly described the board's ruling as "a very genteel and grateful method of repaying our ridiculous and overzealous Loyalty in the course of the late war."[16]

Nor did victory find Virginia in control of the Ohio country, the great prize over which the war had been fought in the first place. The old land companies bestirred themselves and had begun pressing their prewar claims in the trans-Allegheny as soon as the French had been driven from the Ohio Valley. The clamorings were joined by appeals from provincial veterans seeking redemption of the pledge made in 1754 by Governor Dinwiddie promising land bounties in the Ohio country to all those who took up arms against the French. Regardless of their source, these importunings made little impression on the authorities in London. To war-weary policymakers in Whitehall, the Anglo-French conflict in North America had demonstrated at least one clear lesson: stability of the frontier depended on friendship with the Indians. The Board of Trade had signaled its own opposition to further western settlement by the summer of 1760, a position that eventually received the full force of law in the Proclamation of 1763. For all their energetic lobbying, the "gentlemen speculators" of the Ohio and Loyal companies never realized their designs on the lands beyond the Ohio.[17]

Old soldiers fared no better. Writing in July 1762 "in behalf of themselves and the rest of the surviving Officers and Soldiers" of the

Virginia Regiment, George Washington, Adam Stephen, and Andrew Lewis sought the king's "Consideration" of the grants of western lands promised them years before by Dinwiddie. Their petition was never answered. Instead of land in the Ohio country, provincial officers received six months severance pay from the Virginia assembly and a "Gratuity" based on their rank. Enlisted men had received a bonus equivalent to one month's pay when the regiment originally was disbanded in February 1762. When the provincial army was abolished for the second and final time ten months later, those serving in the ranks received their lawful wages and no more.[18]

## TRANSFORMATION IN BEHAVIOR

The Virginia Regiment's role in the Cherokee War was more that of supporting player than of chief actor, and it performed no active role at all during the brief period of heightened tension that followed news of Spain's entry into the war. Nevertheless, in the campaigns of 1760 and 1761, the regiment showed that it still possessed the fighting spirit it had exhibited during the Forbes expedition. As in the campaign of 1758, the provincials' morale and aggressiveness earned them the attention and respect of professional experts: the senior British officers who exercised overall command of military operations in North America. One such discerning judge, Brigadier General Robert Monckton, after April 1760 commander of British forces in the southern colonies, bestowed what may have been for him the ultimate compliment when he informed Jeffery Amherst in July of that year that the Virginia provincials "doo [sic] their Duty as well as any Old Reg't [that is, old British regiment]." Such praise from such a source makes it difficult to discount entirely as boasting one Virginia officer's claim that the "Blues" of the Old Dominion had acquired a reputation for "eclipsing other Provincials, and even vying with the King's Troops, in uniformity, in appearance, exactitude, regularity, firmness and Intrepidity."[19]

Without overstating the case, one could add several additional military virtues to the half-dozen enumerated by Captain Robert Stewart in 1761. Such qualities as resolution, endurance, and a sense of élan were also much in evidence as the Old Dominion's little army went about the various missions it was assigned after 1758. Whether marching against the Cherokees, patrolling the Virginia frontier, or helping clear the final pockets of French resistance from the Ohio country, the men of the Virginia Regiment behaved with the steadiness and aplomb of seasoned veterans.

No less remarkable, given its earlier record in such matters, the Virginia Regiment from 1758 until it was disbanded in December

1762 enjoyed generally low desertion rates, attracted good men, and retained many recruits for more than one enlistment. Five months after the fall of Fort Duquesne, the *Pennsylvania Gazette* printed a "letter from Virginia" that discussed preparations for the 1759 campaign and claimed that "[t]he Levies go on pretty successfully; in a little Time, it is hoped, the Men wanting will be raised." Similar optimism about recruiting was voiced by Governor Fauquier. After inspecting the main provincial encampment at Winchester early in June, Fauquier reported that he had "found the Regiment not so complete as I wish'd . . . [b]ut . . . the Body [of troops] is daily encreasing." By mid-July the provincial army had met over 80 percent of its recruiting goals, a vast improvement over previous years when the regiment seldom operated at more than half of its authorized strength. There were qualitative improvements as well. Unlike the sorry specimens so complained of by provincial officers before 1758, the recruits who signed up in 1759 were described as "generally healthy[,] active[,] likely fellows," the kind of men who could "support the Reputation the Regiment gained in the Campaign of last Year [that is, the Forbes expedition]."[20]

The quality and quantity of provincial soldiers remained reasonably high during the years that followed. "[T]he Recruits enter very fast," Governor Fauquier assured the Board of Trade in June 1760. Using almost identical language, he made that claim again in May 1762 when the regiment, which had been dissolved only two months before, was revived after the assembly learned that Spain had entered the war. A majority of the men who flocked to the colors had seen prior service in the provincial army. According to the governor, three-quarters of those applying for commissions were veteran officers, while "most of our old [enlisted] Men" filled up the ranks. The steady performance of the provincials was underscored in the spring of 1760 when the *Pennsylvania Gazette* reported that the Virginians had "had several Skirmishes with them [Cherokee raiding parties] in which [they had] always repulsed the Enemy, . . . tho' with great Loss of Men." Perhaps the greatest (and certainly the most ironic) testament to the Virginians' dependability came in the same year when detachments of soldiers from the Old Dominion's once desertion-ridden provincial army were employed in capturing deserters from the Pennsylvania provincials in the vicinity of Fort Pitt.[21]

Notwithstanding the transformation in their military behavior, it is likely that the social and economic origins of many of Virginia's provincial soldiers remained just what they had always been. No regimental size rolls could be found for the years after 1757, but there is literary evidence suggesting that provincial military service remained an activity considered fit only for those on the fringes of respectable society. Such sentiments were made strikingly clear in the spring of 1759 when Governor Fauquier directed William Byrd to purchase two shiploads of convicts for impressment into the Virginia Regiment. That recourse ultimately proved unnecessary due to the high number of voluntary enlistments, which soon led the governor to admit that "the Military Ardor of the young Men of this Colony" was only "a little abated" since the heady days of 1758 when bounties were first introduced. Nevertheless, Fauquier's readiness to employ jailbirds as soldiers speaks volumes about the social character of the Virgina Regiment during its last years and the persistent presence of hard-up men in its ranks.[22]

A number of converging factors explain the contrasting behavior of the marginal men who made up Virginia's provincial army before and after 1758. The offer of a generous enlistment bounty obviously was tempting bait for men whose annual income hovered between nothing and a few pounds.[23] Enthusiasm probably was kindled as well by the colony's abandonment of a defensive stance in favor of aggressive, offensive campaigning. As a recruiting device, the shift represented more than just the renunciation of a frustrating and unsuccessful strategy. The change also conveyed an emotional appeal: the suggestion that a great adventure awaited those who dared enlist. The interplay between behavior and events must also be considered, because the regiment's participation in the capture of Fort Duquesne doubtless bequeathed a spirit of confidence to those in the ranks, which helped build a winning momentum and esprit de corps. Attention might be paid as well to the internal dynamics of regimental life as they evolved over a longer term and to the influence of what students of military behavior have come to call "small-unit cohesion."

## SMALL-UNIT COHESION

As a form of group behavior, small-unit cohesion manifests itself in the collective willingness of soldiers to fight and stand steady under fire. The product of intense personal attachments born of shared adversity, mutual dependency, and trust, small-unit cohesion is singled out in modern studies of military performance as the key to combat effectiveness. To the extent that the experience of combat arouses some of the most fundamental human needs and responses, what is true for twentieth-century fighting men likely was true for their eighteenth-century counterparts as well. This suggests another line of argument that may help explain the improved performance of the Virginia Regiment after 1757: that over time various institutional and interpersonal developments had combined to foster the provincials' cohesiveness and hence their effectiveness as a fighting unit.[24]

For some soldiers the process of cohesion building probably started with participation in Washington's basic military training program. Training, discipline, and proper military deportment always were matters of great concern to the regiment's young commander, and during the two years following Braddock's defeat Washington had labored mightily to create an army worth the name. As a related matter, it is worth remembering that initiation into a military organization almost always is an intense experience involving isolation from civilian society and the strenuous imposition of new rules and values. Certainly it is not uncommon for people to emerge from that kind of experience not only with a modicum of military skill but also possessing a measure of personal identification with the military community they have joined. As we have seen, the number of recruits who took one look at Fort Loudoun and promptly decamped was not inconsiderable. But whether motivated by desperation, resignation, fear, or a genuine attraction to military life, there were always some who remained. For those men, the days of training, drilling, patrolling, and simply living together likely nurtured personal friendships and, perhaps, served as a seedbed for unit cohesion.[25]

There are indications that such was the case. Late in 1756 there occurred a particularly conspicuous demonstration of what might be understood as an emerging sense of regimental kinship. Shortly after receiving news that a long-range patrol had been wiped out in the vicinity of Fort Duquesne, provincial officers decided to erect a monument to commemorate their fallen comrades. Located near Fort Cumberland, the monument bore the following inscription:

> To the Memory of Serj. William Shaw, Serj. Joseph Fent, Jeremiah Poor, James Cope, and Timothy Shaw, Soldiers of the Virginia Regiment . . . To testify the Love, Honor and Esteem, paid to them by their Officers, for their great Courage and valiant Behavior.[26]

Enlisted men sometimes had an opportunity to offer reciprocal expressions of esteem for their superiors. In one June 1756 episode, as graphic in its way as the monument at Fort Cumberland, Sergeant William Hughes felt compelled to administer a "sincere Drubbing" to a Winchester innkeeper who had imprudently defamed provincial officers "in the grossest terms."[27] Two events: one formal and presumably decorous; the other spontaneous and violent. But both suggest the formation of emotional ties among at least some members of the provincial army that transcended the distinctions of military rank.

In a somewhat different context, a sense of corporate consciousness and unit pride was clearly conveyed by Lieutenant Colonel Adam Stephen when he boasted in August 1757 about the results of tough training on the men he commanded: "They are well disciplined and have this advantage of all other troops in America that they know the parade as well as Prussians, and the fighting in a Close Country as well as Tartars." Stephen offered that opinion while on detached service at Charleston, South Carolina, with two companies of Virginia provincials. Captain George Mercer, another provincial officer posted in Charleston that summer, echoed Stephen's sentiments and asserted that even British regulars were struck by the "good soldier-like appearance" of the Virginia troops as they boarded their transports at Hampton. Mercer went on to claim that once on station together in Charleston, the British became so impressed with the men sent down from the Old Dominion that "we have lost that comon [sic] Appellation of Provincials, and are known here by the Style and Title of the Detachment of the Virginia Regiment." Although the comments of these Virginia officers doubtless were to some degree self-serving, they nevertheless had the ring of an authentic esprit de corps.[28]

Soldierly appearance alone is not a very reliable gauge of unit cohesion and fighting effectiveness. The real test of such things occurs in combat when awareness of mutual dependency and the need for mutual trust are most acute. It is at that point also that the perceptions of those who bear the brunt of battle, the enlisted men, become crucial. Thus, cohesion and combat effectiveness are much more likely outcomes when enlisted men view their officers as individuals who truly merit respect, confidence, and obedience. That perception, in turn, is largely determined by the willingness of officers to share in the dangers and privations faced by their troops.[29] In speculating about the existence and strength of such perceptions among those in the ranks of the Virginia Regiment, the fact that virtually all provincial officers were line officers takes on special significance.

Unlike twentieth-century armies, wherein a majority of officers perform staff duties in relatively safe and comfortable circumstances, most officers in eighteenth-century armies were troop commanders in line units (that is, fighting units). Put another way, in an age when military technology was low but the requirements for physical courage very high, the officer's primary job was to provide personal and courageous leadership on the battlefield. Such was the principal task of the captains, lieutenants, and ensigns who served in the Virginia

Regiment, and they had the casualties to prove it. Despite the defensive posture of Virginia's forces for much of the period, between the late summer of 1755 and the fall of 1758, over 10 percent of the colony's officers were killed in action. To the ever-watchful men in the ranks, those casualties almost certainly signaled their officers' readiness to bear with them the risks and hardships of active campaigning. On such a sense of solidarity does unit cohesion depend.[30]

Cohesion building also depended upon a measure of stability within the officer corps, the kind of stability that gave the enlisted men sufficient time to observe the conduct of their officers and the officers sufficient time to win the respect of their troops. By provincial standards generally, Virginia officers provided that kind of stable presence. Not counting the three-month tenure of the unfortunate Joshua Fry, the Virginia Regiment had three commanders during its eight-year existence, by no means an inordinate number for a regiment of the line in wartime. Washington provided continuous leadership from June 1754 through 1758 (excepting the eleven-month period between late October 1754 and August 1755 when the Virginia Regiment temporarily was replaced by ten independent companies). Command of the colony's forces next passed to Colonel William Byrd III. Byrd resigned in September 1761 and was succeeded by his (and formerly Washington's) immediate subordinate, Lieutenant Colonel Adam Stephen. By then a veteran of over seven years' continuous service, Stephen led the regiment until it was disbanded in December 1762.[31]

Senior officers made the important operational decisions, established overall standards of discipline, and generally set whatever distinctive tone their regiments happened to possess. But it was the company officers who had the most direct and continuous contact with the men in the ranks. As was the case with those in the field grades, there existed substantial stability among the regiment's company officers. For example, of the forty-eight men who received company-grade commissions when the regiment was reconstituted in August 1755, thirty-six (75 percent) were still at their posts when the provincial army was reduced from sixteen to ten companies almost two years later. (Three of the twelve officers no longer in provincial service had resigned in order to accept regular commissions in British regiments and three others had been killed in action.) Of the twenty-seven officers who survived the reduction, twenty (74 percent) eventually participated in the victorious campaign against Fort Duquesne in 1758.[32]

Information about those who served in the ranks is much more spotty, but what has survived suggests most companies could claim at least a few "veteran" enlisted men, men who served beyond the normal one-year commitment imposed on volunteers and draftees alike. Such men numbered only one or two in some companies but in others constituted one-third or more of those on the rolls. That at least seems the pattern for 1756 and 1757, the only years for which appreciable data exists. During the former year veterans were present in at least eight of the regiment's ten companies. Their number ranged between one apiece in two companies to as many as twenty-three in Captain George Mercer's forty-eight-man company. Useful data from 1757 exists for only four companies. Within those four, the number of veterans ranged from fifteen in Captain Henry Woodward's seventy-three-man company to forty-nine in George Washington's eighty-man company.[33]

Not surprisingly, it was from among the veteran soldiers that many of the regiment's noncommissioned officers were drawn. In keeping with contemporary British practice, each provincial company was authorized three sergeants and three corporals. By 1756 the selection of men for these appointments was subject to considerable scrutiny. In January of that year Washington directed Adam Stephen "to fix upon the proper persons in each Company for Sergeants; having regard to their outward appearances as well as their Moral Characters and Qualifications." The regiment's commanding officer apparently heeded his own advice. By the late summer of 1757 each of the six noncommissioned officers assigned to Washington's company possessed almost two years of continuous military service. Among them were men like Sergeants John Sallard and Reuben Vass, both of whom served with distinction for the duration of the war and whose soldierly qualities eventually won them provincial commissions.[34]

Washington's emphasis on the need for high-quality noncommissioned officers made good sense. Along with the company officers, these were the men whose courage and flair for leadership counted most when the bullets began to fly, the men who would encourage, inspire, or goad those in the ranks amidst all the terrors of combat. And it is possible that their contributions were not confined to tactical leadership on the battlefield. Direct evidence is lacking, but is it not unreasonable to assume that provincial noncommissioned officers, closer in social origin and military rank to the private soldiers, furnished personal role models with whom the privates could easily identify and who, perhaps, they could strive to emulate.[35] Accordingly, provincial sergeants and corporals may have been especially effective at promoting what the best noncommissioned officers have always promoted: pride, confidence, and camaraderie, fundamental building blocks of unit cohesion and thus of improved performance on active service.

Singly and together, the aforementioned factors—hefty enlistment bounties, adoption of an offensive strategy, coalescence of sturdy interpersonal bonds between officers and key segments of the enlisted force—likely contributed to the new fighting spirit and overall effectiveness of the Virginia Regiment. But one senses that no less instrumental in the regiment's dramatic turnabout was the fact that after 1757 men no longer were compelled to serve. They were asked.

## THE SHADOW OF SLAVERY

The Virginia Regiment between 1755 and 1757 was largely a story of marginal men and their determined opposition to the compulsory principle that underlay the Old Dominion's military policy. Among the public figures of the day, none expressed more pronounced distaste for that principle than the Reverend Samuel Davies. In a recruiting sermon preached in Hanover County on 8 May 1757, Davies revealed with striking clarity why the draft was so objectionable to the "lesser sort" and what compulsory service symbolized in the minds of such men. Davies began his homily that day by reminding his listeners that provincial authorities had recently forsaken the draft in favor of bounties and an all-volunteer force. He noted pointedly that the new policy was "not liable to the objections that have been urged against former measures for raising men." Davies then argued that institution of a bounty-volunteer system had eliminated any justification for evading military service. In making that argument he also disclosed the root objection to the draft that had been nursed by men on the margins of Virginia society since 1755, an objection so well known and often employed that Davies set it off in quotation marks in his text. Davies expressed the basis for that opposition in these words: "You cannot any longer object 'that you are *dragged away like slaves* against your wills, while others are without reason exempted': for now it is left to your own honour, and *you may act as free men*." (Italics mine.)[36]

As Davies' language suggests, the antidraft attitudes of poor white Virginians were informed by their familiarity with black slavery. Slavery, after all, was no abstraction to such men. They witnessed daily the hapless and degraded condition of human beings who were owned by others. Surrounded by people in chains, it required no great feat of imagination to see that the terms of the Old Dominion's conscription statutes imposed nothing less than involuntary servitude on poor whites of military age. The parallels between chattel slavery and the draft were obvious: one system was based on the private ownership of human beings, the other on the assumption that people were the property of the state. The savage discipline common to eighteenth-century armies suggested another similarity between the plight of a conscript and the lot of a bondsman. Stories of "common Soldiers" in the Virginia Regiment who were routinely "abused" by their officers served as a reminder that the authority of military superiors over their subordinates was more complete than that in any other human relationship save one: the relationship between master and slave.[37]

The apparently widespread belief that conscripts were a species of slave implies that draft resistance among poor Virginians was inspired by something more than the desire to avoid the dangers and hardships of soldiering. Hardship, danger, and even sudden death, after all, were hardly strangers in the mean world of those who lived on the mudsill in eighteenth-century Virginia. The point is this: as one conjures with the behavior of those the colony tried to conscript, one senses that draft resistance in the Old Dominion was rooted in the fact that, although not full members of the political nation, the "lesser sort" nevertheless shared in the basic values and ideas of a common political culture. Poor Virginians may not have known much about the natural rights theories of John Locke or the libertarian contentions of John Trenchard and Thomas Gordon, but as suggested by Samuel Davies' knowing use of terms like "slaves" and "free men," they understood and prized the meaning of personal freedom.[38] Ultimately, then, the problem was not so much that poor Virginians did not want to be soldiers as it was that they did not want to be forced. Virginia's leaders eventually acknowledged that reality themselves—indeed, they bowed before it—when they turned from compulsion to bribery and replaced conscripts with mercenaries. In so doing, they also revealed something about the fragile nature of government and the boundaries of political deference in mid-eighteenth-century Virginia.

# EPILOGUE

Virginia's military operations in the French and Indian War can be fully understood only when placed in their social and political context. When viewed from that perspective, it can be seen—or at least it has been so argued—that the process of mobilization and war fighting was influenced primarily by the nature of public opinion, the precarious position of the governing elite, the absence of effective mechanisms for enforcing the laws concerning military conscription, and certain broadly shared attitudes about personal freedom that transcended social and economic categories.

Virginia's military policy—the plan of action that encompassed how and for what purpose war was waged—changed over the years of the French and Indian War. In 1754 colonial authorities sought merely to field a small detachment of men for the purpose of guarding the Ohio Company's partially completed fort at the junction of the Allegheny and Monongahela rivers. It was an undertaking that proved much more difficult than they had anticipated. The following year Virginia leaders again faced problems finding auxiliaries to accompany Braddock's British regulars on their march against Fort Duquesne. In the wake of Braddock's defeat in the summer of 1755, Virginia's gentry government turned to the task of formulating a long-term military policy that would deter the colony's enemies at the least possible political and economic cost. In theory, the plan for guarding the frontier with a provincial army of relatively long-service conscripts seemed militarily sound as well as politically and economically expedient. But in spite of a generally more businesslike approach to making war, the military policy devised by colonial authorities proved incapable of securing either the frontier or internal political harmony. Essentially, the gentry's military program foundered because it was rejected by those who had been singled out for service and sacrifice: the men belonging to the lower orders of Virginia society. Accordingly, Virginia's central problem between 1755 and 1758 was one of putting together a military policy that would win acceptance from those on the bottom rung of the social ladder. As demonstrated by their employment of a bounty-volunteer system for raising an army during the years after 1757, provincial authorities eventually did recognize the importance of cultivating those whom they sought to exploit. But such recognition came slowly, and a good deal of blood, treasure, and political goodwill was squandered in the process.

In a general sense, the gentry's disregard for the sensibilities of the "lesser sort" reflected the military and social milieu in which the French and Indian War was fought. The eighteenth century was an age of limited warfare, and politicians seldom found it necessary or even desirable to excite public opinion at any level for military purposes. Recourse to patriotic incantation was particularly rare in Virginia, where during the first half of the eighteenth century at least, a mostly peaceful history had all but eliminated the need for explicit patriotic appeals. But peace came to an end in 1754, and the nine-year struggle that followed pointed up that in late colonial Virginia mobilization for war required more than simply raising and organizing soldiers and supplies. The war and the problems it created disclosed that political mobilization—the process of rallying public opinion and employing the coercive powers of the state to compel cooperation and punish disaffection—had become integral to the task of mobilizing human and material resources. Arguably, political mobilization was the most critical factor of all, particularly for Virginia, where widespread suspicions about the origins and purposes of the war created the need for some kind of artificial stimulation.

The importance of political mobilization was poorly recognized at first and, in the case of testy Governor Robert Dinwiddie, probably not recognized at all. In part for that reason, the attempts of colonial leaders to excite a war spirit were generally uninspired. The colony's single newspaper saw little sustained service as a medium of propoganda. The clergy were employed to a certain extent, but recourse to religion as a device for arousing the populace was fitful and limited. Use of the gentry as agents for mobilizing public opinion was similarly modest. Dinwiddie asked members of the assembly to drum up volunteers for the Virginia Regiment on one or two occasions early in the war, but the gentry themselves were divided over the wisdom and propriety of the governor's aggressive western policy and either ignored his requests or found that their own appeals for recruits went unheeded. In any case, few volunteers stepped forward.

The most dramatic attempt to stimulate public opinion came in the spring of 1756 when Attorney General Payton Randolph organized "an Association of Gent[leme]n" for the announced purpose of helping George Washington determine the best locations for the frontier forts that the colony planned to build. It seems very likely that Randolph and his fellow "Associators" also hoped that "lesser" men might be inspired to follow their example and take up arms in the colony's behalf. If so, that hope went unrealized. The "Associators" arrived on the frontier too late in the campaign season to be of much assistance and soon retired to the safety and comfort of their own plantations. After that one anticlimactic foray, the "Associators" disappeared into the pages of Virginia history. Their disappearance also marked the last real effort at mobilizing Virginians for war by persuasive means until introduction of the bounty-volunteer system in 1758.[1]

Although Governor Dinwiddie had little appreciation for the importance of public opinion, the halfhearted gestures made by the Virginia gentry at arousing broad-based involvement and support for the war turned more on purposeful design. Acting on his own, Dinwiddie had authorized, early in the spring of 1754, a series of actions that made an armed clash with the French all but inevitable. Faced with the governor's fait accompli, the members of the House of Burgesses quickly sensed that most Virginians saw no issues worth fighting over. The gentry also sensed that resort to large-scale mobilization would be socially and economically disruptive and might be politically dangerous. In a society in which men of the "better sort" ruled only by consent, the higher political objective became one of making only minimal military demands on the mass of voters who belonged to the "middling" majority. Under the circumstances, the attractions of a military policy that affected mostly hapless vagrants, landless farmers, and poor artisans were all but irresistible. Moreover, as made clear by frequent employment of terms like the "common herd," the "vulgar herd," and the "ignorant Vulgar," the ruling gentry looked upon their impoverished but presumably tractable countrymen as the kind of beings who were natural candidates in the first place for a provincial army in an age when armies were considered the perfect dumping grounds for economically unproductive and otherwise useless people. In sum, provincial authorities showed little concern about the feelings of the poor when they enacted draft laws.[2] Over time, however, the authorities learned that the feelings of the poor were crucial to military mobilization.

The feelings of the "lesser sort" counted because the governing authorities in mid-eighteenth-century Virginia lacked the instruments of coercion that were needed to force people into doing what they preferred not to do. The militia, for example, was not an embodied armed force that stood poised to impose the gentry's will on their impoverished neighbors. Aside from its part-time slave-patrolling functions, the militia actually was a sprawling and creaky administrative mechanism for raising short-term soldiers in instances of dire emergency; it was a kind of primitive draft board, not a pool of well-trained military policemen.[3] To be sure, every county did have its sheriffs and magistrates, but there was no real constabulary, no body of professional lawmen who could be loosed on deserters and draft dodgers. The provincial government's institutional weaknesses were magnified further by certain geographic and demographic factors: Virginia was vast in size, full of mountains and swamps, its population dispersed. These physical realities conspired against official coercion: there simply were too many places for wanted men to hide and survive. Finally, in the eighteenth century, when the level of military technology was relatively low, governments did not possess the monopoly over the means of violence they enjoy today. Even poor men owned guns in colonial Virginia, a fact that vastly complicated the task of compelling them to do anything. In the final analysis, the gentry abandoned conscription—the cornerstone of their original military policy—because they did not possess the means to impose it on a people inclined to resist compulsory military service. In a time and place where the instrumentalities of government were so feeble, the obedience of even "lesser" men would be forthcoming voluntarily or not at all. Ironically, although they were alternately despised, ridiculed, and ignored in peacetime, the sentiments of the "lesser sort"—indeed, the "lesser sort" themselves—acquired considerable importance in time of war. In this respect, my findings tend to indicate that, in wartime, a correlation exists between the military involvements of particular groups and the social gains that such groups are likely to experience.[4]

Between 1755 and 1758, poor men of military age made their importance felt in hundreds of individual acts of defiance. Many of these individuals flouted the draft laws by running away or simply by ignoring the statutes altogether. Those who were forced on active duty often deserted or gave grudging and halfhearted service. In either case, a sizable number of men on the mudsill of Virginia society refused to behave—and could not be forced to behave—in accordance with received notions of how the "inferior sort" should behave. Because poor Virginians were willing to soldier only on their own terms, the gentry relied after 1758 on generous enlistment bounties to raise the necessary number of men.

In the larger context of the political culture of mid-eighteenth-century Virginia, the military behavior of the less-than-ordinary men caught up in the French and Indian War suggests that the boundaries of political and social deference were, or became, more limited than usually is appreciated. The disregard of marginal men for the laws and policies crafted by their "betters" contrasts sharply with the traditional conception of the Old Dominion as a place where subordination and deference were the primary characteristics of social relationships. The poor may have been deferential enough in peacetime when playing their meager roles in the ordinary rituals of everyday life, but they were notably independent, even assertive, when it came to more fundamental questions involving life and death. They had, of course, plenty of practical reasons for feeling that way.

One of the more obvious conclusions that may be drawn from Virginia's experience in the French and Indian War is that military service on the Amercian frontier was generally unpleasant and always dangerous. Soldiers suffered not only from the enemy and harsh discipline, but equally or more from a perennially weak logistics system that rarely if ever provided food, clothing, and equipment in the requisite amounts. Shortages of basic necessities were joined by all the discomforts afforded by harsh weather and the filth of eighteenth-century camp life. Under such circumstances, the prospect of succumbing to disease or primitive medical practice was an even greater likelihood than dying at the hands of the foe. Perhaps not least, poor men knew as well as anyone else that war disrupted lives and that those who participated in it exposed not only themselves but their families and loved ones to separation, sorrow, and suffering.

Beyond individual calculations of risk and hardship, the resistance of the "lesser sort" to coerced military service was also rooted in their firsthand acquaintance with slavery. That the institution of slavery evoked a series of politically charged images in the minds of eighteenth-century Virginians has been forcefully argued by Edmund S. Morgan. But in contending that the growth of slavery enhanced the valuation that whites placed on freedom for themselves, historians usually have focused on how the contrast of black slavery and white freedom heightened the concern for liberty among those at the top and middle of colonial society.[5] What a study of the military behavior of those at the bottom of the social order reveals is that poor whites valued their liberty no less than did those above them in the social hierarchy. Their esteem for liberty, together with a firsthand appreciation for the degradation of slavery, informed their view—articulated by such dissident spokesmen as the Reverend Samuel Davies—that the draft and compulsory military service in the Virginia Regiment amounted to involuntary servitude, something to be strenuously resisted.

The scale and intensity of popular resistance to the draft in the 1750s made a strong impression on one prominent member of the next generation of Virginia leaders. Twenty years after the events described here, Thomas Jefferson remarked on the enduring symbolic power of conscription in an exchange of letters with John Adams. Writing in May 1777, Jefferson expressed relief that a sufficient number of volunteers for Virginia battalions in the Continental line had made recourse to drafting unnecessary. Adams replied that conscription customarily proceeded with relative ease in Massachusetts, primarily because the authorities there deliberately drafted wealthy men who promptly paid "large Premiums, to their poorer Neighbors, to take their Places." Not so in Virginia. In the 1770s as in the 1750s, conscription in the Old Dominion remained, in Jefferson's words, "the most unpopular and unpracticable thing that could be attempted." As if to underscore how profound was opposition to the draft in his home state, Jefferson then harkened back to the days of the French and Indian War and recalled pointedly that "our people even under the monarchical government had learnt to consider it the last of all oppressions."[6]

Thus, the military behavior of the "lesser sort" may also be seen as a political phenomenon: what appeared to the gentry as lawless and criminal behavior may be understood as well as the actions of poor but spirited people who were jealous guardians of their personal liberty and who were ready to take extralegal action if necessary to defend it. Concerning the importance that even poor Virginians placed on maintaining their independence, it is instructive to recall what John F. Smyth, an eighteenth-century English traveler, had to say of the "plain" people of the American South: "Such is the indolence, folly, and ridiculous pride of these ignorant backwoods men, that they could conceive it an indelible disgrace and infamy to be styled servants, even to his Majesty, notwithstanding they will gladly perform the lowest and most degrading service for hire."[7] The point here is freedom. Smyth found that "ignorant backwoods men" would "gladly perform" demanding and even demeaning labor, but only if hired to do so. The qualification is important. "Only if hired" is simply another way of saying that while poor southerners might "perform the lowest and most degrading services," they would do so only as men who could set, or freely accept, mutually agreed upon terms. In that sense, Virginia's deserters and draft dodgers were conscientious objectors of a special kind. Drawn from a social stratum where life was mean, cheap, and often brief, most of them probably did not object to war and killing on principle. But like the self-consciously independent rustics of whom Smyth spoke, they insisted on the freedom to be violent on their own terms. Seen in that light, the ten-pound enlistment bounty introduced in 1758 took on a significance that went beyond purely mercenary considerations. Again, the essential point is freedom. In addition to the obvious economic appeal of a ten-pound bounty for men of little means, the bounty-volunteer system also represented the gentry's tacit recognition of the "lesser sort" as free men who were at liberty to sell or withhold their services as they themselves saw fit, as men who were free to be soldiers when and if they chose to be so.

The dramatic contrast in the Virginia Regiment's recruiting fortunes before and after the bounty-volunteer system was adopted in 1758 makes clear that if any single premise underlay resistance to coerced military service, it was that men should be free to choose. In the extraordinary circumstances of war, men on the mudsill of Virginia society insisted on thinking and acting for themselves, on deciding for themselves whether the cause was worth their service and sacrifice. That insistence, and their ability to make good on it, likely gave the "lesser sort" a first whiff of their potential power. To that extent, their military behavior may be seen as a harbinger and seedbed for the more drastic reordering of human relationships that overtook and transformed Virginia society during the second half of the eighteenth century.[8] In their own way, the obscure and lowly men in the ranks of the Virginia Regiment were practicing the future.

# NOTES

## 1. "I FOUND THE MILITIA IN VERY BAD ORDER": THE OLD DOMINION ON THE EVE OF WAR

1. Washington to John Campbell, earl of Loudoun, January 1757, in W. W. Abbot et al., eds., *The Papers of George Washington: Colonial Series*, 4 vols. to date (Charlottesville, Va., 1983– ), 3:90.

2. Louis K. Koontz, *The Virginia Frontier, 1754–1763*, Johns Hopkins University Studies in Historical and Political Science, ser. 43, no. 2 (Baltimore, 1925), p. 14.

3. Lee to the Board [of Trade], 20 September 1750, Shelburne Papers, vol. 45, p. 84, original in the Clements Library, University of Michigan (microfilm copy in Colonial Williamsburg Foundation, Research Archives, hereafter referred to as CWFRA). In this study the lieutenant governor of Virginia will be referred to as the governor. During the period under review, the office of governor was held as a sinecure by the earl of Albemarle, the earl of Loudoun, and Sir Jeffery Amherst. The real business of governing fell to a lieutenant governor who was resident in Williamsburg. Three men headed the Virginia government immediately before and during the period of the French and Indian War: William Gooch, 1727–1749; Robert Dinwiddie, 1751–1758; and Francis Fauquier, 1758–1768.

4. William Waller Hening, ed., *The Statutes at Large: Being a Collection of All the Laws of Virginia, from the First Session of the Legislature, in the Year 1619*, 13 vols. (Richmond and Philadelphia, 1809–23), 5:16–17.

5. Percy Scott Flippin, "William Gooch: Successful Royal Governor of Virginia," *William and Mary Quarterly* (hereafter referred to as *WMQ*), 2d ser., 6 (January 1926): 4.

6. Lee to the Board of Trade, 29 September 1750, Shelburne Papers, vol. 45, pp. 84–85 (microfilm copy in CWFRA).

7. Ibid., p. 85.

8. Richard Lee Morton, *Colonial Virginia*, 2 vols. (Chapel Hill, 1960), 2:411; Flippin, "William Gooch," p. 5. See also John W. Shy, *Toward Lexington: The Role of the British Army in the Coming of the American Revolution* (Princeton, 1965), p. 39.

9. Douglas Southall Freeman, *George Washington: A Biography*, 7 vols. (New York, 1948–57), 1:226; Morton, *Colonial Virginia*, 2:618; Fairfax Harrison, "George Washington's First Commission," *Virginia Magazine of History and Biography* (hereafter referred to as *VMHB*), 31 (July 1923): 272.

10. Geoffrey Cousins, *The Defenders: A History of the British Volunteer* (London, 1968), pp. 31, 56.

11. John R. Western, *The English Militia in the Eighteenth Century: The Story of a Political Issue* (London, 1965), pp. 48–74.

12. Douglas Edward Leach, *Arms for Empire: A Military History of the British Colonies in North America, 1607-1763* (New York and London, 1973), pp. 7–13; Frederick Stokes Aldridge, "Organization and Administration of the Militia System of Colonial Virginia" (Ph.D. diss., American University, 1964), pp. 99, 130–33. The most recent study of the vicissitudes of the Virginia militia during its first century of existence is William L. Shea, *The Virginia Militia in the Seventeenth Century* (Baton Rouge, 1983).

13. Jack P. Greene, *The Quest for Power: The Lower Houses of Assembly in the Southern Royal Colonies, 1689-1776* (Chapel Hill, 1963), p. 303.

14. Flippin, "William Gooch," p. 10

15. Aldridge, "Virginia Militia System," pp. 100–101.

16. Francis L. Berkeley, Jr., "The War of Jenkins' Ear," in *The Old Dominion: Essays for Thomas Perkins Abernethy*, ed. Darrett B. Rutman (Charlottesville, Va., 1964), p. 14.

17. The readiness of American colonials of military age to participate in the Cartagena expedition is noted in Leach, *Arms for Empire*, p. 217.

18. Berkeley, "Jenkins' Ear," p. 41; Flippin, "William Gooch," pp. 6–7.

19. Hening, *Statutes*, 5:95; see also Edmund S. Morgan, *American Slavery, American Freedom: The Ordeal of Colonial Virginia* (New York, 1975), p. 340.

20. Berkeley, "Jenkins' Ear," p. 60; Herbert L. Osgood, *The American Colonies in the Eighteenth Century*, 4 vols. (New York, 1924), 3:500.

21. Osgood, *American Colonies*, 3:535; Morton, *Colonial Virginia*, 2:535.

22. "Observations in Several Voyages and Travels in America," from the *London Magazine* for July 1744, reprinted in the *WMQ*, 1st ser., 15 (January 1907): 147–48. One historian believes the militia's military effectiveness had begun to decline as early as the mid-1630s; see Shea, *Virginia Militia*, p. 53. On the deterioration of the Virginia militia, see also Aldridge, "Virginia Militia System," p. 130, and John E. Ferling, *A Wilderness of Miseries: War and Warriors in Early America* (Westport, Conn., 1980), p. 174.

23. Geo[rge] Carrington to N. Walthoe, Cumberland County, Virginia, 13 December 1750, reprinted in William P. Palmer, ed., *Calendar of Virginia State Papers and Other Manuscripts, 1652-1781, Preserved in the Capital at Richmond* (Richmond, 1875; reprint ed., New York, 1968), p. 244. On the "Virtual non-existence" of the Virginia militia see also Shy, *Toward Lexington*, p. 16.

24. Gooch to the Board of Trade, 23 July 1730, C.O. 5/1322, f. 72; Gooch to the Board of Trade, 11 August 1742, C.O. 5/1325, ff. 113–17, in Correspondence of Governor William Gooch (typescript copies in CWFRA).

25. Ibid., Gooch to the Board of Trade, 22 August 1743, C.O. 5/1326, ff. 16–17.

26. Morton, *Colonial Virginia*, 1:20; 2:570, 579–80. The words of Virginia's imperial charter read in part: "We do also Give, Grant, and Confirm, unto the said Treasurer and Co., and their Successors . . . all those Lands . . . situate, lying, and being, in that Part of America called Virginia, from the Point of Land, called Cape of Point Comfort, all along the Sea Coast, to the Northward 200 miles, and from the said Point of Cape Comfort, all along the Sea Coast, to the Southward 200 miles, and all that Space and Circuit of Land, lying from the Sea Coast of the Precinct, aforesaid, up into the Land, throughout from Sea to Sea, West and Northwest; and also all the Islands lying within 100 miles, along the Coast of both Seas of the Precinct aforesaid." Quoted in Louis K. Koontz, "Washington on the Frontier," *VMHB*, 36 (October 1928): 306, 5.

27. Morton, *Colonial Virginia*, 2:570.

28. Hening, *Statutes*, 3:204.

29. Ibid., 5:58, 78–80.

30. Don Higginbotham, *Daniel Morgan: Revolutionary Rifleman* (Chapel Hill, 1961), pp. 2–3.

31. Paul F. Griffin, Robert N. Young, and Ronald L. Chatham, *Anglo-America: A Regional Geography of the United States and Canada* (San Francisco, 1962), pp. 143–44.

32. Jack M. Sosin, *The Revolutionary Frontier, 1763–1784*, vol. 6 of *Histories of the American Frontier*, ed. Ray Allen Billington (New York, 1967), pp. 43–44.

33. Willis DeHass, *History of the Early Settlement and Indian Wars of Western Virginia: Embracing an Account of the Various Expeditions in the West, Previous to 1795* (reprint, Parsons, W. Va., 1960), p. 36; Samuel Kercheval, *A History of the Valley of Virginia*, ed. Oren F. Morton, 4th ed. (Strasburg, Va., 1925), p. 60.

34. Morton, *Colonial Virginia*, 2:550–51.

35. Calculated from: Company Rolls, Virginia Regiment, in George Washington Papers (MSS, Library of Congress, Washington, D.C.), ser. 4, 4:424–35, 452, 461, 463; 6:103–4, 710, 731, 756, 759, 778.

36. Thomas Perkins Abernethy, *Three Virginia Frontiers* (Gloucester, Mass., 1962), p. 57.

37. "A List of Tithables Sent the Lords of Trade," 23 February 1756, in *The Official Records of Robert Dinwiddie, Lieutenant-Governor of the Colony of Virginia, 1751–58, Now First Printed from the Manuscript in the Collections of the Virginia Historical Society*, ed. Robert A. Brock, 2 vols. (Richmond, 1883), 2:352. This document breaks down the population of tithables by age and race. Black-white population figures for the five frontier counties are given as follows:

| County | Whites | Blacks |
|--------|--------|--------|
| Hampshire | 558 | 12 |
| Frederick | 2173 | 340 |
| Augusta | 2273 | 40 |
| Bedford | 357 | 143 |
| Halifax | 629 | 141 |

In mid-eighteenth-century Virginia, only males above age eighteen were counted as white tithables. White women (of any age) and white males below eighteen were not tithed. Black tithables included all persons of both sexes above the age of sixteen. See *Dinwiddie Papers*, p. 353.

38. Kercheval, *Valley of Virginia*, pp. 60–61, 63.

39. John Richard Alden, *John Stuart and the Southern Colonial Frontier: A Study of Indian Relations, War, Trade, and Land Problems in the Southern Wilderness, 1754–1775* (Ann Arbor, 1944), p. 21.

40. F. B. Kegley, *Kegley's Virginia Frontier: The Beginning of the Southwest, the Roanoke of Colonial Days, 1740–1783, with Maps and Illustrations* (Roanoke, Va., 1938), pp. 138, 154–56; Morton, *Colonial Virginia*, 2:533–34.

41. "Journal of Doctor Thomas Walker, 1749–1750," in *Annals of Southwest Virginia, 1769–1800*, ed. Louis P. Summers (Abington, Va., 1929), p. 26.

42. DeHass, *Early Settlement*, p. 37.

43. Kercheval, *Valley of Virginia*, pp. 43–44, 53.

44. Lawrence Henry Gipson, *The British Empire Before the American Revolution*, vol. 4: *Zones of International Friction: North America, South of the Great Lakes Region, 1748–1754* (New York, 1961), pp. 158–60, 225–56.

45. Ibid., pp. 161–62, 255–56.

46. Ibid., pp. 49, 83. See also Leach, *Arms for Empire*, pp. 487–89.

47. Report, Dinwiddie to the Lords Commissioners for Trade and Plantations, January 1755, in *Dinwiddie Papers*, 1:388.

48. Ibid., Dinwiddie to the Lords of Trade, 23 February 1756, 2:339.

49. Gipson, *South of the Great Lakes*, pp. 253; Morton, *Colonial Virginia*, 2:533–34; Kenneth P. Bailey, *The Ohio Company of Virginia and the Westward Movement, 1748–1792: A Chapter in the History of the Colonial Frontier* (Glendale, Calif., 1939), pp. 104–5.

50. Gipson, *South of the Great Lakes*, pp. 251–54; Morton, *Colonial Virginia*, 2:615. The Indian conferees at Logstown were careful to note that the agreement made there was contingent upon the approval of the Onondaga Council of the Six Nations. In fact, because the Six Nations never recognized the agreement, the Treaty of Logstown had no official standing. The Delaware, Shawnee, and Wyandot tribes were vassels of the Iroquois, albeit in a very loose sense.

51. Gipson, *South of the Great Lakes*, pp. 283–85. As was the case with the Treaty of Logstown, the halfhearted agreements made by the Indians at Winchester failed to win support from the Onodaga Council; see Morton, *Colonial Virginia*, 2:615.

52. Dinwiddie to Lord Holderness, 12 March 1754, in *Dinwiddie Papers*, 1:95–96; Bailey, *Ohio Company*, p. 103; Freeman, *Washington*, 1:186–89; Alfred P. James, *The Ohio Company: Its Inner History* (Pittsburgh, 1959), pp. 7–8.

53. For sharing this and many other insights about the workings of colonial Virginia society, I am deeply indebted to Dr. George M. Curtis III, former associate editor of the John Marshall Papers, and to Mr. Harold B. Gill, formerly a member of the Colonial Williamsburg Research Department.

54. Gipson, *South of the Great Lakes*, p. 227; Thomas Perkins Abernethy, *Western Lands and the American Revolution* (New York, 1937), p. 2.

55. Morton, *Colonial Virginia*, 2:540–41; Bailey, *Ohio Company*, pp. 18–19. Rhys Isaac is the leading student of cultural change in late colonial Virginia. His ranging essays on colonial life, some greatly revised, have been collected in *The Transformation of Virginia Society, 1740–1790* (Chapel Hill, 1982), a brilliant reconstruction and analysis of the social history of the Old Dominion during the second half of the eighteenth century. See pp. 12–14 and 311–12 for Isaac's thoughts on the changing valuation eighteenth-century Virginians placed on land.

56. James, *Inner History*, p. 8.

57. "Land Grants for Land between the Alligany and a Line from West Boundary of North Carolina Line to the Confluence of Ohio with the Mississippi," 29 November 1769, in Washington Papers, ser. 4, II:1401–2; Bailey, *Ohio Company*, pp. 35–60; Richard W. Van Alstyne, *The Rising American Empire* (New York, 1960), p. 17.

58. Ibid.; Morton, *Colonial Virginia*, 2:539, 571; Gipson, *South of the Great Lakes*, p. 227.

59. "Land Grants," II:1401.

60. Ibid., 1401-A; Kegley, *Virginia Frontier*, p. 134.

61. Bailey, *Ohio Company*, pp. 66–67. In fact, the Virginia Council granted more than one million acres of land in the trans-Allegheny west on 12 July 1749. In addition to the lands assigned that day to the Loyal and Ohio companies, three other

organizations received grants of 100,000, 50,000, and 40,000 acres respectively (see Morton, *Colonial Virginia*, 2:572).

62. The Ohio Company had the following membership at the time it was organized: Thomas Lee, Thomas Nelson, Thomas Cresap, Francis Thornton, William Nimmo, Daniel Cresap, John Carlyle, Lawrence Washington, Augustine Washington, George Fairfax, Jacob Giles, Nathaniel Chapman, and James Wardrop (see Gipson, *South of the Great Lakes*, p. 228, n.6). John Hanbury, a well-connected merchant of London, was invited to join the Ohio Company four days after Governor Gooch referred the company's petition to the home government (see Lois Mulkearn, comp. and ed., *George Mercer Papers Relating to the Ohio Company of Virginia* [Pittsburgh, 1954], p. xi). The Northern Neck of Virginia is that portion of the Old Dominion that lies between the Rappahannock and Potomac rivers.

63. Bailey, *Ohio Company*, p. 27.

64. *Mercer Papers*, p. xi.

65. Bailey, *Ohio Company*, p. 36.

66. Gipson, *South of the Great Lakes*, pp. 277–29, n. 6.

67. Ibid., pp. 228–29.

68. "Petition of John Hanbury to the King in Council in behalf of the Ohio Company," 11 January 1749, in *Mercer Papers*, pp. 246–48.

69. See, for example, Morton, *Colonial Virginia*, 2:578–79 and Hayes Baker-Crothers, *Virginia and the French and Indian War* (Chicago, 1928), p. 6.

70. *Mercer Papers*, pp. 246–47.

71. Guy Fregault, *Canada: The War of the Conquest*, trans. Margaret M. Cameron (Toronto, 1969), p. 31. The decisive influence of the fears and suspicions of Francophobic policymakers in London is emphasized in T. R. Clayton, "The Duke of Newcastle, the Earl of Halifax, and the American Origins of the Seven Years' War," *Historical Journal* 24 (September 1981): 571–603.

72. Bailey, *Ohio Company*, pp. 27–28, 30–31.

73. Board of Trade to Gooch, 4 March 1749, in C.O. 5/1366, pp. 439–44 (microfilm copy in CWFRA).

74. Bailey, *Ohio Company*, p. 31.

75. Jack M. Sosin, *Whitehall and the Wilderness: The Middle West in British Colonial Policy, 1760-1775* (Lincoln, Neb., 1961), pp. 3–5.

76. Bailey, *Ohio Company*, pp. 18, 31, 116; Alden, *Southern Colonial Frontier*, p. 15.

77. Bailey, *Ohio Company*, pp. 80–87, 104.

78. Report, Dinwiddie to the Lords Commissioners for Trade and Plantations, January 1755, in *Dinwiddie Papers*, 1:386; Alden, *Southern Colonial Frontier*, p. 18.

79. Bailey, *Ohio Company*, p. 205.

80. Washington to the earl of Loudoun, 10 January 1757, in *Washington Papers*, 4:79–80.

81. On popular attitudes in Virginia toward the French and Indian War see Morton, *Colonial Virginia*, 2:579; Baker-Crothers, *French and Indian War*, pp. 22–30; Gipson, *South of the Great Lakes*, pp. 261–62; Bailey, *Ohio Company*, pp. 207–8. The division among the elite on the question of western expansion is examined in Marc Egnal, "The Origins of the Revolution in Virginia: A Reinterpretation," *WMQ*, 3d ser., 37 (July 1980): 401–28; see especially pp. 404–14.

82. A balanced appraisal of Dinwiddie's performance is in Morton, *Colonial Virginia*, 2:602. There are two full-length (and quite favorable) biographies of Din-

widdie: Louis K. Koontz, *Robert Dinwiddie: His Career in American Colonial Government and Western Expansion*, vol. 3 of *The Old Northwest Historical Series* (Glendale, Calif., 1941); and John R. Alden, *Robert Dinwiddie: Servant of the Crown* (Charlottesville, Va., 1973).

83.  Morgan, *American Slavery, American Freedom*, pp. 372–73.

84.  Morton, *Colonial Virginia*, 2:597–98.

85.  Lee to the Board of Trade, 11 May 1750, C.O. 5/1327, f. 84; 12 June 1750, C.O. 5/1327, f. 88; 12 July 1750, C.O. 5/1327, f. 93; 29 September 1750, C.O. 5/1327, f. 110 (microfilm copies in CWFRA).

86.  According to the records of the Ohio Company, Dinwiddie was admitted to membership on 27 March 1750, some fifteen months before he received his appointment as governor (see *Mercer Papers*, p. 5). Richard Morton incorrectly claims that Dinwiddie joined the Ohio Company sometime after he arrived in Virginia (see Morton, *Colonial Virginia*, 2:573); one of Dinwiddie's biographers assigns too early a date to his membership (see Koontz, *Robert Dinwiddie*, p. 159). Dinwiddie's expansionist views are set out in Dinwiddie to Thomas Cresap, 23 January 1752; Dinwiddie to Cresap and [William] Trent, 10 February 1753; Dinwiddie to J[ohn] Hanbury, 12 March [1754]; Dinwiddie to C[apel] Hanbury, 10 May 1754; Dinwiddie to the Lords of the Treasury, 10 May 1754, in *Dinwiddie Papers*, 1:17, 22–23, 102–3, 154–55, 164.

87.  Patrice Louis-Rene Higonnet, "The Origins of the Seven Years' War," *Journal of Modern History*, 40 (March 1968): 60–61.

88.  Dinwiddie to Cresap, 23 January 1752, in *Dinwiddie Papers*, 1:17–18.

89.  Ibid., Dinwiddie to Lord Holderness, 12 March 1754, p. 94.

90.  Ibid., Dinwiddie to the earl of Halifax, 25 October [1754], p. 368. While serving as commander in chief of British-American forces in North America, the earl of Loudoun also came to have doubts about Dinwiddie's rectitude, albeit in another connection. Enraged by Dinwiddie's unauthorized action in lifing a shipping embargo that he had imposed as commander in chief, Loudoun concluded that Dinwiddie had a personal financial stake in the resumption of Virginia's trade (see Stanley M. Pargellis, *Lord Loudoun in North America* [New Haven, 1933], pp. 266–67).

91.  Dinwiddie to Governor Glen, 5 August [1754], in *Dinwiddie Papers*, 1:276.

92.  Washington to the earl of Loudoun, 10 January 1757, in *Washington Papers*, 4:79–80.

93.  Morton, *Colonial Virginia*, 2:602; Bailey, *Ohio Company*, pp. 147–49.

94.  Higonnet, "Seven Years' War," p. 61.

95.  Dinwiddie's address to the general assembly [February 1753], in *Dinwiddie Papers*, 1:26.

96.  Ibid.; Henry Read McIlwaine, ed., *Journals of the House of Burgessess of Virginia, 1752–1755, 1756–1758* (Richmond, 1909), pp. 4–5, 99–100, 103–5, 171, 176–77.

97.  Koontz, *Robert Dinwiddie*, pp. 173, 181; Morton, *Colonial Virginia*, 2:605; McIlwaine, *Burgesses, 1752–1758*, pp. 96, 99.

98.  Hening, *Statutes*, 6:258, 355–56; see above p. 9.

99.  Employing his constitutional powers as Virginia's commander in chief, Dinwiddie did undertake a minor reform of the militia system on his own initiative in November 1752 when he divided the colony into four militia districts, each in the charge of an adjutant responsible for bringing local units "to a more regular discipline." The four districts replaced the single colonywide adjutancy, a post that had been occupied by Lawrence Washington until his death in 1752. This reform also served to introduce George Washington to military affairs as Governor Dinwiddie appointed

him adjutant of the southern district of Virginia. Thus at age twenty, Washington became officially "Major" Washington (see Dinwiddie's Message to the House of Burgessess [October 1752], in *Dinwiddie Papers*, 1:41; Gipson, *South of the Great Lakes*, pp. 265–66; Freeman, *Washington*, 1:266, 268.).

100. Greene, *Quest for Power*, pp. 159–60.

101. McIlwaine, *Burgessess, 1752–1758*, pp. 121, 129, 132, 136, 141, 143–44.

102. On the pistole fee controversy see Glenn C. Smith, "The Affair of the Pistole Fee," *VMHB*, 48 (July 1940): 209–21.

103. Dinwiddie to J[ames] Abercromby, 26 April [1754], in *Dinwiddie Papers*, 1:137–41.

104. Gipson, *South of the Great Lakes*, pp. 262–63.

105. Ibid., pp. 260–61, see especially note 90, p. 261.

106. McIlwaine, *Burgesses, 1752–1758*, pp. 175–77.

107. Leach, *Arms for Empire*, pp. 318–20.

108. Gipson, *South of the Great Lakes*, pp. 189–91, 269–70.

109. Ibid., pp. 191–202; Leach, *Arms for Empire*, pp. 321–22; the inscriptions on the lead plates are quoted in Howard H. Peckham, *The Colonial Wars, 1689–1762*, vol. 2 of *The Chicago History of American Civilization*, ed. Daniel J. Boorstin (Chicago, 1964), p. 123.

110. "Twightee" was the name given by the British to the Miami Indians.

111. Morton, *Colonial Virginia*, 2:616–17; Leach, *Arms for Empire*, pp. 323–24, Gipson, *South of the Great Lakes*, pp. 220–24, 255–56. Gipson describes the fall of Pickawillany as a "momentous event" in the growing crisis between Britons and Frenchmen on the western frontier.

112. Leach, *Arms for Empire*, p. 325; Gipson, *South of the Great Lakes*, pp. 265–75; Peckham, *Colonial Wars*, p. 128.

113. Gipson, *South of the Great Lakes*, pp. 288–90.

114. Ibid., p. 291.

115. Message of Governor Dinwiddie to the House of Burgesses, [November 1753], *Dinwiddie Papers*, 1:39–40.

116. Freeman, *Washington*, 1:309–10. Of this messge to St. Pierre, Dinwiddie's best-known biographer states that it was "so explicit in its claims in behalf of the English people that the governor of the Virginia colony must have known that he committed himself to hostilities if the French commandant rejected his demands" (see Koontz, *Virginia Frontier*, p. 49).

117. Gipson, *South of the Great Lakes*, p. 298.

118. Washington was selected after the council's first two choices, Colonel Joshua Fry and Major William Russell, declined this dangerous assignment. On this point see ibid., pp. 295–96. Bernhard Knollenberg believes that Washington's selection was due primarily to the influence of his patron, William Fairfax (see Knollenberg, *George Washington: The Virginia Period, 1732–1775* [Durham, N. C., 1964] pp. 11–12).

119. The best account of Washington's epic trek to Fort Le Boeuf is in Freeman, *Washington*, 1:274–326. See also James Thomas Flexner, *George Washington: The Forge of Experience (1732–1775)* (Boston, 1965), pp. 55–80; Gipson, *South of the Great Lakes*, pp. 294–99; and Morton, *Colonial Virginia*, 2:638–42.

120. The contents of Washington's journal have been reprinted in *The Diaries of George Washington, 1748–1799*, ed. Donald Jackson, 6 vols. (Charlottesville, Va., 1976–79), 1:118–61, and in *The Diaries of George Washington, 1748–1799*, ed. John C. Fitzpatrick, 4 vols. (Boston and New York, 1925), 1:73–102.

121. Morton, *Colonial Virginia*, 2:642.

122. Ibid., pp. 31–32.

123. Washington to the earl of Loudoun, 10 January 1757, in *Washington Papers*, 4:79.

## 2. "THE DISAGREEABLE SUBJECT OF DEFENCE": THE POLITICS OF MOBILIZATION

1. Such is the conclusion reached by R. R. Palmer and Joel Colton, *A History of the Modern World* (New York, 1960), p. 249; Max Savelle, *The Origins of American Diplomacy: The International History of Angloamerica, 1942–1763* (New York and London, 1967), p. 386; Richard L. Morton, *Colonial Virginia*, 2 vols. (Chapel Hill, 1960), 2:635–37; Douglas Edward Leach, *Arms for Empire: A Military History of the British Colonies in North America: 1607–1763* (New York, 1973), pp. 307–8; and more recently by W. Stitt Robinson, *The Southern Colonial Frontier, 1607–1763* (Albuquerque, 1979), p. 202. For a contrasting view see Lawrence Henry Gipson, *The British Empire before the American Revolution*, vol. 6: *The Great War for Empire: The Years of Defeat, 1754–1757* (New York, 1946), pp. 9–10, 16–17, 20.

2. [John Mercer?], "Dinwiddiane," November 1757, in *The Colonial Virginia Satirist: Mid-Eighteenth Century Commentaries on Politics, Religion and Society*, ed. Richard Beale Davis (Philadelphia, 1967), pp. 17–18. On this point see also Morton, *Colonial Virginia*, 2:579; Kenneth P. Bailey, *The Ohio Company of Virginia and the Westward Movement, 1748–1792: A Chapter in the History of the Colonial Frontier* (Glendale, Calif., 1939), p. 35; David John Mays, ed., *The Letters and Papers of Edmund Pendleton, 1743–1803*, 2 vols. (Charlottesville, 1976), 1:81.

3. The widespread belief that the governor's aggressive western policy was driven mainly by his personal financial stake in the Ohio Company was emphasized by George Washington when he tried to explain the apathy that greeted Dinwiddie's early warnings about the French threat at the back of Virginia. See Washington to John Campbell, earl of Loudoun, January 1757, in W. W. Abbot et al., eds., *The Papers of George Washington: Colonial Series*, 4 vols. to date (Charlottesville, Va., 1983– ), 4:79. Another contemporary of Dinwiddie's used verse to point up the distinction between the governor's public professions and private intentions:

"In words the public good affecting,
to private views, your deeds directing."

(Quoted in Davis, *Colonial Virginia Satirist*, p. 29.)

4. Dinwiddie to Thomas Cresap, 23 January 1752, in *The Official Records of Robert Dinwiddie, Lieutenant-Governor of the Colony of Virginia, 1751–1758, Now First Printed from the Manuscript in the Collections of the Virginia Historical Society*, ed. Robert A. Brock, 2 vols. (Richmond, 1883), 1:17–18. Louis K. Koontz, whose admiration for Dinwiddie is evident on every page of his biography of the Virginia governor, acknowledges that Dinwiddie's interest in the Ohio Company was inextricably bound up in the circumstances that occasioned the French and Indian War. See Koontz, *Robert Dinwiddie: His Career in American Colonial Government and Westward Expansion* (Glendale, Calif., 1941) p. 241. On another occasion Koontz termed Dinwiddie "one of England's most imperially-minded colonial officials." See Koontz, "Washington on the Frontier," *Virginia Magazine of History and Biography* (hereafter cited as VMHB), 36 (October 1928): 307. Dinwiddie's role in instigating the crisis in the Ohio Valley also receives major emphasis in John R. Alden, *Robert Dinwiddie: Servant of the Crown* (Charlottesville, 1973), p. 42. Alden is a sympathetic biographer but minces no words when describing Dinwiddie's role in the coming of the French and Indian War. According to Alden, Dinwiddie "precipitated" that conflict. See ibid., p. 2. For a detailed analysis of the provocative actions of both Dinwiddie and his

principal French protagonist, the Marquis Duquesne, see Partice Louis-Rene Higonnet, "The Origins of the Seven Years' War," *Journal of Modern History*, 40 (March, 1968): 57–90. Higonnet contends that the Anglo-French conflict over the Ohio country was largely instigated by the Virginia governor. For a vigorous critique of Higonnet, see T. R. Clayton, "The Duke of Newcastle, the Earl of Halifax, and the American Origins of the Seven Years' War," *Historical Journal*, 24 (September 1981): 571–603.

5. Dinwiddie to the Board of Trade, P.R.O., C.O. 5/1327, ff. 274 (microfilm copy in Colonial Williamsburg Foundation, Research Archives, hereafter cited as CWFRA); Dinwiddie to Captains [Michael] Cresap and [William]Trent, 10 February 1754, in *Dinwiddie Papers*, 1:23; Dinwiddie to Governor James Glen, 25 October 1754, in ibid., p. 377. Francis Jennings offers a detailed analysis of Anglo-Iroquois relations down to the mid-eighteenth centruy in *The Ambiguous Iroquois Empire* (New York, 1984). See especially chapters 2, 18, and 19. Iroquois pretensions to dominion in the Ohio country are addressed more summarily in Anthony F. C. Wallace, *The Death and Rebirth of the Seneca* (New York, 1969), pp. 111–14. Other new scholarship on the Iroquois includes Richard Aguila, *Iroquois Restoration: Iroquois Diplomacy on the Colonial Frontier* (Detroit, 1982), and Daniel K. Richter and James H. Merrell, eds., *Beyond the Covenant Chain: The Iroquois and Their Neighbors in Indian North America, 1600–1800* (Syracuse, 1987). I am grateful to Professor Fred Anderson for calling my attention to these important studies.

6. Lawrence Henry Gipson, *The British Empire before the American Revolution*, vol. 4: *Zones of International Friction: North America, South of the Great Lakes Region, 1748–1754* (New York, 1961), pp. 269–75, 295–99.

7. Dinwiddie to the Board of Trade, 16 June 1753, P.R.O., C.O. 5/1327, ff. 292–94 (microfilm copy in CWFRA). See also Dinwiddie to Governor James Hamilton, 22 May 1753, P.R.O., C.O. 5/1327, ff. 306–7 (microfilm copy in CWFRA).

8. Board of Trade to the king, 16 August 1753, P.R.O., C.O. 5/1367, (microfilm copy in CWFRA).

9. Halifax to the duke of Newcastle, 15 August 1753, British Museum, Add. MSS. 33,029 (microfilm copy in CWFRA).

10. The earl of Holderness to Dinwiddie, 28 August 1753, P.R.O., C.O. 5/211, ff. 21–40 (microfilm copy in CWFRA).

11. This point is made more fully in Higonnet, "Origins of the Seven Years' War," p. 65.

12. Dinwiddie to Lord Fairfax, [January 1754] in *Dinwiddie Papers*, 1:49.

13. Ibid.; Dinwiddie to Patton, January 1754, in ibid., pp. 50–51.

14. Washington's adjutancy had been transferred from the Southern to the Northern Military District in November 1753; see Morton, *Colonial Virginia*, 2:643, n. 14.

15. Dinwiddie to Trent, January 1754, in *Dinwiddie Papers*, 1:55–57.

16. Ibid., Dinwiddie to the governors of South Carolina, Pennsylvania, North Carolina, New York, Maryland, New Jersey, and Massachusetts, January 1754, 61–71.

17. See note 3, above.

18. Dinwiddie to the governors of Massachusetts, New Jersey, and South Carolina, January 1754, in *Dinwiddie Papers*, 1:70, 68, 62. For a further discussion of this point, see Higonnet, "Origins of the Seven Years' War," p. 63.

19. John Richard Alden, *John Stuart and the Southern Colonial Frontier: A Study of Indian Relations, War, Trade, and Land Problems in the Southern Wilderness, 1754–1775* (Ann Arbor, 1944), pp. 31–32, 42–43. Dinwiddie's correspondence with the Cherokee and Catawba chieftans is in *Dinwiddie Papers*, 1:60–61.

20. Gipson, *Zones of International Friction*, p. 24; Hayes Baker-Crothers, *Virginia and the French and Indian War* (Chicago, 1928), p. 40.

21. Baker-Crothers, *French and Indian War*, pp. 42–43; Douglas Southall Freeman, *George Washington: A Biography*, 7 vols. (New York, 1948–57), 1:418–19.

22. Dinwiddie to the earl of Albemarle, 18 June 1754; Dinwiddie to Governor Horatio Sharpe, 6 September 1754, in *Dinwiddie Papers*, 1:209, 304. A full account of the ludicrous proceedings involving the North Carolinians is in Gipson, *The Years of Defeat*, pp. 46–47.

23. Baker-Crothers, *French and Indian War*, p. 45. Douglas Edward Leach attributes the absence of "unified action" to the general malaise of "colonial particularism" (see Leach, *Arms for Empire*, p. 331). In fact, each of Virginia's neighboring colonies seems to have had substantial reasons for refusing its aid.

24. Douglas Southall Freeman and Richard L. Morton believe that Fairfax's personal disinclination to comply with Dinwiddie's directive accounts for the refractory behavior of the Frederick militia. See Freeman, *Washington*,1:331, and Morton, *Colonial Virginia*, 2:643. That opposition to Dinwiddie's orders came from within the Frederick militia itself is suggested in Dinwiddie to Lord Fairfax, 23 February 1754, in *Dinwiddie Papers*, 1:82.

25. Washington to Dinwiddie, 20 March 1754, in *Washington Papers*, 1:78.

26. William Waller Hening, ed., *The Statutes at Large: Being a Collection of All the Laws of Virginia from the First Session of the Legislature, in the Year 1619*, 13 vols. (Richmond and Philadelphia, 1809–23), 6:113, 350. The applicable statute was an act of 1748 entitled "An Act for making provision against Invasions and Insurrections."

27. Daniel J. Boorstin, *The Americans: The Colonial Experience* (New York, 1958), pp. 351–57; Don Higginbotham, *The War of American Independence: Military Attitudes, Policies, and Practice, 1763–1789* (New York and London, 1971), pp. 7, 10–11; Leach, *Arms for Empire*, p. 21; Richard H. Kohn, *Eagle and Sword: The Beginnings of the Military Establishment in America* (New York, 1975), pp. 7–9; John E. Ferling, *A Wilderness of Miseries: War and Warriors in Early America* (Westport, Conn., 1980), p. 16.

28. Dinwiddie to the House of Burgesses [November 1753], in *Dinwiddie Papers*, 1:41.

29. Traditional interpretations regarding the nature of the political system of eighteenth-century Virginia may be found in Charles S. Sydnor, *Gentlemen Freeholders: Political Practices in Washington's Virginia* (Chapel Hill, 1952); Carl Bridenbaugh, *Myths and Realities: Societies of the Colonial South* (Baton Rouge, 1952), pp. 1–53; and Boorstin, *The Colonial Experience*, pp. 92–143. Richard L. Morton's richly detailed *Colonial Virginia* also supports this point of view; see especially volume 2, pp. 120–21. Dissenting interpretations are available in Thomas J. Wertenbaker, *Patrician and Plebian in Colonial Virginia, 1698–1750* (Charlottesville, 1910) and in the same author's *The Planters of Colonial Virginia* (Princeton, 1922). A more recent argument on behalf of democratic tendencies in eighteenth-century Virginia is made by Robert E. and B. Katherine Brown in *Virginia, 1705–1786: Democracy or Aristocracy?* (East Lansing, 1964). The newest major interpretive study of eighteenth-century Virginia is Rhys Isaacs' *The Transformation of Virginia, 1740–1790* (Chapel Hill, 1982). In this highly original study, Isaacs charts Virginia's transition from a traditional, hierarchical political and social system to a more open and complex cultural order.

30. Jackson Turner Main, *The Social Structure of Revolutionary America* (Princeton, 1965), p. 62; Brown, *Democracy or Aristocracy?* pp. 12, 15; Jack P. Greene, "Society, Ideology, and Politics: An Analysis of the Political Culture of Mid-Eighteenth Century Virginia," in Richard M. Jellison, ed., *Society, Freedom, and*

*Conscience: The Coming of the Revolution in Virginia, Massachusetts, and New York* (New York, 1976), p. 17.

31.  Hugh Jones, *The Present State of Virginia From Whence Is Interred A Short View of Maryland and North Carolina* (London, 1724), ed. Richard L. Morton (Chapel Hill, 1956), p. 130; Main, *Social Structure*, p. 66; Greene, "Society, Ideology, and Politics," p. 17. In spite of the fact that some "landless" whites were relatred to men of property, enjoyed free access to their holdings, and might someday come to possess those lands themselves, there is ample reason for supposing that about one-fifth of the white population was made up of truly poor men. On this point see Main, *Social Structure*, pp. 49–51, 54. According to Main's definition, "truly poor men" were those who were landless and lacked more than fifty pounds in personal property (ibid., p. 62).

32.  The numerical dominance of the "middling sort" in eighteenth-century Virginia is noted in, among other places, Main, *Social Structure*, p. 65; Greene, "Society, Ideology, and Politics," p. 17; and Richard Hofstadter, *America at 1750: A Social Portrait* (New York, 1973), p. 158. On the middle-class orientation of the militia, see *Dinwiddie Papers*, 2:345. Historians agree that franchise requirements in eighteenth-century Virginia were not very restrictive. All adult white males owning twenty-five acres of improved land or one hundred acres of unimproved land were qualified to vote. Even tenants could vote if they held a lifetime lease on enough land to meet the established suffrage requirements. James A. Henretta estimates that 60 percent of the adult white males possessed sufficient property to vote (Henretta, *The Evolution of American Society, 1700–1815: An Interdisciplinary Analysis* [Lexington, Mass., 1973], p. 92). Charles Sydnor, Jack Greene, J. R. Pole, and Robert and Katherine Brown also agree that the franchise was widespread in prerevolutionary Virginia (Sydnor, *Gentlemen Freeholders*, p. 75; Greene, "Society, Ideology, and Politics," p. 20; Pole, "Historians and the Problem of Early American Democracy," *American Historical Review*, 47 (April 1962): 635; Brown, *Democracy or Aristocracy?* p. 131). Evidence that eighteenth-century Virginians themselves were aware of the existence of three general orders or ranks in their society is to be found in contemporary references to the "rich" or "better sort," the "middling sort," and the "poor." On this point see Main, *Social Structure*, p. 232.

33.  Sydnor, *Gentlemen Freeholders*, p. 23. Election to the lower house was a very serious business since that institution was, by common agreement, "the chief support of the Liberty and Property of the Subject" (ibid., p. 26). J. R. Pole notes that elections "were almost invariably between members of the gentry" (Pole, "Early American Democracy," p. 635).

34.  Sydnor, *Gentlemen Freeholders*, p. 95.

35.  Even Robert and Katherine Brown admit that Virginia voters customarily chose "men above average in their economic and social status" for their representatives (*Democracy or Aristocracy?* p. 227); see also Greene, "Society, Ideology, and Politics," p. 23. On the influence of slavery on white solidarity, see Edmund S. Morgan, *American Slavery, American Freedom: The Ordeal of Colonial Virginia* (New York, 1975), chapter 17, and Wertenbaker, *Patrician and Plebian*, p. 212.

36.  Sydnor, *Gentlemen Freeholders*, p. 42.

37.  Douglas Adair, ed., "James Madison's Autobiography," *William and Mary Quarterly* (hereafter cited as *WMQ*), 3d ser., 2 (April 1945): 199.

38.  John Pendleton Kennedy, ed., *Journals of the House of Burgesses of Virginia, 1761–1765* (Richmond, 1909), pp. 269–71; Sydnor, *Gentlemen Freeholders*, pp. 47–48.

39.  Jack P. Greene, ed., *The Diary of Colonel Landon Carter of Sabine Hall, 1752–1778*, 2 vols. (Charlottesville, 1965), 2:1009.

40. Jones, *Present State of Virginia*, p. 77; Ferling, *Wilderness of Miseries*, p. 121.

41. Dinwiddie to Lord Holdernesse, 12 March 1754, in *Dinwiddie Papers*, 1:93–94.

42. Ibid., Dinwiddie to Lord Fairfax, 23 February 1754, p. 82.

43. Ibid., Dinwiddie to Holdernesse, 12 March 1754, p. 93–94.

44. Hening, *Statutes*, 5:417–18.

45. Dinwiddie to Holdernesse, 12 March 1754, in *Dinwiddie Papers*, 1:94.

46. Greene, *Carter Diary*, 1:123.

47. Message of Governor Dinwiddie to the council and burgesses, [14 February 1754], in *Dinwiddie Papers*, 1:74; Henry Read McIlwaine, ed., *Journals of the House of Burgesses of Virginia, 1752–1755, 1756–1758* (Richmond, 1909), p. 176.

48. Message of Governor Dinwiddie to the council and burgesses, [14 February 1754], in *Dinwiddie Papers*, 1:73–75; ibid., "Message of Governor Dinwiddie to the House of Burgesses," pp. 75–76; ibid., p. 76; McIlwaine, *Burgesses, 1752–1758*, pp. 176–77.

49. Ibid., Message of Governor Dinwiddie to the council and burgesses, 14 February 1754, p. 75.

50. Address of the burgesses to Governor Dinwiddie, 15 February 1754, in *Dinwiddie Papers*, 1:78.

51. Greene, *Carter Diary*, 1:123.

52. Dinwiddie to J[oh]n Hanbury, 12 March 1754, in *Dinwiddie Papers*, 1:102.

53. Greene, *Carter Diary*, 1:123. Carter's reference was to the oblique title of the military supply bill: "An Act for the encouragement and protection of the settlers upon the waters of the Mississippi." Commenting on the reluctance of the House to support Dinwiddie's call to arms, one historian terms the bill's title a "pretext" for granting a supply (Joseph A. Waddell, *Annals of Augusta County, Virginia, From 1726 to 1871* [Staunton, Va., 1902; reprint, Bridgewater, Va., 1958], p. 100)

54. Dinwiddie to the Lords of Trade, 12 March 1754, in *Dinwiddie Papers*, 1:98; ibid., Dinwiddie to James Abercromby, 26 April 1754, p. 141.

55. Ibid., Dinwiddie to Captain [Adam] Stephen, 11 August 1755, 2:150.

56. Ibid., Dinwiddie to Speaker [of the House of Burgesses] John Robinson, 24 January 1755, 1:477–78.

57. Hening, *Statutes*, 6:418.

58. Washington to Dinwiddie, 29 April 1757, in *Washington Papers*, 4:147–48; Jack Greene claims that Dinwiddie took it upon himself to "persuade the House to include four councilors among the commissioners" (see Greene, *The Quest for Power: The Lower Houses of Assembly in the Southern Royal Colonies, 1689–1776* [Chapel Hill, 1963], p. 104). However, in a letter to the Board of Trade, the governor implied that those appointments had been made unilaterally by the House of Burgesses and "contrary to the Desire" of the councilors themselves. In fact, the House's presumptuousness was cited by the governor as one reason why he would have preferred to disallow the appropriations act (see Dinwiddie to the Lords [of] Trade, 10 May 1754, in *Dinwiddie Papers*, 1:161). The original members of the appropriations committee were councilors William Nelson, Thomas Nelson, Philip Grymes, and Peter Randolph. Representing the burgesses were John Robinson, Charles Carter, Carter Burwell, Benjamin Waller, Richard Bland, James Power, William Digges, Dudley Digges, John Page, and John Chiswell. Any nine members constituted a quorum (Hening, *Statutes*, 6:418).

59.  Hening, *Statutes*, 6:418. Dinwiddie to the Lords of Trade, 10 May 1754, in *Dinwiddie Papers*, 1:161. Dinwiddie questioned the constitutionality of the appropriations bill on the grounds that it deprived the governor of "his undoubted [right] of directing the Application of all Monies rais'd for the Defence and security of the Country."

60.  Hening, *Statutes*, 5:401–4.

61.  Greene, *Quest for Power*, pp. 103, 304.

62.  The process by which the lower houses of assembly in the southern provinces increased their authority at the expense of the colonial executive is carefully deliniated in Greene, *Quest for Power*. For legislative encroachment in the area of military affairs, see especially pp. 297–309.

63.  Hening, *Statutes*, 7:69–87, 163–69, 171–231, 251–53, 255–65, 331–37, 347–53, 357–63, 369–72, 381–83, 463–65, 495–502. Jack Greene emphasizes that the decision made in the spring of 1758 not to continue the committee was based on the relatively high cost of its operations (Greene, *Quest for Power*, p. 306). Greene fails to note that this decision was made by the first session of the assembly to be convened after Dinwiddie left office. The coincidence between the departure of the distrusted governor and the lapse of the committee seems too neat to be just that.

64.  Dinwiddie to Washington, 25 May 1754, in *Dinwiddie Papers*, 1:172.

65.  Ibid., Dinwiddie to Governor [James] Hamilton, 21 March 1754, p. 120; see also Dinwiddie to Horatio Sharpe, 1 March 1754, in *Dinwiddie Papers*, 1:86.

66.  Freeman, *Washington*, 1:339.

67.  On George Muse see Freeman, *Washington*, and Peter Walne, ed., "A Mystery Resolved: George Washington's Letter to Governor Dinwiddie, June 10, 1754," *VMHB*, 79 (April 1971): 138, n. 16. At the time of his appointment, Muse was serving as militia adjutant for the Middle Neck Military District (the region between the Rappahannock and York rivers. Ironically, Muse was later cashiered for cowardice during the Battle of the Great Meadows; see Greene, *Carter Diary*, 1:115.

68.  Douglas Southall Freeman notes that Dinwiddie had a "certain partiality for his fellow Scots"; Freeman, *Washington*, 1:339.

69.  Adam Stephen, "The Ohio Expedition of 1754" in Benjamin Rush Papers (MSS, Historical Society of Pennsylvania, Philadelphia, Pa.) reprinted in *Pennsylvania Magazine of History and Biography*, 18 (1894): 43–44.

70.  Biographical sketches of most of the original officers in the Virginia Regiment are available in *Dinwiddie Papers*, 1:112–15, notes 83–91.

71.  In his *History of the United States Army*, for example, Russell F. Weigley makes no distinction at all between Virginia's provincial forces and militiamen called up for temporary periods of active service. He chooses rather to incorporate the two different institutions by referring to them jointly as Virginia's "militia army." See Weigley, *History of the United States Army* (New York, 1976), pp. 14–16. Similar confusion regarding the differences between provincials and militia is to be found in Howard H. Peckham's *The Colonial Wars*. The forces under Washington's command in 1754 are mistakenly called "Virginia militia," and one chapter is misleadingly entitled "French Militia vs. Virginia Militia" (see Peckham, *The Colonial Wars, 1689–1762* [Chicago, 1964], pp. 120–38. In *Arms for Empire*, Douglas Edward Leach's truly sweeping survey of the colonial military experience, the existence of provincial forces is recognized, but their distinctive role in the colonial military structure is largely ignored. Significant similarities notwithstanding, provincial armies were not exact replicas in miniature of the regular British army, identical at every point but size. For example, provincial troops served comparatively short enlistments and rarely if ever were used to control or coerce the civilian population. Most significantly, provincial armies were

not permanent institutions; they were created in response to a specific military requirement and existed only for the duration of hostilities.

72. Hening, *Statutes*, 5:16.

73. Washington to Dinwiddie, 9 March 1754, in *Washington Papers*, 1:73–74.

74. John W. Shy, "A New Look at Colonial Militia," *WMQ*, 3d ser., 20 (April
1963): 181–83; Ferling, *Wilderness of Miseries*, pp. 77, 92.

75. Washington to Captain Joshua Lewis, 18 September 1755, in *Washington
Papers*, 2:48.

76. "A Roll of Captain Christopher Gist's company[,] July 13th, 1756," in George
Washington Papers (MSS, Library of Congress, Washington, D.C.), ser. 4, 4:472. Gist,
a native of Maryland and later a resident of western Pennsylvania, no doubt had traded
on his connections in both places to raise these men.

77. "A Roll of Capt. Robert Stewart's Troop," 11 May 1756, in Washington
Papers, MSS ser. 4:354. See also ibid., "A Roll of Capt. Henry Harrison's Company,"
13 July 1756; "A Roll of Capt. Joshua Lewis's Company," 13 July 1756; "A Roll of
Capt. William Peachy's Company," 13 July 1756; "A Roll of Capt. Robert Spotswoods'
Company," 13 July 1756; "A Roll of Capt. Robert Stewart's Troop of Light Horse," 30
July 1756, items 428, 430, 432, 433, 452.

78. Hening, *Statutes*, 6:438–440; 7:44–46; 163–69. The military supply bills that
authorized the enlistment of men in provincial service were not always explicit about
the duration of such enlistments. If not otherwise stated, soldiers presumably were
expected to serve during the period a particular bill was in force. Most supply bills
had a legislative life of one year. However, in commenting on a troop bill enacted in
March 1756, Dinwiddie gave it as his opinion that men who agreed to enlist as paid
substitutes (that is, men who in effect volunteered for duty and accepted the ten-pound
fine imposed on draftees who wished to avoid service) had made themselves liable for
an indefinite term of service. *Dinwiddie Papers*, 2:423.

79. Washington to the earl of Loudoun, 10 January 1757, in *Washington Papers*,
4:84. On this point see also Freeman, *Washington*, 2:136.

80. Fear of the harsh penalties authorized by the British Mutiny Act was not the
only thing that promoted reasonably good behavior among Washington's troops while
on the march to and from Fort Necessity. During their first campaign the men of the
Virginia Regiment simply had nowhere to desert unless it was into the arms of the
French or hostile Indians. Fear of capture as much as fear of punishment kept the men
in the ranks. Once returned to the relative safety of Wills Creek, they deserted in
droves.

81. Hening, *Statutes*, 6:114.

82. Ibid., p. 546.

83. Ibid., p. 560

84. Ibid., 7:87–92.

85. Ibid., pp. 106–16. See especially sections 4 and 6.

86. Pay rates for Virginia militiamen called to active duty customarily were
calculated in pounds of tobacco. During the first two years of the French and Indian
War, the following pay rates were in force:

| CAVALRY Pounds of Tobacco Per Day | | INFANTRY Pounds of Tobacco Per Day | |
|---|---|---|---|
| Colonel | 60 | Colonel | 50 |
| Lieutenant Colonel | 50 | Lieutenant Colonel | 40 |
| Major | 50 | Major | 40 |
| Captain | 30 | Captain | 30 |
| Lieutenant | 30 | Lieutenant | 25 |
| Cornet | 25 | Ensign | 20 |
| Quartermaster | 25 | Sergeant | 18 |
| Corporal | 22 | Drummer | 18 |
| Trumpeter | 22 | Soldier | 15 |
| Trooper | 20 | | |

Virginia's provincial forces received their wages in money (provincial currency) rather than tobacco. Pay rates for most grades remained unchanged throughout the years of the French and Indian War. As of 1754 the regimental pay table was established as follows:

| RANK | WAGES PER DAY |
|---|---|
| Colonel | 15 *s.* |
| Lieutenant Colonel | 12 *s.* |
| Major | 10 *s.* |
| Captain | 8 *s.* |
| Lieutenant | 4. *s.* |
| Ensign | 3 *s.* |
| Sergeant | 2 *s.* |
| Drummer | 1. *s.* |
| Soldier | 8 *p.* |

In October 1754, when the Virginia assembly agreed that a recently enacted poll tax might be paid in either cash or tobacco, it was deemed that one pound of tobacco had an equivalent cash value of one penny. By using this figure as a conversion factor, it can be seen that provincial officers received a considerably higher salary than their tobacco-earning counterparts in the militia. For example, if converted into shillings and pence, the daily pay of an infantry major in the militia would be 3*s.* 4.*d.*, less than half of what was paid to a major in the Virginia Regiment. The same or even greater differentials applied to other officer ranks. Throughout the war, however, militiamen in the lowest enlisted grades who were called to active duty continued to be favored over their provincial counterparts by a pay differential of at least 4*p.* per day.

87. Main, *Social Structure*, p. 130. Wages are shown in provincial currency, worth about 40 to 70 percent of sterling. It should be noted that wages paid to common laborers typically were not "found" wages; that is, all ordinary living expenses had to be borne by the worker himself. The fact that the lower wages paid to provincial soldiers were "found" and thus included at least the promise of free food and certain items of apparel, theoretically served to diminish the salary differential between common soldiers and their civilian counterparts. In reality, the promises made to provincial soldiers often went unredeemed.

88. Reply of Governor Dinwiddie to the . . . [Governor's Council], [16 February 1754], in *Dinwiddie Papers*, 1:78; ibid., Dinwiddie to J[ames] Abercromby, 26 April 1754, pp. 137–38; Greene, *Carter Diary*, 1:123.

89. Washington to Dinwiddie, 9 March 1754, in *Washington Papers*, 1:73–74.

90. In his study of early American military institutions and ideas, Lawrence Delbert Cress notes that Virginia lawmakers were particularly disposed to employ

vagrants and social misfits as soldiers (see Cress, *Citizens in Arms: The Army and the Militia in American Society to the War of 1812* [Chapel Hill, 1982], p. 6).

### 3. "POMPOUS UNDERTAKINGS AND INGLORIOUS RESULTS": THE CAMPAIGNS OF 1754 AND 1755

1. Dinwiddie to Halifax, 12 March 1754; Dinwiddie to Governor [James] Glen, 15 April 1754, in *The Official Records of Robert Dinwiddie, Lieutenant-Governor of the Colony of Virginia, 1751–1758, Now First Printed from the Manuscript in the Collections of the Virginia Historical Society*, ed. Robert A. Brock, 2 vols. (Richmond, 1883), 1:100, 127.

2. Ibid., Dinwiddie to the earl of Holdernesse, 12 March 1754, p. 96. The land grant proclamation is reprinted in William Waller Hening, ed., *The Statutes at Large: Being a Collection of All the Laws of Virginia from the First Session of the Legislature, in the Year 1619*, 13 vols. (Richmond and Philadelphia, 1809–23), 7:661–62. The text of the proclamation implies that bounty lands on the Ohio were intended only for enlisted men. Bernhard Knollenberg makes much of this point in discussing how former Virginia Regiment officers, George Washington chief among them, came to obtain the lion's share of the property (see Knollenberg, *George Washington: The Virginia Period, 1732–1775* [Durham, N.C., 1964], pp. 91–100). Knollenberg fails to appreciate that in spite of the wording of the proclamation, Dinwiddie did intend to award tracts of land to provincial officers as well as to enlisted men. The governor made that point clear in his letter of 12 March 1754 to Lord Holdernesse. The existence and amount of the enlistment bounty is mentioned in Dinwiddie to Governor [James] Hamilton, 21 March 1754, in *Dinwiddie Papers*, 1:121. Private John Shaw's testimony is contained in an affidavit he submitted to the South Carolina Council on 6 September 1754. The affidavit is reprinted in Hays Baker-Crothers and Ruth Allisan Hudnut, "A Private Soldier's Account of Washington's First Battles in the West: A Study in Historical Criticism," *Journal of Southern History*, 8 (May 1942): 23.

3. Baker-Crothers and Hudnut, "Washington's First Battles," p. 23.

4. Washington to Dinwiddie, 9 March 1754, in W. W. Abbot, et al., eds., *Papers of George Washington: Colonial Series*, 4 vols. to date (Charlottesville, Va., 1983–   ), 1:73–74.

5. Ibid., Washington to Dinwiddie, 20 March 1754, p. 32. The population figures were derived from "A List of Tithables Sent to the Lords of Trade," 23 February 1756, in *Dinwiddie Papers*, 2:345, 352–53. The list of tithables included the governor's "Observations" on the total population of the colony.

6. Washington to Dinwiddie, 20 March 1754, in *Washington Papers*, 1:78. During this period it seems that Washington was reduced to promising potential recruits that "whatever they carried as soldiers" on the expedition should be their "own" to keep (ibid., Captain James Mackay to Washington, 27 August 1754, pp. 194–95). Perhaps if he had been aware of this commitment, Governor Dinwiddie would have thought it less "strange that the Officers shou'd have allow'd them [the provincial] troops to Desert with their Guns" (ibid., Dinwiddie to Washington, 3 August 1754, p. 182).

7. Ibid., Dinwiddie to Fairfax, [January 1754], p. 52; see also Louis K. Koontz, *Robert Dinwiddie: His Career in American Colonial Government and Western Expansion* (Glendale, Calif., 1941), p. 247.

8. "Commission of John Carlyle," 26 January 1754, in *Dinwiddie Papers*, 1:54; see also ibid., Dinwiddie to Carlyle, 27 January 1754, p. 53.

9. Carlyle to Washington, 17 June 1754, 28 June 1754, in *Letters to Washington and Accompanying Papers*, ed. Stanislaus Murray Hamilton, 5 vols. (Boston and New York, 1898–1902), 1:4–5, 18–20. Washington himself had harsh words for backcountry

provisioners; see Washington to William Fairfax, 11 August 1754, in *Washington Papers*, 1:186–87.

10. Dinwiddie to Colonel [William] Fairfax, 27 June [1754]; Dinwiddie to Carlyle, 27 June [1754]; Dinwiddie to Charles Dick, 4 December [1754], in *Dinwiddie Papers*, 1:220, 418–19.

11. Ibid., Dinwiddie to Sharpe, 17 December 1754, pp. 424–26. Another dubious incident involved the activities of Carlyle's deputy, Christopher Gist. Gist, a renowned explorer and frontiersman, had been retained by Carlyle to let contracts with farmers living in the Virginia and Maryland backcountry. Dinwiddie later complained that Gist's reported expenditures for beef cattle were so high that when joined with a bill for the same item submitted independently by Carlyle, the total amount was sufficient to provide every Virginia soldier with four barrels of beef a day (ibid., Dinwiddie to Carlyle, 20 February 1755, pp. 510–11).

12. Ibid., Dinwiddie to [William] Fairfax, 19 February 1755, pp. 509–10. Five months later Dinwiddie faulted Carlyle for charging commissions on the public transactions he performed while serving as commisary. In mid-1755 the governor rebuked him by saying: "W[he]n I appointed You Commissary I never imagin'd You w[oul]d have charg'd Com[m]is[sion]s as You had a stand'g Salary, and all You did was for the Public Service." This subsequent complaint notwithstanding, the governor was true to his promise and continued making use of Carlyle on an ad hoc basis (ibid., Dinwiddie to Carlyle, 9 July 1755, 2:97).

13. John W. Shy, *Toward Lexington: The Role of the British Army in the Coming of the American Revolution* (Princeton, 1965), p. 336.

14. On the regiment's continuing supply problems, see, for example, the letter of complaint from Colonel William Byrd III to Governor Francis Fauquier, 14 June 1758, in *The Correspondence of the Three William Byrds of Westover, Virginia 1684–1776*, ed. Marion Tinling, 2 vols. (Charlottesville, 1977), 2:659.

15. Dinwiddie to Washington, 15 March 1754, in *Dinwiddie Papers*, 1:106; ibid., "Governor Dinwiddie's Instructions to Major Washington," [January 1754], p. 59.

16. *The Diaries of George Washington, 1732–1799*, ed. Donald Jackson, 6 vols. (Charlottesville, 1976–79), 1:174–75. The Swedish volunteer was Carolus Gustavus de Splitdorph, later commissioned in the Virginia Regiment and killed in 1755 at the Battle of the Monongahela (see ibid., p. 175, note 23).

17. Washington to the earl of Loudoun, 10 January 1757, in *Washington Papers*, 4:80.

18. Douglas Southall Freeman, *George Washington: A Biography*, 7 vols. (New York, 1948–57), 1:347.

19. Washington to Dinwiddie, 25 April 1754, in *Washington Papers*, 1:88–89.

20. Ibid., Washington to Dinwiddie, [10 June 1754], 132–33.

21. Jumonville's party had been sent to warn the Virginians off "French territory" and to ascertain what they could about British intentions and strength. There are numerous accounts of Washington's skirmish with Jumonville; see, for example, Lawrence Henry Gipson, *The British Empire Before the American Revolution*, vol. 6: *The Great War for Empire: The Years of Defeat, 1754–1757* (New York, 1946), p. 31; and Douglas Edward Leach, *Arms for Empire: A Military History of the British Colonies in North America, 1607–1763* (New York and London, 1973), p. 335. The Jumonville Affair quickly became an international cause celebre with the French arguing that Jumonville had been a diplomatic emissary on his way to peacefully request the departure of the British and that the circumstances of his death were equivalent to an "assassination." Washington strongly defended his conduct, and Dinwiddie and the British government agreed that his attack on Jumonville had been justified. For

comments by the principals and other contemporaries on this controversial episode, see Jackson, *Washington Diaries*, 1:194–98; Dinwiddie to Sir Thomas Robinson, 18 June 1754; Dinwiddie to the earl of Albemarle, 18 June [1754], in *Dinwiddie Papers*, 1:202–3, 208–10; the earl of Albemarle [British Ambassador at Paris] to Sir Thomas Robinson, 2 September and 12 September 1754 in Shelburne Papers MSS, vol. 36, pp. 35, 48, original in the Clements Library, University of Michigan (microfilm copy in Colonial Williamsburg Foundation, Research Archives; hereafter cited as CWFRA). According to Lawrence Henry Gipson, this "insignificant encounter [between Washington and Jumonville] in an isolated mountain ravine on the western slopes of the Alleghenies" signaled the real start of the "Great War for Empire" (see Gipson, *The Years of Defeat*, p. 32). The most lyrical appreciation of the Jumonville affair was penned by Thackeray: "It was strange that in a savage forest of Pennsylvania a young Virginia officer should fire a shot and waken up a war which was to last for sixty years . . . and of all the myriads engaged in the vast contest to leave the prize of the greatest fame with him who struck the first blow!" (William Makepeace Thackeray, *The Virginians*, 2 vols. [London 1857–59; reprint New York and London, 1951], 1:52–53).

22. Narrative accounts of the 1754 campaign are available in Freeman, *Washington*, 1:327–411; Gipson, *The Years of Defeat*, pp. 20–43; and Leach, *Arms for Empire*, pp. 331–42. On Washington's hastily constructed fortification at the Great Meadows, see J. C. Harrington, *New Light on Washington's Fort Necessity: A Report of the Archeological Explorations at Fort Necessity National Battlefield Site* (Richmond, 1957). On the battle itself, see Freeman, *Washington*, 1:400–11; Gipson, *The Years of Defeat*, pp. 38–43; and Leach, *Arms for Empire*, pp. 339–42. The surrender proceedings are closely scrutinized in Gipson, *The Years of Defeat*, pp. 39–49; Leach, *Arms for Empire*, 340–41; Richard L. Morton, *Colonial Virginia*, 2 vols. (Chapel Hill, 1960), 2:655–56. An English translation of the surrender agreement signed by Washington at Fort Necessity is in the Virginia Colonial Papers, 1753–1754, folder 44, item 14, original in the Virginia State Library, Richmond (microfilm copy in CWFRA). In the uproar that followed publication of the surrender terms, few Virginians were inclined to hold Washington personally responsible for making the embarrassing admissions concerning Jumonville's death and French claims to the Ohio Valley. Most of the criticism was directed instead at Captain Van Braam, who was accused by some of having deliberately misled his commander (see Jack P. Greene, *The Diary of Colonel Landon Carter of Sabine Hall, 1752–1778*, 2 vols. [Charlottesville, 1965], 1:111; and Dinwiddie to Albemarle, 12 February 1755, in *Dinwiddie Papers*, 1:497–98). Historians are now generally agreed that the Dutchman's French was weak and that his English was even more limited. Thus the prevailing view is that Van Braam's translation of the surrender terms was simply faulty, not deceitful. It seems that Van Braam's contemporaries later came to share this view themselves. When he capitulated to the French at Fort Necessity, Washington agreed to leave Van Braam and one other officer, Captain Robert Stobo, behind as hostages to guarantee that Virginia would fulfill the terms of surrender. After his eventual release and in addition to his back pay, the burgesses voted Van Braam a bonus of five hundred pounds in recognition of his "Sufferings during a long and painful confinement" (Henry Read McIlwaine, ed., *Journals of the House of Burgesses of Virginia, 1752–1758* [Richmond, 1909], pp. 227, 238). The lower house also urged Governor Francis Fauquier to seek an appointment for Van Braam on the regular British establishment. The governor agreed to recommend Van Braam for a King's commission (ibid., p. 246).

23. Lawence Henry Gipson decried the campaign of 1754 for having been "faulty both in its planning and execution" (see Gipson, *Years of Defeat*, p. 43).

24. Washington to Dinwiddie, [10 June 1754], 20 August 1754, in *Washington Papers*, 1:131, 190–91.

25. Adam Stephen, "The Ohio Expedition of 1754," in Benjamin Rush Papers (MSS, Historical Society of Pennsylvania, Philadelphia, Pennsylvania), reprinted in *Pennsylvania Magazine of History and Biography*, 18 (1894): 47; Baker-Crothers and Hudnut, "Washington's First Battles," p. 24.

26. Harrington, "New Light on Fort Necessity," p. 13.

27. Freeman, *Washington*, 1:405.

28. Ibid., p. 400; Leach, *Arms for Empire*, pp. 339–40.

29. In March 1754 Dinwiddie estimated that one volunteer was the equivalent of almost three men "forc'd on the Service" (see Dinwiddie to Holdernesse, 12 March 1754, in *Dinwiddie Papers*, 1:94.

30. Ibid., Dinwiddie to Lord Halifax, 17 March 1755, p. 528.

31. By the middle of the eighteenth century, the free white adult male population of Virginia was almost forty-four thousand; three hundred volunteers accompanied Washington on the march to Fort Necessity, and not all of them were Virginians. The population estimates were derived from "A List of Tithables Sent to the Lords of Trade," 23 February 1756, in *Dinwiddie Papers*, 2:352–53.

32. Peter Fontaine to Moses Fontaine, 7 June 1754, in Ann Maury, ed. and trans., *Memoirs of a Huguenot Family: Translated and Compiled from the Original Autobiography of the Rev. James Maury* (New York, 1853; reprint, Baltimore, 1967), p. 361.

33. Dinwiddie to Secretary of State for the Southern Department Thomas Robinson, 23 September 1754, in *Dinwiddie Papers*, 1:326.

34. McIlwaine, *Burgesses, 1752–1758*, pp. 52–58, 202–3. Desperate for money, the governor, in return for a riderless supply bill, promised to sign a bill that would authorize a twenty-five hundred-pound payment to Randolph contingent upon the king's approval (see Dinwiddie to Secretary [of State for the Southern Department], Sir [Thomas] Robinson, 23 September [1754], in *Dinwiddie Papers*, 1:324.

35. Greene, *Carter Diary*, 1:114. McIlwaine, *Burgesses, 1752–1758*, p. 205.

36. Dinwiddie to Washington, 3 August 1754, in *Dinwiddie Papers*, 1:31.

37. Dinwiddie to Washington, 11 September 1754, in *Letters to Washington*, 1:44–45.

38. Washington to Dinwiddie, 20 August 1754, in *Dinwiddie Papers*, 1:287–89.

39. "A Morning Return for Col. Washington's Regiment," 1 June 1754; "A Return of the Virginia Regiment," 14 August 1754, in George Washington Papers (MSS, Library of Congress, Washington, D.C.), ser. 4, 4:172, 195; Baker-Crothers and Hudnut, "Washington's First Battles," p. 26.

40. Dinwiddie to Sharpe, 6 September 1754; Dinwiddie to Hamilton, 6 September 1754, in *Dinwiddie Papers*, 1:304–5, 308; Dinwiddie to Washington, 11 September 1754, in *Letters to Washington*, 1:42–45. Fort Cumberland was built at the fork formed by the junction of Wills Creek and the Potomac River; it was on the Maryland shore (see Samual Kercheval, *A History of the Valley of Virginia*, ed. Oren F. Morton, (4th ed.; Strasburg, Va., 1925), p. 69n.

41. Dinwiddie to Carlyle, 11 September [1754], in *Dinwiddie Papers*, 1:318–19. For a contemporary description of the diet of slaves, see Hunter Dickinson Farish, ed., *Journal and Letters of Philip Vickers Fithian, 1773–1774: A Plantation Tutor in the Old Dominion* (Charlottesville, 1957), p. 199.

42. Dinwiddie to Holdernesse, 10 May 1754; Dinwiddie to the Lords of the Treasury, 10 May 1754; Dinwiddie to Robinson, 18 June 1754; Dinwiddie to Secretary [at War Henry] Fox, 15 August [1754], in *Dinwiddie Papers*, 1:158–59, 164, 204–5, 280–81. Concerning Dinwiddie's calls for British aid, see ibid., Dinwiddie to Holder-

nesse, 12 March 1754; Dinwiddie to James Abercromby, 24 July [1754]; Dinwiddie to the Lords of Trade, 25 October 1754; Dinwiddie to Horace Walpole, 25 October 1754, pp. 235–39, 93–98, 235–39, 362–65, 370–72.

43. A point that was agreed upon in a meeting of the British Cabinet, 20 February 1755, quoted in Stanley M. Pargellis, *Lord Loudoun in North America* (New Haven, 1933; reprint, New York, 1968), p. 20.

44. Quoted in Max Savelle, *The Origins of American Diplomacy: The International History of Angloamerica, 1492–1763* (New York and London, 1967), p. 400.

45. Thomas Robinsòn to the earl of Albemarle, British Ambassador to Paris, 12 September 1754, Shelburne Papers MSS, vol. 36, p. 48, original in the Clements Library, University of Michigan (microfilm copy in CWFRA).

46. Ibid., Robinson to Albemarle, 3 October 1754, p. 61.

47. On Braddock's selection as commander of the British forces, see Thad W. Riker, "The Politics Behind Braddock's Expedition," *American Historical Review* 13 (July 1908): 742–52. For a sketch of Braddock's military career see John W. Fortesque, *A History of the British Army*, 13 vols. (London and New York, 1899–1930), 2:274–75.

48. "Sketch for the Operations in North America," 16 November 1754, in *Military Affairs in North America, 1748–1765: Selected Documents From the Cumberland Papers in Windsor Castle*, ed. Stanley Pargellis (New York, 1936; reprint, New York, 1969), pp. 45–48.

49. Dinwiddie to Robinson, 25 October [1754], in *Dinwiddie Papers*, 1:352–55; McIlwaine, *Burgesses, 1752–1758*, pp. 209–10. Dinwiddie neglected to mention that this financial assistance was only a loan and that the Crown expected to be reimbursed (see Dinwiddie to Robinson, 25 October [1754], in *Dinwiddie Papers*, 1:353; Freeman, *Washington*, 1:442).

50. Greene, *Carter Diary*, 1:114.

51. Dinwiddie to the earl of Halifax, 25 October [1754]; Dinwiddie to Robinson, 16 November [1754], in *Dinwiddie Papers*, 1:367, 405.

52. McIlwaine, *Burgesses, 1752–1758*, p. 222; Hening, *Statutes*, 6:438–40.

53. The draft law is reprinted in Hening, *Statutes*, 5:94–96.

54. Greene, *Carter Diary*, 1:123.

55. Hening, *Statutes*, 6:440; Edmund S. Morgan, *American Slavery, American Freedom: The Ordeal of Colonial Virginia* (New York, 1975), p. 141. Gloria Main provides a carefully crafted account of the time-consuming, labor-intensive nature of tobacco culture in her *Tobacco Colony: Life in Early Maryland, 1650–1720* (Princeton, 1982), see especially pp. 31–47.

56. Hening, *Statutes*, 6:439–40. As provided by an act of 1736, the qualifications for voting in a general election were possession of at least one hundred acres of unimproved land, twenty-five acres "with a house and plantation," or ownership of a house and lot in a town (see Hening, *Statutes*, 4:475–78.)

57. Dinwiddie to the Lords of Trade, 16 November 1754; Dinwiddie to Robinson, 12 February [1755], in *Dinwiddie Papers*, 1:401; 493–94; Gipson, *The Years of Defeat*, p. 51; Freeman, *Washington*, 1:439.

58. Dinwiddie to Robinson, 25 October, 16 November [1754]; Dinwiddie to the Lords of Trade, 25 October 1754; Dinwiddie to Halifax, 25 October [1754]; Dinwiddie to Washington, 4 May, 4 June 1754, in *Dinwiddie Papers*, 1:355, 403–4, 365, 369, 149, 193–94; Washington to Dinwiddie [10 June 1754], in *Washington Papers*, 1:129–30, 135–38; William Fitzhugh to Washington, 4 November 1754, in *Letters to Washington*, 1:54–55; Wahington to Fitzhugh, 15 November 1754, in *Washington Papers*, 1:225–26.

59. Dinwiddie to Sharpe, 6 September 1754; Dinwiddie to Hamilton, 6 September 1754; Dinwiddie to Innes, 11 September [1754]; Dinwiddie to Washington, 11 September [1754], in *Dinwiddie Papers*, 1:304–6, 308, 315, 316–17.

60. Dinwiddie's commissions to Walker and Dick were dated 28 December 1754 (see ibid., p. 436).

61. Keith Ryan Nyland, "Doctor Thomas Walker (1715–1794) Explorer, Physician, Statesman, Surveyor and Planter of Virginia and Kentucky" (Ph.D. diss., Ohio State University, 1971), pp. 58–74.

62. Dinwiddie to Carlyle, 12 December 1754, in *Dinwiddie Papers*, 1:424. Dick to Washington, 6 September 1755, in *Letters to Washington*, 1:87–88; Freeman, *Washington*, 2:112, 116, 130. Dick resigned his post in the fall of 1755, apparently because of an inability to collect money owed him by the colonial government for provisions he had purchased at his own expense. This major grievance was accompanied by "50" other irritations "too tedious to mention." Dick to Washington, 6 September 1755, in *Letters to Washington*, 1:87.

63. Dinwiddie to Sharpe, 17 December 1754, in *Dinwiddie Papers*, 1:424–25. Ibid., Dinwiddie to Charles Dick and Thomas Walker, 28 December 1754, p. 440. In return for their services, Walker and Dick received two hundred pounds a year plus expenses, "a handsome appointment" in the governor's opinion. The two men accepted Dinwiddie's offer and soon were headed for the Virginia backcountry. Walker carried with him a sizable amount of money for reimbursing frontier contractors. Apprehensive about exciting any larcenous tendencies in the social undesirables who manned the ranks of the Virginia Regiment, Dinwiddie sent advance notice to Colonel James Innes (then serving at Wills Creek as "camp Master General") that Walker was on his way up, taking care to add that "he has a pretty Sum of Money. I wish You to take him into Y[ou]r Tent for Safety" (see ibid., Dinwiddie to Dick, 12 December 1754; Dinwiddie to Sharpe, 17 December 1754; Dinwiddie to Dick and Thomas, 28 December 1754, pp. 421, 425, 440; F. B. Kegley, *Kegley's Virginia Frontier: The Beginning of the Southwest, the Roanoke of Colonial Days, 1740–1783, with Maps and Illustrations* [Roanoke, Va., 1938], p. 209). The salary of two hundred pounds per annum was equivalent to a major's pay in the Virginia Regiment. Dinwiddie's cautionary statement about the need to safeguard Walker and his funds is in Dinwiddie to Innes, 28 December 1754, in *Dinwiddie Papers*, 1:442.

64. Ibid., Dinwiddie to Dick, 28 December 1754, 29 December 1754, 25 January 1755; Dinwiddie to Walker, 10 February 1755, 15 February 1755; Dinwiddie to Dick, 18 February 1755, pp. 440–41, 442–43, 479–80, 489, 503, 505.

65. Ibid., Dinwiddie to Dick, 4 December [1754], 12 December 1754, 19 December 1754, pp. 418–19, 420–21, 431. The central role played by geography, communications, and supply on the outcome of military operations in the French and Indian War is handled with customary deftness by John Shy in *Toward Lexington*, pp. 86–89.

66. Ibid., Dinwiddie to Innes, 12 December 1754; Dinwiddie to Dick and Walker, 28 December 1754; Dinwiddie to Sharpe, 2 January 1755, 7 January 1755; Dinwiddie to Arthur Dobbs, 17 January 1755; Dinwiddie to Stephen, 10 February 1755, pp. 422, 439–40, 447–48, 448–52, 468, 490. On Dinwiddie's progress in recruiting troops, see ibid., Dinwiddie to Halifax, 17 March 1755, p. 528; ibid., Dinwiddie to Walker, 29 March 1755, 2:11–12.

67. Ibid., Dinwiddie to Robinson, 25 October 1754; Dinwiddie to Governor [James] DeLancey, 8 November 1754; Dinwiddie to the Lords of the Treasury, 16 November [1754]; Dinwiddie to Robinson, 16 November [1754]; Dinwiddie to Innes, 12 November, 12 December 1754; Dinwiddie to Governor [Horatio] Sharpe, 2 January 1755, pp. 355, 393, 402–3, 396, 422, 447.

68. Washington to Loudoun, 10 January 1757, in *Washington Papers*, 4:81.

69. Dinwiddie to Charles Dick, 25 January 1755; Dinwiddie to the earl of Halifax, 12 February 1755; in *Dinwiddie Papers*, 1:480, 496.

70. Ibid., Dinwiddie to Stewart, 26 November, 4 December 1754; Dinwiddie to Captains George Mercer, [Andrew] Waggener, and [Robert] Stewart, 15 January [1755], pp. 414, 462.

71. The Petersburg-Fredericksburg impressment riots are mentioned briefly in Gipson, *The Years of Defeat*, p. 54. Richard L. Morton's comprehensive history of colonial Virginia relegates mention of this episode to a footnote (see Morton, *Colonial Virginia*, 2:664, n. 3). The riots are ignored altogether in Freeman, *Washington;* and Hays Baker-Crothers, *Virginia and the French and Indian War* (Chicago, 1928).

72. Alan Rogers, *Empire and Liberty: American Resistance to British Authority, 1755–1763* (Berkeley, 1974), see especially chapter 4. A similar argument is made in Leach, *Arms for Empire*, pp. 504–8. For more on the often strenuous American opposition to British recruiting practices, see also Douglas Leach, *Roots of Conflict: British Armed Forces and Colonial Americans, 1677–1763* (Chapel Hill, 1986), pp. 83–86.

73. Dinwiddie to Mercer, Waggener, and Stewart, 15 January [1755], in *Dinwiddie Papers*, 1:462.

74. Braddock to Robinson, 18 March 1755, in W.O. 34/73, ff. 23–27, Amherst Papers (Colonial Virginia Records Project microfilm copy in CWFRA).

75. Braddock to William Morris, 24 May 1755, quoted in Freeman, *Washington*, 2:44–45. Dinwiddie was quite embarrassed by Braddock's difficulties in the Old Dominion (see Dinwiddie to Braddock, 23 May, 3 June 1755; Dinwiddie to Robinson, 6 June 1755; Dinwiddie to the Lords of Trade, 6 June 1755, in *Dinwiddie Papers*, 2:40–42, 48–49, 50–51, 52–53.

76. Braddock to [Sir Thomas Robinson], 5 June 1755, quoted in William Livingston, *A Review of the Military Operations in North America; From the Commencement of the French Hostilities on the Frontiers of Virginia in 1753, to the Surrender of Oswego, on the 14th of August, 1756* (Dublin, 1757), p. 251.

77. Strictly speaking, during the ten months from November 1754 to August 1755, the Virginia Regiment ceased to exist. Throughout that period the colony's provincial troops were assigned to unregimented (or independent) companies that lacked field-grade officers. On this point see Franklin Thayer Nichols, "The Organization of Braddock's Army," *William and Mary Quarterly* (hereafter cited as *WMQ*), 3d. ser., 4 (April 1947):130.

78. As used by Braddock, the term "rangers" did not connote a party of men that had been trained and equipped for a special mission, for example, woods fighting. Rather, the Virginia "rangers" were used by Braddock as flankers whose function it was "to cover the Main Body of the Army, and shelter it from all Manner of Surpize" (quoted in Nichols, "The Organization of Braddock's Army," p. 131). The organization of Braddock's army is also discussed in Pargellis, *Cumberland Papers*, p. 78; see also the troop return on pp. 88–89.

79. Braddock to Robert Napier, 8 June 1755, in Pargellis, *Cumberland Papers*, p. 84.

80. Quoted in Freeman, *Washington*, 2:44. British opinion of the provincials had not improved by the time Braddock's army had marched up to Fort Cumberland early in June. Noting that approximately half of his two thousand effectives were men furnished by the southern colonies, Braddock derided these auxiliaries as men of "so little courage and good disposition, that scarce any military service can be expected from them, although I have employed the best officers to form them." The "best officers" were, of course, British officers. To one Ensign Allen fell the task of transforming the Virginia troops into "as like soldiers as it was possible." What the Virgi-

nians must have felt as they were drilled by a young Briton scarce out of his teens hardly requires much imagination (see Braddock to [Robinson], 5 June 1755, in Livingston, *Military Operations in North America*, p. 250; Freeman, *Washington*, 2:44).

81. "Sketch of an Order about the Rank etc. of the Provincial Troops in North America," [12 November 1754], reprinted in Pargellis, *Cumberland Papers*, pp. 43–44.

82. Ibid., "Sketch of Regulations & Orders Proposed Relating to Affairs of North America. November, 1754 and Queries Relating to the Same," (reprint) pp. 34–36. For the background of the decision to subordinate men holding provincial commissions to regular officers, see Pargellis, *Lord Loudoun* (New Haven, 1933; reprint, New York, 1968), pp. 85–87.

83. Mercer to Washington, 17 August 1757, in *Letters to Washington*, 2:177.

84. Charles M. Clode, *The Military Forces of the Crown; Their Administration and Government*, 2 vols. (London, 1869), 1:181; Pargellis, *Lord Loudon*, pp. 85–86. The mutiny act, first approved by Parliament in 1689, was a piece of annual legislation by which that body authorized the existence of the British army and regulated its discipline.

85. Braddock's bleak reputation owes much to Horace Walpole's description of him as a man "desperate in his fortune, brutal in his behavior, and obstinate in his sentiments" (quoted in Francis Parkman, *Montcalm and Wolfe: The Decline and Fall of the French Empire in North America* (Boston, 1892; reprint, New York 1962), p. 146. The British army's best known historian generally agrees with Walpole's assessment (see Fortesque, *British Army*, 2:274–75, 277). More balanced appraisals are in Gipson, *Years of Defeat*, pp. 83–85; and Nichols, "Organization of Braddock's Army," pp. 144–45; see also Leach, *Roots of Conflict* p. 79.

86. Charles Hamilton, ed., *Braddock's Defeat: The Journal of Captain Robert Cholmley's Batman; The Journal of a British Officer; Halkett's Orderly Book* (Norman, Okla., 1959), p. 71. Private Anderson's crime was unspecified, but his offense must have been a serious one since the "dreaded cat" normally was employed only in extreme cases; a conventional lash was the usual form of punishment. On the latter point see Nichols, "Organization of Braddock's Army," p. 142, n. 94.

87. Hamilton, ed., *Braddock's Defeat*, pp. 64, 93–94, 94, 98; Nichols, "Organization of Braddock's Army," p. 144. Despite his blunt warning, Braddock put few, if any, men to death for desertion; soldiers were simply too scarce a resource to waste for the sake of redeeming a threat. Instead of hanging them, Braddock customarily punished captured deserters with a severe whipping.

88. Hening, *Statutes*, 5:16–26; 4:112–18. "Tying Neck and heels" consisted of lashing a rope around the neck of the victim, trailing it down his back, and then securing it tightly around his ankles. This form of punishment was authorized by the Militia Act of 1738. No mention of it was made in a revised statute approved in August 1755, but "tying neck and heels" was reinstated less than two years later by the Militia Act of 1757 (see Hening, *Statutes*, 7:96). For detailed explanations of this and other juridicial punishments, see Davis Y. Paschall, "Crime and Its Punishment in Colonial Virginia, 1607–1776," (Master's thesis, College of William and Mary, 1937).

89. Soon after being reappointed as commander of the Virginia Regiment, Washington instructed his second in command to "be particularly careful in seeing that strict Order is observd among our Soldiers, as that is the Life of Military discipline" (Washington to Stephen, 19 November 1755, in *Washington Papers*, 2:172). Stephen's comments about the two unsuccessful deserters and the sympathetic response of the spectators who witnessed their punishment are in Stephen to Washington, 25 July 1756, in *Letters to Washington*, 1:321. The unflattering characterization of provincial enlisted men was offered by the Reverend James Maury (see Maury to John Fontaine, 15 June 1756, in Maury, *Memoirs of a Huguenot Family*, p. 404).

90. Washington to Stephen, 18 November 1755, 1 February 1756, in *Washington Papers* 2:172, 310. Information about the punishments imposed by provincial military courts in the late spring and early summer of 1757 was derived from the following sources: "At a General Court Martial held by order of Coll. George Washington at Fort Loudoun [,] May 7 1757," in Washington Papers MSS, ser. 4, 6:216; ibid., "At a Regimental Court martial held at Fort Loudoun[,] June 19[,] 1757," item 221; ibid., "The Proceedings of a General court martial held at Fort Loudoun on the 25 and 26 Days of July 1757," item 225. Data on British military punishments during the second half of the eighteenth century may be found in Arthur N. Gilbert, "The Changing Face of British Military Justice, 1757–1783," *Military Affairs*, 49 (April 1985): 80–84.

91. The valor of the provincials is singled out for praise in Joseph Bell to Washington, 5 September 1755, *Letters to Washington*, 1:85; and in Hamilton, *Braddock's Defeat*, p. 29.

92. Captain Robert Orme to Henry Fox, [undated 1755], in Pargellis, *Cumberland Papers*, p. 100; McIlwaine, *Burgesses, 1752–1758*, p. 294.

93. Sir John St. Clair to Napier, 22 July 1755, in Pargellis, *Cumberland Papers*, pp. 105–6.

94. The argument that Braddock was duly vigilant up until what were virtually the final moments of his march on Fort Duquesne is made in Stanley M. Pargellis, "Braddock's Defeat," *American Historical Review*, 41 (January 1936): 265; Gipson, *The Years of Defeat*, pp. 86, 94; Leach, *Arms for Empire*, p. 364; and Peter E. Russell, "Redcoats in the Wilderness: British Officers and Irregular Warfare in Europe and America, 1740 to 1760," *WMQ*, 3d ser., 35 (October 1978): 642–43. As for the battle itself, in his closely reasoned analysis, Stanley Pargellis flatly denies that the British lost because of inappropriate tactics. As Pargellis sees it, they lost because "Braddock and his staff, on the day of the battle, neglected to follow fundamental rules laid down in European manuals, . . . and never gave their soldiers a chance to demonstrate that Old World methods, properly applied, might have won the day" (Pargellis, "Braddock's Defeat," p. 253). Gipson supports the Pargellis thesis in its main points and absolves Braddock of personal blame for the British defeat. Gipson goes on to claim that it was Lieutenant Colonel Thomas Gage who made the most critical violation of conventional tactical principles. As commander of the advance guard, Gage had the special responsibility to secure all strategic points adjoining the line of march. That assignment he manifestly failed to carry out (see Gipson, *Years of Defeat*, pp. 94–98, especially page 95, n. 92). More recently, both John Shy and Peter E. Russell have affirmed the general suitability of European military tactics to the American frontier (see Shy, *Toward Lexington*, p. 127; and Russell, "Redcoats in the Wilderness," pp. 629–52).

95. "Anonymous Letter on Braddock's Campaign," 25 July 1755, reprinted in Pargellis, *Cumberland Papers*, pp. 123, 118.

96. Dinwiddie later claimed that Dunbar's retreat enraged the people of Virginia while Braddock's defeat had merely surprised them (see Dinwiddie to [William] Shirley, 18 October 1755 and Dinwiddie to Henry Fox, 20 August 1755, in *Dinwiddie Papers*, 2:245, 164).

97. Ibid., Dinwiddie to Dunbar, 26 July 1755, pp. 118–20. Dinwiddie even promised to furnish four hundred reinforcements if Dunbar would agree to mount a second expedition. Whether the governor could have made good on that promise may be doubted. Dunbar's plans to go into winter quarters eventually were disapproved by Major General William Shirley, Braddock's successor as commander in chief of British forces in North America. Shirley gave Dunbar the option of renewing the Ohio campaign or marching his troops to New York for employment on the northern frontier. Dunbar chose the latter alternative (Gipson, *Years of Defeat*, p. 133). Seizing on his complaint of poor health as an excuse to "kick him upstairs," the War Office removed Dunbar from North America in November 1755 and named him lieutenant-governor

of Gibralter (see Secretary of War Henry Fox to Dunbar, November 1755, in War Office—Out Letters, Secretary of War, 1755–1757, W.O. 4/51, p. 37 [Colonial Virginia Records Project microfilm copy in CWFRA]).

98. Dinwiddie to St. Clair, 11 August 1755, in *Dinwiddie Papers*, 2:147.

99. Ibid., Dinwiddie to Fox, 20 August 1755; Dinwiddie to Sharpe, 25 August 1755; Dinwiddie to Shirley, 18 October 1755, pp. 147, 170, 245.

100. Ibid., Dinwiddie to Robinson, 23 July 1755, p. 113; James Maury to _____ , 9 August 1755, in Maury, *Memoirs of a Huguenot Family*, p. 380; Washington to Dinwiddie, 11 October 1755, in *Washington Papers*, 2:105. For a grisly narrative account of the war on the Virginia frontier, see Kercheval, *Valley of Virginia*, pp. 72–108.

101. Hening, *Statutes*, 6:463, 461.

102. On this point, see the remark made in the fall of 1754 by Landon Carter concerning Virginia's need to "excite" military assistance from Britain. Greene, *Carter Diary*, 1:123. See also James Maury to Moses Fontaine, 11 June 1759, in Maury *Memoirs of a Huguenot Family*, p. 410.

103. Samuel Davies, "Religion and Patriotism: The Constituents of Good Soldiers," in *Sermons on Important Subjects. By the Late Reverend and Pious Samuel Davies, A.M. Sometime President of the College of New Jersey*, 5 vols. (Philadelphia, 1818), 3:213.

## 4. "BAD NEWS FROM EVERY QUARTER": THE COLONY BESIEGED

1. James Maury to _____ , 9 August 1755, in Ann Maury, ed. and trans., *Memoirs of a Huguenot Family: Translated and Compiled from the Original Autobiography of the Rev. James Maury* (reprint, Baltimore, 1967), p. 380. Pierre de Rigand de Vandreuil, the governor-general of New France, encouraged the Indians in their excesses because he believed "there is no surer way to sicken the people of the English colonies of war" (quoted in Guy Fregault, *Canada: The War of the Conquest*, trans. Margaret M. Cameron [Toronto: Oxford University Press, 1969], p. 120). The comments about the hastily abandoned home are in the "Journal of Captain Charles Lewis, October 10–December 10, 1755," in the *Proceedings* of the Virginia Historical Society, 9 (1891): 208. The estimate that over one hundred frontier residents had been killed or kidnapped during the fall of 1755 is in Robert Dinwiddie to Sir Charles Hardy, 18 October 1755, in *The Official Records of Robert Dinwiddie, Lieutenant-Governor of the Colony of Virginia, 1751–1758, Now First Printed from the Manuscript in the Collections of the Virginia Historical Society*, ed. Robert A. Brock, 2 vols. (Richmond, 1883), 2:251. Maury's comment about the contraction of the Virginia frontier is in Maury to John Fontaine, 15 June 1756, in Maury, *Memoirs of a Huguenot Family*, p. 403.

2. Charles Steuart to Walter Tullideph, 23 September 1751, in Charles Steuart Letter Book, original in the Historical Society of Pennsylvania (microfilm copy in Colonial Williamsburg Foundation Research Archives, hereafter referred to as CWFRA). On the relatively tranquil relationship between masters and slaves in Virginia during the first half of the eighteenth century, see also Hugh Jones, *The Present State of Virginia From Whence Is Interred A Short View of Maryland and North Carolina* (London, 1724), ed. Richard L. Morton (Chapel Hill, 1956), p. 93; Edmund S. Morgan, *Virginians at Home: Family Life in the Eighteenth Century* (Williamsburg, 1952), pp. 60–61; and Gerald W. Mullin, *Flight and Rebellion: Slave Resistance in Eighteenth Century Virginia* (New York, 1972), p. 124. On the militia's internal security role, see Frederick Stokes Aldridge, "Organization and Administration of the Militia System of Colonial Virginia," (Ph.D. diss., American University, 1964), pp. 115–22, 231–33; and Lawrence Henry Gipson, *The British Empire before the Ameri-*

*can Revolution*, vol. 6: *The Great War for Empire: The Years of Defeat, 1754–1757* (New York, 1946), p. 15.

    3.  Dinwiddie to Charles Carter, 18 July 1755; Dinwiddie to the earl of Halifax, 23 July 1755; Dinwiddie to Henry Fox, 24 May 1756; Dinwiddie to the earl of Loudoun, 9 August 1756; in *Dinwiddie Papers*, 2:102, 114, 414–15, 474. In August 1756 Dinwiddie calculated that the number of slaves in Virginia stood at 120, 156 (see ibid., p. 474). In further recognition that Virginia had fallen upon dangerous times, one month after Braddock's defeat, the provisions in the militia statute that dealt with slave patrolling were tightened up (see William Waller Hening, ed., *The Statutes at Large: Being a Collection of All the Laws of Virginia from the First Session of the Legislature, in the Year 1619*, 13 vols. (Richmond and Philadelphia, 1809–23), 6:543. To insure that an adequate number of militiamen would be on hand in their home counties, in August 1755 the Virginia assembly forbade "the governor or commander in chief, to lead or march the militia of this colony, . . . more than five miles beyond" the Old Dominion's western border (see Hening, *Statutes*, 6:548).

    4.  Maury to Fontaine, 15 June 1756, in Maury, *Memoirs of a Huguenot Family*, p. 406. Additional comments on the economic disruption caused by the large-scale militia call-up are in Francis Jerdone to Duncan Maclane, 15 May 1756, in Letter Copy Book of Francis Jerdone, 1756–1763, original in the Swem Library, College of William and Mary (microfilm copy in CWFRA).

    5.  Maury to _____ , 9 August 1755; Maury to Fontaine, 15 June 1756, in Maury, *Memoirs of a Huguenot Family*, pp. 380, 401.

    6.  Dinwiddie to Halifax, 24 February 1756, in *Dinwiddie Papers*, 2:346.

    7.  Thomas J. Wertenbaker, *Patrician and Plebian in Colonial Virginia, 1698–1750* (Charlottesville, 1910), p. 204; on the legacy of Bacon's Rebellion, see also Charles Willard Hoskins Warner, *Road to Revolution: Virginia's Rebels from Bacon to Jefferson 1676–1776* (Richmond, 1961), p. 92; and Edmund S. Morgan, *American Slavery, American Freedom: The Ordeal of Colonial Virginia* (New York, 1975), p. 328.

    8.  The political aftermath of Bacon's Rebellion is discussed in detail in Stephen Saunders Webb's revisionist study of Anglo-American relations; see Webb, *The Governors-General: The English Army and the Definition of Empire, 1569–1681* (Chapel Hill, 1979), chapter 7, especially pp. 368–72.

    9.  Henry Read McIlwaine, ed., *Journals of the House of Burgesses of Virginia, 1752–1755, 1756–1758* (Richmond, 1909), p. 297.

    10.  Ibid., pp. 297–98.

    11.  Hoping not to alienate those few neighboring tribes who were not already "in the interest of the French," the assembly ruled that anyone who "knowingly and willfully" killed a friendly Indian would be guilty of a felony (see ibid., pp. 300, 305, and Hening, *Statutes*, 6:500–502.

    12.  McIlwaine, *Burgesses, 1752–1758*, p. 300; Hening, *Statutes*, 6:521–30.

    13.  The research of Aubrey C. Land in eighteenth-century Maryland history points up the socially selective character of the ten-pound draft exemption fee. According to Land, the annual income of poor farmers in Maryland did not exceed fifteen pounds and ranged downward to as low as six pounds. Land's "clear impression" is that the social and economic differences between eighteenth-century Maryland and Virginia were "not very great" (see Land, "Economic Base and Social Structure: The Northern Chesapeake in the Eighteenth Century," in Gary B. Nash, ed., *Class and Society in Early America* [Englewood Cliffs, 1970], pp. 120–21). On the matter of jail terms for reluctant draftees, see Hening, *Statutes*, 6:527.

    14.  Maury to Fontaine, 15 June 1756, in Maury, *Memoirs of a Huguenot Family*, p. 404; William Fairfax to George Washington, 3 September 1756, in *Letters to Wash-*

*ington and Accompanying Papers*, ed. Stanislaus Murray Hamilton, 5 vols. (Boston and New York, 1898-1902), 1:361–62.

15. Jackson Turner Main, *The Social Structure of Revolutionary America* (Princeton, 1965), pp. 61–62; the growing number of landless men in eighteenth-century Virginia is also discussed in Willard F. Bliss, "The Rise of Tenancy in Virginia," *Virginia Magazine of History and Biography* (hereafter cited as *VMHB*), 43 (October 1950): 427–41. For an analysis of this phenomenon in one Virginia county, see Darrett and Anita Rutman, *A Place in Time: Middlesex County, Virginia, 1650–1750* (New York, 1984), pp. 236–39.

16. "Message of the Governor to the Council and Burgesses," [March or April] 1752, *Dinwiddie Papers*, 1:30–31.

17. For the purposes of calculation, it was assumed that "planter" and "farmer" were interchangeable terms denoting a common occupation rather than a distinctive social or economic niche.

18. According to Jackson Turner Main, the non-farm population on the frontier was "no more than 1 percent" while non-farm workers comprised only 6 or 7 percent of the white male population in the Virginia piedmont and no more than 10 percent in the tidewater (see Main, *Social Structure*, pp. 46–47, 52, 55–56). The income of Virginia farmers varied considerably, but Main's study of colonial tax lists leads him to believe that artisans generally earned considerably less. In terms of social and economic status, Main assigns artisans an intermediate place between farmers and laborers (ibid., pp. 72, 79, 83). For further evidence of the contempt in which laborers and most artisans were held by those above them in the social hierarchy, see Main, pp. 198–99. Willard F. Bliss finds that farmers in colonial Virginia ranged from wealthy men to those who were poverty-stricken and usually in debt (see Bliss, "Rise of Tenancy in Virginia," pp. 434–40).

19. Annotations noting the presence in the Virginia Regiment of a soldier of mixed Negro-Indian ancestry were found in a size roll for Captain Henry Harrison's Company, dated 13 July 1756; mention of two mulattoes in the provincial ranks is made in a December 1757 size roll for Captain Robert McKenzie's company. Both size rolls are in the George Washington Papers (MSS, Library of Congress, Washington, D.C.), ser. 4, 4: item 428, and 6: item 103. There is evidence to show that blacks were serving in the Virginia Regiment by no later than 1755. In February of that year, the *Virginia Gazette* carried a notice offering one pistole for the capture of William Holmes, "a Mullatoe, about 45 Years of Age," who had deserted from the Virginia Regiment (see *Virginia Gazette* [Hunter], 28 February 1755). Later that year, Captain Peter Hog reported that his company included "two Neg[r]o[e]s & 2 Multatoes [sic]" (see Hog to Washington, 29 November 1755, in *Letters to Washington*, 1:137). A little less than two years later, the *Virginia Gazette* reported that two mulattoes had recently deserted from the regiment (see *Virginia Gazette* [Hunter], 2 September 1757). On the use of blacks as soldiers during the colonial period, see Benjamin Quarles, "The Colonial Militia and Negro Manpower," *Mississippi Valley Historical Review*, 45 (March 1959): 643–52. According to Quarles, colonial officials employed blacks as soldiers only in "unusual emergencies" when a "paucity of manpower" caused the authorities to abandon their "customary caution" about arming Negroes. This pattern was evident in Virginia during the French and Indian War. In the same letter in which he mentioned the presence of several blacks in his company, Captain Peter Hog implied that if he could find a sufficient number of white replacements, the blacks would be dismissed.

20. "Instructions for Colonel Washington," [14 August 1755], in W. W. Abott et al., eds., *The Papers of George Washington: Colonial Series*, 4 vols. to date (Charlottesville, 1983-    ), 2:185; ibid., "General Instructions for the Recruiting Officers of the Virginia Regiment," 1–3 September 1755, 2:13–14.

21. Ibid., Hog to Washington, 14 May 1756, 3:131–33; "A Roll of Capt. William Bronaugh's Company," 13 July 1756; "A Roll of Capt. Thomas Cocke's Company," 13 July 1756; "A Roll of Capt. William Peachy's Company," 13 July 1756; "A Size Roll of Capt. [George] Mercer's Company," 2 August 1756; "A Size Roll of Capt. Robert Spotswood's Company, 4 October 1757, in Washington Papers MSS, ser. 4, 4: items 425–26, 432, 436; 6: item 731. After learning that many new recruits were "being judged Useless and discharg'd," Washington had urged in April 1756 that: "great Care shou'd be observed in choosing active Marksmen; the manifest Inferiority of inactive Persons, unused to Arms, in this kind of Service, although equal in Numbers; to lively Persons who have practised [sic] Hunting, is inconceivable. The Chance against them is more than two to one." His recommendation went unheeded. A few months later Washington himself was complaining of the unsuitability of the men being enlisted. See Stephen to Washington, 31 January 1756, in *Letters to Washington*, 1:194; Washington to Dinwiddie, 16 April 1756, 25 June 1756, in *Washington Papers*, 3:1–3, 222–24.

22. It seems that Catlet avoided both a hanging and a stint in the provincial army. Once released from prison, he apparently absconded and later returned to his home in Prince William County. He lived in Prince William undisturbed until he was arrested in 1762 for passing counterfeit money. Catlet's deposition is in the Virginia Colonial Papers, 1762–1767 (MSS, Virginia State Library, Richmond), folder 46, item 4 (microfilm copy in CWFRA). In another instance, a Virginia physician named James Roy used military service as a means of escaping his creditors (see Jerdone to George Brown, 10 June 1758, in Jerdone Letter Book, CWFRA). Since the kinds of records (for example, detailed census reports) that would provide a basis for a truly definitive analysis are lacking, the precise social composition of the Virginia Regiment remains somewhat speculative. Even the quantitative data contained in the size rolls are open to varying interpretation. Thus, in contrast to my reading of this source, John Ferling believes the size rolls reveal that enlisted men in the provincial army represented a fair cross-section of Virginia society. Those in the ranks of Ferling's Virginia Regiment are about evenly divided between skilled artisans rendered unemployable by the Old Dominion's growing number of slave craftsmen and aspiring young farmers lured by the promise of a western land bounty. It is indisputable that over half of the individuals listed in the size rolls identified themselves as practitioners of some kind of craft. But since the rolls show only general occupational categories and not the status of individual soldiers within their respective trades (that is, apprentice, journeyman, or master craftsman), it is impossible to determine how many men were truly skilled craftsmen and how many simply claimed an occupational status they did not, in fact, possess. As Ferling himself points out, it was not unknown for common laborers in eighteenth-century Virginia to boast of skills they lacked. (On this point see, for example, Washington to Tench Tilghman, 24 March, 4 August 1784, in *The Writings of George Washington from the Original Manuscript Sources, 1745–1799*, ed. John C. Fitzpatrick, (39 vols. (Washington, D.C., 1931–44), 27:367–68, 452–53.) On the other hand, if the skills of artisan-soldiers were real, why did they not, in the generally prosperous middle years of the eighteenth century, simply move to another colony where the economic prospects were more congenial? It is certainly possible that skilled men who lacked the resources to move to, say, Philadelphia, may well have preferred a soldier's pay to starvation. But skilled or not, such unfortunates perforce would have occupied not a middling but a distinctly inferior economic and social position. As for Ferling's would-be farmers, while some hard-up souls with pastoral ambitions may have been attracted by a private's modest pay, it is uncertain whether many were drawn into military service after 1754 by the promise of free land. Although such a promise had been made by Governor Dinwiddie during the first year of the war, land bounties were never mentioned in any subsequent legislation. Accordingly, whether the terms of Dinwiddie's 1754 proclamation applied to those whose service began after that date at least is open to question. In sum, conclusions about the kinds of men who fought

for Virginia during the French and Indian War are almost inevitably tentative. My own sense is that, taken as a whole, the surviving evidence points to a provincial army that, down to 1758 at least, was composed mostly of poor and politically vulnerable men. For a different view, see John C. Ferling, "Soldiers For Virginia: Who Served in the French and Indian War?" *VMHB*, 94 (July 1986): 307–28.

23. Hening, *Statutes*, 6:525–26.

24. Washington to Stephen, 28 November 1755, in *Washington Papers*, 2:184–85; Robert Stewart to Washington, 5 December 1755, in *Letters to Washington*, 1:143.

25. Washington to McCarty, [22 November 1755], in *Washington Papers*, 2:176–77. Sternly reprimanded by Washington in November 1755, McCarty nevertheless received his ensign's commission less than two months later. On the irrepressible McCarty's later exploits, see Dinwiddie to Washington, 10 December 1755, and Dinwiddie to McCarty, 10 December 1755, in *Dinwiddie Papers*, 2:561–62. The exchange between Governor Sharpe and Washington concerning the recruiting practices of Christopher Gist is in *Letters to Washington*, 2:161–63, and *Washington Papers*, 4:318–19; see also the "Deposition of Thomas Hudson," 27 August 1757, in *Letters to Washington*, 2:184–85. An account of the drunken march from Fredericksburg is in the "Journal of Captain Charles Lewis," pp. 205–7.

26. Washington to Dinwiddie, 29 April 1757, [17 September 1757], in *Washington Papers*, 4:145, 406; Brokenbrough to Washington, 29 September 1755, in *Letters to Washington*, 1:100–101.

27. The original (1748) version of the statute on invasions and insurrections is reprinted in Hening, *Statutes*, 6:112–18. The statute was renewed without change in 1753. The revised statute of 1755 is in Hening, pp. 544–50. The militia act of 1738 had authorized "tying neck and heels" as punishment for disobedience; the militia act of 1755 established a fine of 7s.6p. (10 shillings if the offender belonged to a cavalry unit) for the same offense. The militia acts of 1738 and 1755 are reprinted in Hening, 5:16–24 and 6:530–44.

28. Dinwiddie's remarks about the need for increased discipline are in McIlwaine, *Burgesses, 1752–1758*, p. 319; Washington's call for a more stringent military code is in Washington to Dinwiddie, 11 October 1755, in *Washington Papers*, 2:101–7. Dinwiddie's order reappointing Washington as commander of the Virginia Regiment is in *Dinwiddie Papers*, 2:184.

29. Hening, *Statutes*, 6:559–64. The most significant procedural limitations stipulated that: (1) general military courts (which could impose the death penalty) could be convened only on Virginia soil; (2) no fewer than nine officers could decide a captial case and that a two-thirds majority was necessary for conviction; (3) a written transcript of the proceedings had to be made; and (4) death sentences had to be confirmed by the governor (see ibid., pp. 560–62). Additional evidence exists for believing that during the dark days of 1755, Virginia politicians were anxious to keep Washington happy. While Washington was weighing Dinwiddie's offer to take command of the reconstituted Virginia Regiment, the assembly approved a number of new prerogatives for the colony's senior soldier. The enticements included the right to appoint an aide-de-camp, a personal secretary, an adjutant, and a quartermaster. After he accepted the appointment, Washington also was entrusted with a military chest and given descretion to use its contents "as . . . the Nature and Good of the Service requires" (see "Instructions for Colonel Washington," [14 August 1755], in *Dinwiddie Papers*, 2:186; see also Washington to Andrew Lewis, 6 September 1755, in *Washington Papers*, 2:23–24.

30. McIlwaine, *Burgesses, 1752–1758*, pp. 320–21; Hening, *Statutes*, 6:564–65.

31. Dinwiddie had dissolved the assembly of 1752–1755 after the October 1755 session in hopes that a general election would return a more cooperative group of burgesses. About 38 percent of the members lost their seats, but there were few changes

in the leadership of the lower house. It is doubtful whether the election resulted in a more pliable legislature. On this matter, see Dinwiddie to Halifax, 1 October 1755, in *Dinwiddie Papers*, 2:266; McIlwaine, *Burgesses, 1752–1758*, p. xxv; and Morton, *Colonial Virginia*, 2:684. The assembly's refusal to support the Crown Point expedition is covered in McIlwaine, *Burgesses, 1752–1758*, pp. 336–37, 345.

32. McIlwaine, *Burgesses, 1752–1758*, pp. xxvi, 345, 351, 370; Dinwiddie to Fox, 10 May 1756, in *Dinwiddie Papers*, 2:408.

33. The act for "disarming Papists" also prohibited Roman Catholics from owning horses valued at more than five pounds; the act is reprinted in Hening, *Statutes*, 7:35–39.

34. Washington's warning about the deteriorating military situation is in Washington to Dinwiddie, 7 April 1756, in *Washington Papers*, 2:332–35; the Indian threat in the spring of 1756 is also discussed in Washington to Robinson, 7 April 1756, and Washington to Robert Hunter Morris, 9 April 1756 in ibid., pp. 337–39, 345–46. Washington's plans for a two thousand-man regiment divided into two battalions of ten companies each are described in Washington to Dinwiddie, 16 April 1756, and Washington to Robinson, 16 April 1756, in ibid., 3:1–6, 6–8. The complaints about foot dragging by the burgesses are in Fairfax to Washington, 26 April 1756, in *Letters to Washington*, 1:230.

35. McIlwaine, *Burgesses, 1752–1758*, p. xxvi.

36. Hening, *Statutes*, 7:17–18; Dinwiddie to Washington, 8 May 1756, [_____ June 1756], in *Dinwiddie Papers*, 2:406, 434. For the locations of the forts and details on their size and construction, see Joseph A. Waddell, *Annals of Augusta County, Virginia, From 1726 to 1871* (Staunton, Va., 1902; reprint, Bridgewater, Va., 1958), p. 115; Louis K. Koontz, "Washington on the Frontier," *VMHB*, XXXVI (October 1928): 314–21; Roy Bird Cook, "Virginia's Frontier Defenses, 1719–1795," *West Virginia History* (hereafter cited as WVH), 1:(1940):119–20; Otis K. Rice, "The French and Indian War in West Virginia," *WVH*, XXIV (1963): 144

37. Washington to Dinwiddie, 17 September 1757, in *Washington Papers*, 4:411–12; and Washington to Dinwiddie, 24 October 1757, in *Writings of Washington*, 2:151.

38. If possible, the costs of building the Cherokees a fort were to be met with funds that Dinwiddie had received earlier from England. The assembly did, however, agree to provide up to two thousand pounds if building expenses exceeded what the governor had on hand, see McIlwaine, *Burgesses, 1752–1758*, pp. 368, 370. Dinwiddie's motives and initial diplomatic overtures toward the Cherokees are discussed in "Minutes of a Council with the Cherokees," 5 September 1755; Dinwiddie to Sir Thomas Robinson, 24 November 1755; "Commission from Governor Dinwiddie to Messrs. Randolph and Byrd, Commissioners to the Catawba and Cherokee Indians," 23 December 1755; "Governor Dinwiddie's Message to the Catawbas," 23 December 1755; "Governor Dinwiddie's Message to the Cherokee Indians," 23 December 1755; "Governor Dinwiddie's Instruction to Messrs. Randolph and Byrd," 23 December 1755; Dinwiddie to Robinson, 24 December 1755, in *Dinwiddie Papers*, 2:187–88, 283, 292–93, 298–305, 306–7. Virginia-Cherokee relations during the first half of the eighteenth century are examined in W. Stitt Robinson, "Virginia and the Cherokees: Indian Policy from Spotswood to Dinwiddie," in *The Old Dominion: Essays for Thomas Perkins Abernethy*, ed. Darrett B. Rutman (Charlottesville, 1964), pp. 21–40; for the period of the French and Indian War, see David H. Corkran, *The Cherokee Frontier: Conflict and Survival, 1740–1762* (Norman, 1962).

39. Dinwiddie's instructions to Randolph and Byrd are reprinted in *Dinwiddie Papers*, 2:301–3. Dinwiddie's "Message to the Cherokee Indians" voiced hope for a British-Cherokee alliance "as long as the Sun and Moon gives Light." Comparable sentiments were expressed in the governor's message to the Catawbas (see ibid., pp. 299–301). For a contemporary account of the Sandy Creek expedition, see [William

Maxwell, ed.] "[Lieutenant Thomas] Morton's Diary," *The Virginia Historical Register and Literary Note Book*, 4 (January 1851): 143–47; the lament about having "Enter'd in to a Soldier's life," is in "Morton's Diary," p. 144. Other contemporary comments on the expedition are in Thomas Lloyd to Edmund Hector, 10 October 1756, Public Record Office H.C.A. 30/258, High Court of Admiralty—Misc. 1750–1756, SR 5703 (typescript copy in CWFRA), and Edmund Pendleton to William Preston, 12 May 1756, in David John Mays, ed., *The Letters and Papers of Edmund Pendleton, 1743–1803*, 2 vols. (Charlottesville, 1952), 1:8. Dinwiddie's campaign instructions to Major Andrew Lewis are in *Dinwiddie Papers*, 2: 320–22. The expedition is briefly described in Morton, *Colonial Virginia*, 2:689; Waddell, *Annals of Augusta*, pp. 129–30; and Rice, "The French and Indian War in West Virginia," pp. 141–43.

40. Washington's analysis of the Sandy Creek expedition is in Washington to Robinson, 24 April 1756, in *Washington Papers*, 3:48–51. The Cherokees' military prowess is noted in "Morton's Diary," pp. 144–45, and in Washington to Dinwiddie, 7 April 1756, in *Washington Papers*, 2:332–35. For details concerning construction of the fort for the Cherokees, see "Governor Dinwiddie's Instructions to Major Andrew Lewis," 24 April 1756, and Dinwiddie to Halifax, 24 September 1756, in *Dinwiddie Papers*, 2:389–91, 520.

41. Maury to Fontaine, 15 June 1756; Maury to Philip Ludwell, [1756], in Maury, *Memoirs of a Huguenot Family*, pp. 406, 439–40.

42. The Cherokees' participation in the 1756 campaign is discussed in Dinwiddie to [William H.] Lyttelton, 2 September 1756, in *Dinwiddie Papers*, 2:495; see also Dinwiddie to Lyttelton, 20 November 1756, in William H. Lyttelton Papers, 1756–1760, original in the Clements Library, University of Michigan (microfilm copy in CWFRA). For Governor Francis Fauquier's critique of the Cherokees as allies, see Fauquier to Byrd, 17 August 1758, in *The Official Papers of Francis Fauquier, Lieutenant Governor of Virginia, 1758–1768*, ed. George Reese, 3 vols. (Charlottesville, 1980–83, 1:61. Washington's comment about the Cherokees' appreciation of their own importance is in Washington to Henry Bouquet, 16 July 1758, in *Writings of Washington*, 2:238. The disdain of most white Virginians for Indians is noted in Jones, *Present State of Virginia*, p. 60. According to Jones, the average Virginian looked upon all Indians as "savage, idolatrous, unbelieving, numerous, monstrous, idle and delighting in war and cruelty" (see Jones, *Present State of Virginia*, p. 51). For Washington's analysis of Virginia's handling of her Indian allies, see Washington to Dinwiddie, 5 November 1757, in *Writings of Washington*, 2:157–58.

43. Hening, *Statutes*, 7:14–17.

44. Ibid., 6:527; 7:14–15.

45. Ibid., 7:14–16; 6:527; estimates on the relative value of ten pounds are in Land, "Economic Base and Social Structure: The Northern Chesapeake in the Eighteenth Century," pp. 120–21; see also the same author's "Economic Behavior in a Planting Society: The Eighteenth Century Chesapeake," *Journal of Southern History*, XXXIII (November 1967): 483.

46. Hening, *Statutes*, 7:69–71.

47. Ibid., 7:72–73.

48. On Virginia's defense appropriations between May 1755 and June 1757, see Hening, *Statutes*, 6:463, 521–30; 7:18, 62–63, 81. In its September 1756 session, the assembly met to consider recruiting strategies for the Royal American Regiment, a newly organized component of the regular British army. During that session the members transacted no business pertaining to the Virginia Regiment.

49. For Washington's handling of recruiting matters, see ibid., "General Instructions for the Recruiting Officers of the Virginia Regiment," [3] September 1755; Washington to Captain Robert Stewart, 18 November 1755; Washington to Lieutenant

Austin Brockenbrough, 18 November 1755; Washington to Ensign Dennis McCarthy, 22 November 1755; Washington to Lieutenant Colonel Adam Stephen, 28 November, 3 December 1755; Washington to Captain Peter Hog, 27 December 1755; Washington to Captain John McNeill, 21 July 1756, in *Washington Papers*, 2:13-15, 169, 176, 184-85, 197, 236-37; 3:275-76; Washington to Sharpe, 20 July 1757; Washington to Dinwiddie, 27 August, 4:318-19, 384-87. Information on Washington and logistical matters is in ibid., Washington to Dinwiddie, 11 September 1755; Washington to Charles Dick, 20 September 1755; Washington to John Carlyle, 16 October 1755; Washington to Hog, 28 November 1755; Washington to Thomas Walker, 3 December 1755, 10 January 1756, Washington to Robert Stewart, 10 May 1756, 27 July 1756, 2:29-31, 55-56, 118, 186-87, 198-99, 269-70; 3:112-13, 297-98; ibid., Washington to Loudoun, 10 January 1757; Washington to Dinwiddie, 29 April 1757, 10 June 1757; Washington to John Robinson, 10 July 1757; Washington to Dinwiddie, 10 July 1757; Washington to Thomas Bullitt, 24 July 1757, 4:79-90, 144-48, 192-95, 287-89, 291-93, 327-29; Washington to John Blair, 17 April 1758; Washington to Sir John St. Clair, 23 June 1758, in *Writings of Washington*, 2:177, 221. Examples of the range of administrative details that Washington contended with are in Washington to John Ashby, 28 December 1755; Washington to Stewart, 8 May 1756; Washington to Dinwiddie, 10 October 1756, in *Washington Papers*, 2:241-42; 3:100-101, 430-34. Ibid., Washington to Stephen, 17 April 1757; "Instructions for Captain Joshua Lewis," 6 June 1757; Washington to Major Andrew Lewis, 29 July 1757; "General Instructions to all the Captains of Companies," 29 July 1757, 4:138, 179-82, 346-48, 341-45.

50. Ibid., Washington to Dinwiddie, 13 January 1756; 27 April 1756; 3 May 1756; 23 May 1756; 25 June 1756; 4 August 1756; 23 September 1756; 28 September 1756; 10 October 1756; 2:278-80; 3:58-61, 81-84, 171-73, 222-24, 312-18, 414-18, 420-21, 430-34; ibid., Washington to Dinwiddie, 5 April 1757; 29 April 1757; 10 June 1757, 4:128-29, 144-48, 192-95. On training and discipline, see, for example, Washington's "Orders" for 1 May and 2 May 1756, in ibid., 3:70-71, and his "General Instructions to all the Captains of Companies," 29 July 1757, in ibid., 4:341-45.

51. Ibid., Washington to Charles Lewis, 27 January 1756, in ibid., 2:297-98; see also Washington's "admonition" of 8 January 1756, in ibid., pp. 256-58. Washington also put great stock in the appearance of his officers. Shortly after he was reappointed colonel of the Virginia Regiment in August 1755, Washington ordered "Every Officer . . . to provide himself as soon as he can conveniently, with a Suit of Regimentals of good blue Cloath: the Coat to be faced and cuffed with Scarlet, and trimmed with Silver; a Scarlet waistcoat, with silver Lace; blue Breeches, and a silver-laced Hat" (see ibid., Washington's "Orders" for 17 September 1755, pp. 40-41). Personal improvement was encouraged, too. When the regiment went into winter quarters in 1755-56, Washington pointedly suggested "that there ought to be a time appropriated" for professional reading and study (see ibid., Washington's "Orders" for 8 January 1756, p. 257). In that regard Washington singled out for special mention Humphrey Bland's, *A Treatise of Military Discipline*. First published in 1727, Bland's *Treatise* was probably the best-known military handbook of its day. Washington reportedly sent to London for a copy of Bland's book shortly after Braddock's defeat. For information about Washington's professional military studies, see John W. Wright, "Pickering's Letter on Washington," *Tyler's Historical Quarterly and Geneological Magazine*, 7 (July 1925): 18-19; and Oliver L. Spaulding, Jr., "The Military Studies of George Washington," *American Historical Review*, 29 (July 1924): 675-80.

52. William Allason to William Walker, 8 November 1757, in Letter Book of William Allason, 1757-1770, original MS in the Virginia State Library (microfilm copy in CWFRA). The "other" Virginia merchant was Francis Jerdone, who made the glum prediction cited here in a letter to Hugh Crawford on 10 September 1757 (Jerdone Letter Book, CWFRA). Pendleton's comment is in Pendleton to William Preston, 26 September 1757, *Papers of Pendleton*, 1:12-13. The Reverend James Maury's prediction that his fellow parson would prefer unemployment to possible mutilation is in Maury

to William Douglas, 31 May 1758, quoted in Robert E. and B. Katherine Brown, *Virginia, 1705–1786: Democracy or Aristocracy?* (East Lansing, 1964), p. 250. For other doleful assessments of Virginia's prospects, see Jerdone to Samuel Richards, Israel Manduil & Company, 2 June 1756; Jerdone to Alexander Speirs and Hugh Brown, 20 May 1757, in Jerdone Letter Book, CWFRA; and Peter Fontaine, Jr., to Moses Fontaine, 11 June 1757, in Maury, *Memoirs of a Huguenot Family*, p. 367.

53. Washington to Dinwiddie, 24 October 1757; 5 October 1757, in *Dinwiddie Papers*, 2:151, 142; see also Washington to Stanwix, 8 October 1757, and Washington to Robinson, 25 October 1757, in ibid., pp. 145, 154. By mid-1757 Governor Dinwiddie had come to share similar views about the futility of a defensive strategy (see Dinwiddie to Lyttelton, 24 September 1757, in Lyttelton Papers, CWFRA; and Dinwiddie to Washington, 16 November 1757, 10 December 1757, in *Dinwiddie Papers*, 2:552, 559).

54. "Proposal for Frontier Forts," [9 November 1756], in *Washington Papers*, 4:10–11. Intended as bastions for safeguarding the "[frontier] inhabitants in their lives and properties," the backcountry forts sometimes proved uncertain places of refuge. For example, in June 1756 Vaux's fort on the Holston River in Augusta County was overrun with the loss of all twenty-eight people who had sought protection within its walls. Built about twenty miles apart and always undermanned, the forts were even less effective "as a barrier against incursions of the barbarians" into the colony's more settled regions. By the end of 1756, Washington concluded that, in a strictly military sense, the forts were "doing no Singular Service to our Country" (see Hening, *Statutes*, 7:18; *Pennsylvania Gazette*, 29 July 1756; Washington to Loudoun, 10 January 1757, in *Washington Papers*, 4:83).

55. Information on the Virginia Regiment's troop strength in 1756 and 1757 was obtained from the following sources: Dinwiddie to the Lords of Trade, 23 February 1756; Dinwiddie to Halifax, 24 February 1756; Dinwiddie to Fox, 20 March 1757; Dinwiddie to Washington, [_____ June 1756], 24 June 1757, in *Dinwiddie Papers*, 2:345, 348, 372, 434, 655; Washington to Stanwix, 8 October 1757, in *Writings of Washington*, 2:145; Washington Papers MSS, ser. 4, 4: items 425–35, 452, 461, 463; 6: items 103–4, 710, 731, 756, 759, 778. Manpower levels in the Virginia Regiment were at particularly low ebb during the spring and early summer of 1757 when, on orders from the earl of Loudoun, then commander in chief of all British forces in North America, several companies of Virginia provincials were sent to South Carolina. (At that time it was feared that South Carolina was about to be invaded by a large enemy force; in fact, the attack never materialized.) On 16 June 1757, shortly after the 200-man Virginia contingent had left for Charleston, Washington noted that the regiment's total effective strength consisted of 384 men scattered among 9 frontier forts (see Washington to Dinwiddie, 16 June 1757, in *Washington Papers*, 4:221). On the deployment to South Carolina, see Dinwiddie to Lyttelton, 2 April 1757; Dinwiddie to Sharpe, 5 April 1757; Dinwiddie to Loudoun, 5 April 1757, in *Dinwiddie Papers*, 2:602–5; Dinwiddie to Lyttelton, 26 May 1757, in Lyttelton Papers, CWFRA.

56. Washington to Morris, 1 January 1756, in *Washington Papers*, 2:249; Dinwiddie to Washington, [_____ June 1756], 19 August 1756, in *Dinwiddie Papers*, 2:434, 480.

57. Landon Carter's complaint about the men of his county taking to the swamps is in Carter to Washington, [April 1756], in *Letters to Washington*, 1:236. On the refusal of draftable men to attend the lotteries, see ibid., William Fairfax to Washington, 3 September 1756, pp. 361–62; and Dinwiddie to Washington, 13 September 1756, in *Dinwiddie Papers*, 2:506. Complaints about sloppy administration of the draft laws are in Dinwiddie to Washington, 19 August 1756, in *Letters to Washington*, 1:343, and Washington to Henry Lee, 30 June 1757, in *Washington Papers*, 4:275.

58. Mention of the Fredericksburg jail break is made in Dinwiddie to Lord [Thomas] Fairfax, 18 October 1755, in *Dinwiddie Papers*, 2:248. Early in 1757 Washington observed that "many" of those unable to pay the ten-pound draft-exemption fee

simply absconded (see Washington to Loudoun, 10 January 1757, in *Washington Papers*, 4:81); on those men who collected bounty money and ran, see Washington to Dinwiddie, 17 September 1757, in *Dinwiddie Papers*, 2:126.

59.  Late in 1755 there were less than 340 men serving in the Virginia Regiment (see Stephen to Washington, 22 November 1755, *Letters to Washington*, 1:127–29). Dinwiddie's offer to pardon deserters who returned to the ranks by 20 September 1755 is printed in the 29 August 1755 issue of the *Virginia Gazette* (Hunter); the governor's admission that "few have taken Advantage of the Offer . . . of Indemnity," and his order to begin a colonywide search for deserters, appeared in the *Virginia Gazette* (Hunter) for 26 September, 3 October, and 10 October 1755. Surviving issues of the *Virginia Gazette* for the two-year period between Braddock's defeat and the fall of 1757 contain numerous advertisements for runaway soldiers; see, for example, the *Virginia Gazette* (Hunter), 22 August; 3, 10, 24 October; 7, 28 November; 5, 12, 19, 26 December 1755; 2, 9 January; 27 August; 3 September 1756; 2 September 1757.

60.  Dinwiddie's order to imprison both known and suspected deserters was issued in a public letter to all county lieutenants, militia officers, and justices of the peace. The letter appeared in the 3 September 1756 issue of the *Virginia Gazette* (Hunter). For estimates of desertion rates during the summer of 1757, see Washington to John Robinson, 10 July 1757, and Washington to Stanwix, 30 July 1757, in *Washington Papers*, 4:287–89, 353–54. The difficulty of estimating the regiment's supply needs and Dinwiddie's despairing remark about the need to suspend recruiting are both contained in Dinwiddie to Washington, 10 September 1757, in *Dinwiddie Papers*, 2:693–94.

61.  Dinwiddie to Washington, 8 May 1757, in *Dinwiddie Papers*, 2:406; Washington to Andrew Lewis, 1 July 1757, in *Washington Papers*, 4:277–78.

62.  These sentences were handed down "at a General Court Martial held by order of Col. George Washington at Fort Loudoun, May 7[,] 1757." A copy of these proceedings is in the Washington Papers MSS, ser. 4, 6: item 216. Five captured deserters were subjected to similar punishment in December 1755, "each receiving a thousand lashes" (quoted in "Journal of Captain Charles Lewis," p. 215). On occasion, the lash was applied liberally for lesser crimes as well. In September 1755 a soldier named Sullivan was given six hundred lashes for "uttering treasonable Expressions" (see Stephen to Washington, 27 September 1755, in *Letters to Washington*, 1:99–100).

63.  Dinwiddie to Washington, 27 May 1757, in *Dinwiddie Papers*, 2:423; Washington to Dinwiddie, 3 August 1757, in *Washington Papers*, 4:360. For additional instances when recourse was made to capital punishment, see Washington to Stanwix, 15 July 1757, 30 July 1757, in *Washington Papers*, 4:306–7, 353–54; "Minutes of a Court-Martial Held at Winchester," 2 May 1756, in *Dinwiddie Papers*, 2:399–401; "At a General Court Martial held by order of Col. George Washington at Fort Loudoun, May 7[,] 1757," in Washington Papers MSS, ser. 4, 6: item 216. Washington's record as a disciplinarian in both the French and Indian War and the War of Independence is evaluated in Stuart L. Bernath, "George Washington and the Genesis of American Military Discipline," *Mid-America: An Historical Review*, 2 (April 1967): 83–100.

64.  Washington to Dinwiddie, 27 August, 17 September 1757, in *Washington Papers*, 4:385, 406; Dinwiddie to Sharpe, 14 June 1757, in *Dinwiddie Papers*, 2:639. Dinwiddie readily approved Washington's requests to execute captured deserters.

65.  Washington to Loudoun, 10 January 1757, in *Washington Papers*, 4:83.

66.  Washington to Dinwiddie, 11 October 1755, in *Washington Papers*, 2:101–7; Dinwiddie to Sharpe, 8 May 1756, in *Dinwiddie Papers*, 2:241; Washington to Loudoun, 10 January 1757, in *Washington Papers*, 4:79–90. Thomas Lloyd's comments are in Lloyd to Hector, 10 October 1756, in P.R.O. H.C.A. 30/258 High Court of Admiralty—Misc. 1750–1756 SR 5703 (typescript copy in CWFRA). One telling episode that illustrated the continuing logistics mess occurred late in 1758 when Governor

Francis Fauquier received a message from Colonel William Byrd III announcing that the long-awaited march on Fort Duquesne had begun. In making that news known to his council, Fauquier also informed them that Byrd had "laid out near £200 for underwaistcoats for his men, the weather being extremely cold, which he hopes the Assembly will allow" (Fauquier to the council, 1 November 1758, in *The Correspondence of the Three William Byrds of Westover, Virginia, 1684–1776*, ed. Marion Tinling, 2 vols. [Charlottesville, 1977], 2:667). Thus, after four years of fighting, the normal provincial supply channels could not even furnish long underwear for Virginia troops partcipating in what for the Old Dominion was the crucial campaign of the French and Indian War.

67. [John Mercer?], "Pro Patria," _____ 1756, in *The Colonial Virginia Satirist: Mid-Eighteenth Century Commentaries on Politics, Religion, and Society*, ed. Richard Beale Davis (Philadelphia, 1967), p. 29.

68. On the six thousand pounds owed to provincial soldiers, see Robinson to Washington, 21 April 1757, in *Letters to Washington*, 2:66–67; the financial distress of the Virginia provincials serving in South Carolina is discussed in Dinwiddie to Stephen, 24 November 1757, in *Dinwiddie Papers*, 2:718. The military pay problem is also mentioned in "Governor Dinwiddie's Address to the House of Burgesses," 14 April 1757; Dinwiddie to Loudoun, 6 May 1757, in *Dinwiddie Papers*, 2:611, 618; and in Washington to Dinwiddie, 27 June 1757; Washington to Hog, 24 July 1757, in *Washington Papers*, 4:325–26. Complaints about the assembly's treatment of wounded veterans are in Washington to Loudoun, 10 January 1757, and Washington to Dinwiddie, 27 April 1757, in *Washington Papers*, 4:85–86, 145–46. What the lack of an organized pension system for disabled provincial veterans meant on a human level is reflected in the story of one William Saunders. Saunders was thrown into jail in Chester, Pennsylvania, late in August 1757 on suspicion of robbing and raping "a poor dumb Woman." For his part, Saunders claimed he was a veteran of the Virginia Regiment who had lost his left hand while fighting for the Old Dominion. Since his discharge he allegedly had scrounged for his living as a peddler. (Saunders' assertion about the nature of his occupation may have been an artful claim designed to explain the assorted pieces of silver plate found in his possession at the time of his arrest.) Saunders' case is described in the *Pennsylvania Gazette*, 25 August 1757.

69. On the usefulness of connections in high places, see John Martin to Washington, 30 August 1755, and George Mason to Washington, 12 June 1756, in *Letters to Washington*, 1:84–85, 277–78. The point relating poverty and exclusion from the political process is that if men were too poor to pay the ten-pound draft-exemption fee, they probably were too poor to qualify for enfranchisement. The fact that so many common soldiers were immigrants (European immigrants comprised almost half of the regiment's enlisted strength in 1756 and 1757) likely did nothing to increase their personal identification with Virginia's cause. (See table 2 for date on the birthplaces of provincial soldiers.)

70. On the inclination of provincial deserters to head for the nearest neighboring colony, see Peter Hog and John McNeill to Washington, 13 October 1755, in Washington Papers MSS, ser. 4, 4: item 72; Washington to Loudoun, 10 January 1757, and Washington to Dinwiddie, 10 June 1757, in *Washington Papers*, 4: 85, 194.

71. On the stated mission of the Virginia Regiment, see "Commission from Governor Dinwiddie to Colonel George Washington," 14 August 1755, and Dinwiddie to Shirley, 20 September 1755, in *Dinwiddie Papers*, 2:184, 210. Turmoil within the regiment is noted in Washington to Loudoun, 10 January 1757, in *Washington Papers*, 4:86. The various weaknesses of the regiment were held up to sharp and public criticism by the anonymous author of "The Virginia Centinel, No. X," in the *Virginia Gazette* (Hunter), 3 September 1756.

## 5. "OUR PEOPLE ARE MUCH UNEASY": DISSENSION AND VICTORY

1. James Maury to John Fontaine, 15 June 1756; Peter Fontaine to Moses Fontaine, 11 June 1757, in Ann Maury, ed and trans., *Memoirs of a Huguenot Family: Translated and Compiled from the Original Autobiography of the Rev. James Maury* (reprint, Baltimore, 1967), pp. 403, 366; Samuel Davies, "The Crisis: Or, The Uncertain Doom of Kingdoms at Particular Times," "The Curse of Cowardice," in *Sermons on Important Subjects. By the Late Reverend and Pious Samuel Davies, A.M. Sometime President of the College of New Jersey,* 5 vols. (Philadelphia, 1818), 5:251, 280.

2. John Robinson to Washington, 3 November 1757, in *Letters to Washington and Accompanying Papers,* ed. Stanislaus Murray Hamilton, 5 vols. (Boston and New York, 1898–1902), 2:230; Robert Dinwiddie to Washington, 23 January, 8 April, June, 19 August 1756; 26 January, 1 June 1757; Dinwiddie to [Peter] Hog, 8 September 1756; Dinwiddie to [Horatio] Sharpe, 30 July 1757; Dinwiddie to [Andrew] Lewis, 1 December 1757, in *The Official Records of Robert Dinwiddie, Lieutenant-Governor of the Colony of Virginia, 1751–1758, Now First Printed from the Manuscript in the Collections of the Virginia Historical Society,* ed. Robert A. Brock, 2 vols. (Richmond, 1883), 2:326–28, 381, 431, 480, 585, 635–36, 504, 677, 719; [John Mercer?], *The Colonial Virginia Satirist: Mid-Eighteenth-Century Commentaries on Politics, Religion, and Society,* ed. Richard Beale Davis (Philadelphia, 1967), p. 32.

3. "Philo Patria" presented his arguments in the form of a letter written to a "friend" who sat in the House of Burgesses. From all appearances, the letter was intended for publication in the *Virginia Gazette* and presumably appeared in one of the now missing issues. A manuscript copy of the letter is in the George Washington Papers (MSS, Library of Congress, Washington, D.C.), ser. 4, 6: item 855. The MS bears the following notation by Washington: "Written It is supposed by Colo. Richard Bland[,] 1756." Bland was a respected member of the House of Burgesses for more than thirty years (1742–1775). Along with leading men like John Robinson, Charles Carter, and Payton Randolph, Bland served on the series of "Country Committees" convened during the French and Indian War to oversee the expenditure of defense appropriations. Such service doubtless made him an informed critic of provincial military policy. Bland's political career and contributions as an eighteenth-century political thinker are evaluated in Clinton Rossiter, "Richard Bland: The Real Whig in America," *William and Mary Quarterly* (hereafter cited as *WMQ*), 3d ser., 10 (January 1953): 33–79.

4. For a recent examination of the origins and influence of anti-army ideology in eighteenth-century America, see John Phillip Reid, *In Defiance of the Law: The Standing-Army Controversy, The Two Constitutions, and the Coming of the American Revolution* (Chapel Hill, 1981).

5. Washington to Dinwiddie, 11 October 1755, in *Dinwiddie Papers,* 2:236–37; Adam Stephen to Washington, 7 November 1755, in *Letters to Washington,* 1:123.

6. Washington to Dinwiddie, 9 October 1757, in *The Writings of George Washington from the Original Manuscript Sources, 1745–1799,* ed. John C. Fitzpatrick, 39 vols. (Washington, D.C., 1931–44.), 2:147–48; other complaints of conniving magistrates are in Washington to Dinwiddie, 5 October 1757; Washington to John Stanwix, 8 October 1757, in ibid., pp. 141, 144. During the spring and summer of 1756, Captain Robert Stewart, commanding a detachment of provincial troops in the Hampshire County hamlet of Maidstone, also had difficulties with a politically well-connected innkeeper (see Stewart to Washington, 20 June 1756, in *Letters to Washington,* 1:280–82).

7. Joseph Wolgamote's letter is in the Washington Papers MSS, ser. 4, 7: item 93; the letter is reprinted in *Letters to Washington,* 2:326–27. Ensign Gordon's death is discussed in [Horatio] Sharpe to Dinwiddie, 30 March 1756, in *Letters to Washington,* 1:219, and Washington to David Bell, 8 April 1756, in W. W. Abbot et al., eds.

*The Papers of George Washington: Colonial Series*, 4 vols. to date (Charlottesville, 1983–      ), 2:342–43. Toward the end of the war, Governor Francis Fauquier made passing reference to a provincial corporal accused of killing a civilian (see Fauquier to Stephen, 25 January 1762, in *The Official Papers of Francis Fauquier, Lieutenant Governor of Virginia, 1758–1768*, ed. George Reese, 3 vols. (Charlottesville, 1980–83), 2:668. For another instance of high-handed military behavior toward civilians, see Washington to John Forbes, 30 December 1758, in *Writings of Washington*, 2:317–18.

    8.  Dinwiddie to Washington, 8 April 1756; Charles Carter to Washington, 27 April 1756; Robinson to Washington, 17 April 1756, in *Letters to Washington*, 1:213, 233, 221. On this subject see also ibid., Landon Carter to Washington, 21 April 1756, p. 223. These allegations apparently had substance. Washington insisted that most members of his command conducted themselves with "morality and Good Behavior" but did acknowledge that "a few" officers were guilty of "inadvertance and miscon-duct" (see Washington to Dinwiddie, [18 April 1756]; Washington to Robinson, 24 April 1756, in *Washington Papers*, 3:13–15, 48.

    9.  The "Virginia-Centinel No. X" originally appeared in the *Virginia Gazette* (Hunter) for 3 September 1756. Reprints of this strongly worded indictment appeared shortly thereafter in the *Pennsylvania Journal and Weekly Advertiser* of 4 November 1756 and in the *Maryland Gazette* for the same date. The "Centinel" may have au-thored as many as sixteen articles, but only two survive, numbers "IX" and "X." Number "IX," which appeared in the *Virginia Gazette* of 28 August 1756, was tem-perate in tone, offered a rather conventional detailing of French perfidy, and was generally sanguine about the chances for an ultimate British victory. The identity of the author of the "Centinel" series remains a mystery, although Douglas Southall Freeman speculates that he may have been an aggrieved militia officer. For discussion of the "Centinel" affair, see Douglas Southall Freeman, *George Washington: A Biog-raphy*, 7 vols. (New York, 1948–57), 2:208–12.

    10.  Davies, "The Crisis: Or, the Uncertain Doom of Kingdoms at Particular Times" (28 October 1756) and "The Curse of Cowardice" (8 May 1758) in *Sermons on Important Subjects*, 5:251, 282.

    11.  The estimate of the monthly costs of maintaining the Virginia Regiment is in Dinwiddie to the earl of Halifax, 24 May 1756, in *Dinwiddie Papers*, 2:418. Provin-cial military expenditures as of January 1757 were tallied up in a letter from James Abercromby, the colony's London agent, to the Board of Trade (see Abercromby to the Board of Trade, 12 January 1757, in C.O. 5/1329); the letter's contents are summarized in Richard Lee Morton, *Colonial Virginia*, 2 vols. (Chapel Hill, 1960), 2:706. In 1773 the *Virginia Gazette* estimated that the Old Dominion had raised £539,962 10s. for the war (see *Virginia Gazette* [Purdie and Dixon] 29 January 1773). On Virginia's war expenditures see also "A State of Paper Money Emitted in Virginia for the Years 1755, 1756, 1757, 1758, 1759, 1760, 1762," in Shelburne Papers MSS, vol. 46, p. 176, original in the Clements Library, University of Michigan (microfilm copy in Colonial Williams-burg Foundation Research Archives; hereafter cited as CWFRA).

    12.  Maury's complaint about the proliferation of taxes is in Maury to Fontaine, 15 June 1756, in Maury, *Memoirs of a Huguenot Family*, p. 401. High war taxes and other economic woes brought petitions for relief from various counties (see Henry Read McIlwaine, ed., *Journals of the House of Burgesses of Virginia, 1752–1755, 1756–1758* [Richmond, 1909], pp. 339, 357, 362, 364); on the subject of high war taxes see also Andrew Burnaby, *Travels through the Middle Settlements in North-America in the Years, 1759 and 1760* (London, 1775), p. 39. An analysis of the tax structure of prere-volutionary Virginia and other southern colonies is in Robert A. Becker, "Revolution and Reform: An Interpretation of Southern Taxation, 1763 to 1783," *WMQ*, 3d ser., 32 (July 1975): 417–42, see especially pp. 418–22. The regressive character of the Virginia poll tax and other of the Old Dominion's public levies is one of Becker's main points (the comment about war taxes falling "heavily" on poor Virginians is in Maury

to Fontaine, 15 June 1756, in Maury, *Memoirs of a Huguenot Family*, p. 402). Becker claims that prior to 1754, public expenses were met by "tobacco export taxes, quit rents and occasional minor poll taxes" (p. 421). In 1751 merchant Charles Steuart described taxes in the Old Dominion as "moderate" (see Steuart to Walter Tullideph, 23 September 1751, in Charles Steuart Letter Book, original in the Historical Society of Pennsylvania [microfilm copy in CWFRA]. There is a short discussion of poll tax rates during the first half of the eighteenth century in Edmund S. Morgan, *American Slavery, American Freedom: The Ordeal of Colonial Virginia* (New York, 1975), p. 345. The legislative action taken during the assembly session of February–August 1755 to institute a land tax and increase the poll tax rates is recorded in William Waller Hening, ed., *The Statutes at Large: Being a Collection of All the Laws of Virginia from the First Session of the Legislature, in the Year 1619*, 13 vols. (Richmond and Philadelphia, 1808–23), 6:463–64, 522. For the other kinds of taxes that were enacted during the French and Indian War, see "Additional Taxes laid on the Virginians to Redeem & Sink the Paper Money Emitted in the Colony for the aid of the War," in Shelburne Papers MSS, vol. 46, p. 177 (microfilm copy in CWFRA). The land tax was particularly resented by the larger land owners because it applied to all the land "they hold when not near one Seventh of it is in Cultivation" (ibid). On the unpopularity of the land tax, see also David John Mays, ed., *The Letters and Papers of Edmund Pendleton, 1734–1803*, 2 vols. (Charlottesville, 1967), 1:91. The assertion that the land tax impaired the land owner's ability to meet his other financial obligations is in Louis Morton, *Robert Carter of Nomini Hall: A Virginia Tobacco Planter of the Eighteenth Century* (Charlottesville, 1945), p. 127. In spite of the plethora of taxes, the provincial government soon found it necessary to anticipate the collection of tax revenues by issuing treasury notes. These notes were issued for a specific period of time, and provision was made for their redemption at the end of that time by the imposition of additional special taxes. The notes were not only receivable for taxes but also were made legal tender for all private monetary transactions, a measure that later embroiled the colony in a heated controversy with British merchants and the Board of Trade. The notes were first issued in May 1755, and every assembly session thereafter (save two) down to October 1760 authorized further emissions. There was no need for further emissions because after that date the British Crown reimbursed the colony for most of its military expenses. The laws concerning the emission of paper money are in Hening, ed., *Statutes*, 6:435–38, 522–30; 7:69–87, 163–69, 171–79, 255–65, 347–53, 357–63, 495–502. For a discussion of Virginia's wartime financial policies and a convenient summary of the colony's currency emissions during the French and Indian War, see Joseph Albert Ernst, "The Robinson Scandal Redivivus: Money, Debts, and Politics in Revolutionary Virginia," *Virginia Magazine of History and Biography* (hereafter cited as *VMHB*), 77 (April 1969): 146–73. A more complete study of the complex financial issues is in Ernst, "Genesis of the Currency Act of 1764: Virginia Paper Money and the Protection of British Investments," *WMQ*, 3d ser., 23 (January 1965): 33–74, and the same author's *Money and Politics in America, 1755–1775: A Study in the Currency Act of 1764 and the Political Economy of Revolution* (Chapel Hill, 1973).

13. The evidence for concluding there was a division in the House of Burgesses between those favoring vigorous (and expensive) prosecution of the war and those who favored a more modest approach (and lower taxes) is in Jack P. Greene, ed., *The Diary of Landon Carter of Sabine Hall, 1752–1778*, 2 vols. (Charlottesville, 1965), 1:107–14; Landon Carter to Washington, April 1756; William Fairfax to Washington, 9 May, 13 May 1756; [Richard Bland?] to Washington, [1756]; Bland to Washington, 7 June 1757; William Ramsey to Washington, 17 October 1758, in *Letters to Washington*, 1:236, 251, 256–57, 391; 2:87–89; 3:117; Fauquier to the Board of Trade, 14 April 1759, in *Fauquier Papers*, 1:207–9.

14. Dinwiddie's report of growing unhappiness in the assembly over the large number of provincial officers is in Dinwiddie to Washington, 26 January 1757, in *Dinwiddie Papers*, 2:585. Throughout the latter half of 1756, Dinwiddie frequently

fumed about "how far short the Officers have been in comply'g w'th y'r Promises [to find recruits] w'n Comiss'd" (see ibid., Dinwiddie to Washington, [June 1756], 19 August, 16 November 1756, pp. 434, 480, 552. Complaints of a swollen and self-serving provincial military establishment appeared at about the same time in the satirical "O Dinwiddiane," whose anonymous author bemoaned the "needless offices . . . [that] to crush us are contriving" (quoted in Davis, *Colonial Virginia Satirist*, p. 21). Manpower figures from July 1756 were derived from the Washington Papers MSS, ser. 4, 4: items 425–35, 452, 461, 463. The Virginia Regiment's rank structure as of July 1756 is given in "Formation of the Virginia Regiment," [12 July 1756], in *Letters to Washington*, 1:297–99. At that time each company was authorized four to six noncommissioned officers in addition to its complement of commissioned officers (see ibid., pp. 299–300).

15. Ex-Captain Peachey's comments are in Peachey to Washington, 14 November 1757, in *Letters to Washington*, 2:235. See also Dinwiddie to Washington, 19 August 1756; "Instructions to Colonel George Washington, Commander-In-Chief of the Virginia Regiment," 16 May 1757, in *Dinwiddie Papers*, 2:482, 622–23. In his letter advising Washington of the assembly's decision, Dinwiddie stated that the lawmakers acted because of "the great Expence the Virg'a Regim't has cost the Country from the No. of Companys . . . not complea't in proportion to the vast Charge of Officers" ("Instructions to Colonel George Washington," in *Dinwiddie Papers*, 2:622). The details of the reduction are also given in Hening, *Statutes*, 7:74–75.

16. Washington to the earl of Loudoun, 10 January 1757 in *Washington Papers*, 4:83–84; Thomas Waggener to Washington, 19 June 1757, in *Letters to Washington*, 2:106. For other complaints from provincial officers regarding what they considered shabby treatment, see Robert McKenzie to Washington, 18 February 1757; John Hall to Washington, [November 1757]; George Mason to Washington, 16 May 1758, in *Letters to Washington*, 2:46, 249, 299; Washington to Dinwiddie, 10 July 1757, in *Washington Papers*, 4:291.

17. "Coppy [sic] of the Officers of the Virginia Regim't Letter to Lieut. Coll. Adam Stephen Command[ing] at Fort Cumberland[,] . . . October 4, 1756," in Washington Papers MSS, ser. 4, 4:item 756; "Officers of the Virginia Regiment" to Washington, 12 November 1756, in *Letters to Washington*, 1:382–85. Washington's threat to resign is in Washington to Robinson, December 1756, in *Writings of Washington*, 1:531–33. The letter to Robinson also forwarded the third written protest by provincial officers angered by the "Virginia-Centinel's" accusations. The protest is in ibid., pp. 533–35.

18. Landon Carter to Washington, [April 1756], in *Letters to Washington*, 1:235. Carter huffed that the officers' remonstrances were believed by "perhaps one man in a hundred." Robinson's consoling remarks are in Robinson to Washington, 16 November 1756, in ibid., 2:1–2; William Fairfax made his supportive comments in Fairfax to Washington, ibid., p. 38.

19. Writing as "Philo Patria," Bland insisted that most officers had "given sufficient Proofs of their Resolution in their Country's Cause" (see Bland to Washington, [1756], in ibid., 1:386). The "Remonstrance" of April 1757 is in "Remonstrance of [the] Officers of the Virginia Regiment to Governor Dinwiddie," [16 April ?] 1757, in *Writings of Washington*, 2:25–27. The general antagonism between soldiers and civilians was reflected in the growing personal estrangement between Washington and Governor Dinwiddie. Relations between the two had never been close, but down to the spring of 1757, their dealings had been marked by a fair measure of mutual confidence. However, by early summer there were signs that mutual confidence had given way on both sides to mutual distrust. In June Washington confided to John Robinson his belief that "it wou'd give pleasure to the Governor to hear that I was involved in trouble: however undeservedly, such are his dispositions toward me" (Washington to Robinson, 10 June 1757, in *Washington Papers*, 4:198–99). Washington continued voicing such

sentiments as the summer progressed; see, for example, Washington to Robinson, 10 July 1757; Washington to Dinwiddie, [17 September 1757], in ibid., pp. 287–89, 405–9. There is little in the record to sustain the worst of these suspicions, although during his final months in America, Dinwiddie did accuse Washington of "ingratitude," upbraided him for careless reporting, and refused a request for leave (Dinwiddie to Washington, 15 August, 24 September, 19 October 1757, in *Dinwiddie Papers*, 2:684, 703, 707–8). In part, the governor's ill-temper may be attributed to the effects of a stroke he suffered in the fall of 1756. By the following year, the governor's "Paralytick Disorder" no doubt had made him more crotchety than usual. During his last year in office (he sailed home to England in January 1758), Dinwiddie's patience, never great in any case, had been all but exhausted by the cares of a long and frustrating war. Resentful of the public criticism directed at his army and clearly hurt by his failure to win a royal commission, Washington himself by 1757 was unusually sensitive to real and imagined slights. On Dinwiddie's failing health see Dinwiddie to the earl of Loudoun, 28 October [1756]; Dinwiddie to Abercromby, 22 March 1757; Dinwiddie to Washington, 2 November 1757; Dinwiddie to Richard Corbin, November 1758, in *Dinwiddie Papers*, 2:535, 601, 713, 723. The squabbling between Dinwiddie and Washington is discussed in Freeman, *Washington*, 2:260–61, 270–72.

20.  Information on the level of literacy in eighteenth-century Virginia and an imaginative analysis of the oral culture of its "common folk" is in Rhys Isaac, *The Transformation of Virginia, 1740–1790* (Chapel Hill, 1982), pp. 121–24; the rhyme maliciously attributed to "Governor Dinwiddie" and the observations of "Timothy McOates" are both the work of the anonymous author of the *Virginia Satirist* (see *The Colonial Virginia Satirist*, pp. 24, 31).

21.  For Washington's complaints of civilian connivance with deserters, see Washington to Dinwiddie, 8, 23 September 1756, 11 July 1757, in *Washington Papers*, 3:396, 399, 417; 4:295–97. Dinwiddie's admission of helplessness regarding this problem is in Dinwiddie to Washington, 30 September 1756, in *Dinwiddie Papers*, 2:523.

22.  Captain Peter Hog's account of his patrol's violent encounter with the deserters and their civilian friends is in Hog to Washington, 17 December 1755, in *Letters to Washington*, 1:154–55; the allegations of the captured deserter are in "The Proceedings of a General court martial held at Fort Loudoun on the 25[th] & 26[th] Days of July 1757," in Washington Papers MSS, ser. 4, 6:item 284. For additional reports of complicity in desertion on the part of civil magistrates, see Washington to Dinwiddie, 8 September 1756, in *Washington Papers*, 3:396; Dinwiddie to the earl of Loudoun, 6 October 1756, in *Dinwiddie Papers*, 2:524.

23.  Washington to Dinwiddie, 24 April 1756, in *Washington Papers*, 3:46; Peachey to Washington, 22 August 1757, *Letters to Washington*, 2:182.

24.  Davies, "The Crisis: Or, the Uncertain Doom of Kingdoms at Particular Times," in *Sermons on Important Subjects*, 5:274. In the fall of 1755, a notice "To the Printer" of the *Virginia Gazette* criticized "Some that lay at Home in inglorious Ease" while the frontier was besieged by hostile Indians. The notice was unsigned, but the language was Davies's. The notice appeared in the *Virginia Gazette* (Hunter) for 7 November 1755.

25.  That prerevolutionary Virginia was beset by social disintegration and change is the key theme in the writings of Rhys Isaacs. The fruits of Isaacs's research and thinking are gathered in his provocative *The Transformation of Virginia, 1740–1790*. The growth of social anxiety in the 1760s and 1770s is also noted and discussed in Jack P. Greene, "Society, Ideology, and Politics: An Analysis of the Political Culture of Mid-Eighteenth Century Virginia," in Richard M. Jellison, ed., *Society, Freedom, and Conscience: The Coming of the Revolution in Virginia, Massachusetts, and New York* (New York, 1976); see especially pp. 57–76.

26. Pitt's personal background and political career are summarized in Lawrence Henry Gipson, *The British Empire before the American Revolution*, vol. 7: *The Great War for Empire: The Victorious Years, 1758–1760* (New York, 1949), pp. 3–26.

27. Washington to Stephen, [23 October 1756], in *Washington Papers*, 3:441. Major General James Abercromby exercised formal command of British military forces in North America as the campaign of 1758 began. Abercromby was more the choice of King George II than of Pitt, but the latter's control of the war had become so complete that Abercromby was little more than an order-taker in any event. Forbes and Jeffery Amherst were handpicked by Pitt as Abercromby's subcommanders. Pitt was particularly taken with Amherst, whom he promoted from colonel to major general. Pitt's overall plan of operations for 1758 was as follows: Amherst was to move against Louisburg as the first stage of the advance on Quebec; Abercromby was to lead an expedition against Fort Ticonderoga; Forbes was to relieve the southern frontier and march on Fort Duquesne. The earl of Loudoun's operations in 1757 had failed completely. On top of Braddock's defeat in 1755 and the loss of Oswego in 1756, came Loudoun's aborted expedition against Louisburg and Montcalm's successful attack on Fort William Henry in 1757. The loss of Fort William Henry with almost its entire garrison was a particularly humiliating defeat and placed the French squarely astride the strategic land bridge between the Hudson and Lake Champlain. Pitt and Loudoun were never on good terms to begin with, and the defeats of 1757 did nothing to endear the latter to the former. Loudoun's failure to submit an overall plan of operations for 1758 was the immediate cause for his removal from command. On the relationship between Loudoun and Pitt, see Stanley M. Pargellis, *Lord Loudoun in North America* (New Haven, 1933; reprint, New York, 1968), pp. 252, 347, 356. The defeats of 1757 and British strategy for 1758 are discussed in Gipson, *The Victorious Years*, pp. 174–79, 247–49, and Douglas Edward Leach, *Arms for Empire: A Military History of the British Colonies in North America, 1607–1763* (New York and London, 1973), pp. 393–404, 415–19.

28. "Pitt's circular letter of 30 December 1757 to the Governors of Pennsylvania[,] Maryland[,] Virginia[,] South Carolina[,] North Carolina[,]" is in Gertrude Selwyn Kimball, ed., *Correspondence of William Pitt When Secretary of State with Colonial Governors and Military and Naval Commissioners in America*, 2 vols. (New York and London, 1906), 1:140–43. In terms of its military objectives, Pitt stated that the Forbes campaign was aimed at "removing & repelling the Dangers, that threaten the Frontiers of any of the Southern Colonies" (ibid., p. 141). In the meantime, John Blair received a letter from General Abercromby that, "Tho not in express words, . . . clearly" made known that Fort Duquesne was Forbes's primary target. As Blair later put it, "This [the reduction of Fort Duquesne] was a favorite Scheme with us" (see Blair to Pitt, 29 June 1758, in ibid., pp. 288–91). On the general consensus in Virginia on the necessity of taking the forks of the Ohio, see Dinwiddie to Abercromby, 20 June 1757, in *Dinwiddie Papers*, 2:650–51; Bland[?] to Washington, [1756]; John Baylor to Washington, 20 June 1757; Robinson to Washington, 3 November 1757, in *Letters to Washington*, 1:386–95; 2:115, 229–30. On the important influence of Pitt's promise of reimbursement, see McIlwaine, *Burgesses, 1752–1758*, p. 497; and Fauquier to Forbes, 8 June 1758, in *Fauquier Papers*, 1:19. The Virginia assembly had reason to believe that Pitt would make good on his promise of reimbursement; the colony had recently received a reimbursement of thirty-two thousand pounds from Parliament for its military expenses in 1757 (see Hays Baker-Crothers, *Virginia and the French and Indian War* [Chicago, 1928], p. 129).

29. The military bill of April 1758 is reprinted in Hening, *Statutes*, 7:163–69. While the provincials were marching against Fort Duquesne, defense of the Old Dominion was entrusted to three companies of rangers and "so many [militia] men . . . as . . . shall appear necessary to garrison the [frontier] forts" (ibid., pp. 164–65, 169). Command of the Second Virginia Regiment was given to William Byrd III, scion of one of the colony's most affluent families and a man who, whatever his other faults,

had demonstrated considerable talent at Indian diplomacy. The twenty-nine-year-old Byrd had served as a volunteer with Lord Loudoun in 1757. Forbes was quite taken with Byrd and praised his "noble example" to William Pitt (see Forbes to Pitt, 10 July 1758, in *Pitt Correspondence*, 1:295–96).

30. Hening, *Statutes*, 7:164. John Blair later acknowledged there was a general consensus among the lawmakers that the bounty offered the most promising "means to compleat [the provincial army] with greater dispatch and better men." As a further recruiting inducement for the 1758 campaign, the assembly promised that all volunteers would be discharged by 1 December. Blair's comments are in Blair to Pitt, 29 June 1758, in *Pitt Correspondence*, 1:289–91; the promise of a short campaign is in Hening, *Statutes*, 7:168.

31. Blair's comments are in McIlwaine, *Burgesses, 1752–1758*, p. 506; Washington's appraisal of the new bounty system is in Washington to Waggener, 25 April 1758, in *Writings of Washington*, 2:186. The estimate on the relative value of ten pounds in mid-eighteenth-century Virginia is from Aubrey C. Land, "Economic Behavior in a Planting Society: The Eighteenth Century Chesapeake," *Journal of Southern History* 33 (November 1967):483. Recruiting progress in the spring of 1758 is discussed in Washington to Andrew Lewis, 21 May 1758, in *Writings of Washington*, 2:202; Fauquier to the Board of Trade, 11 June 1758; Fauquier to Washington, 25 June 1758, in *Fauquier Papers*, 1:23–26, 41–42. By all accounts, Fauquier was one of the best and best liked of Virginia's colonial governors. Like his predecessor Robert Dinwiddie, Fauquier actually was the lieutenant-governor, but to him fell all of the responsibilities and virtually all of the authority that normally accrued to the full-fledged "governors" of royal colonies. During Fauquier's ten-year term (1758–1768), the office of governor was held as a sinecure by (consecutively) the earl of Loudoun and Jeffery Amherst. A sketch of Fauquier is in Morton, *Colonial Virginia*, 2:714–15; see also Percy Scott Flippin, *The Royal Government in Virginia* (New York, 1919).

32. The Forbes expedition is closely examined in Parker King Lawrence, "Anglo-American Wilderness Campaigning, 1754–1764: Logistical and Tactical Developments" (Ph.D. diss., Columbia University, 1970), especially chapter 7; Lawrence Henry Gipson accords a chapter to Forbes's march in *The Victorious Years*, pp. 247–86. Virginia's part in the Forbes campaign is described in Nellie Norkus, "Virginia's Role in the Capture of Fort Duquesne, 1758," *The Western Pennsylvania Historical Magazine* 45 (December 1962): 291–308; also useful is Paul H. Giddens, "The Co-Operation of the Southern Colonies in the Forbes Expedition Against Fort Duquesne," *VMHB* 36 (January, April 1928): 1–16, 145–61. Shorter summaries of the campaign are in Leach, *Arms for Empire*, pp. 438–44; and Morton, *Colonial Virginia*, 2:714–18, 722–25. Forbes's army numbered almost 7,000 men and included the following major elements: the 1,200-man Highland Regiment, 350 troops from the Royal American Regiment, 40 members of the Royal Regiment of Artillery, and about 5,000 provincial troops from Virginia, Pennsylvania, and North Carolina. Additional details on the composition and strength of Forbes's army are in Alfred Procter, James, ed., *Writings of General John Forbes Relating to His Service in North America* (Menasha, Wis., 1938), p. x.

33. Forbes's initial inclination to march up from Fort Cumberland along the Braddock Road was strongly influenced by the earl of Loudoun's provisional "Plan of Operations on the Mississippi, Ohio, Etc.," 1 February 1758, reprinted in *Writings of Forbes*, p. 35. The first indication that Forbes was reconsidering his original plan to use Braddock's Road came early in May when Washington received a letter from Forbes's aide-de-camp hinting at a possible shift to the Pennsylvania route (see Francis Halkett to Washington, 4 May 1758, in *Letters to Washington*, 2:285). The real moving force behind the change was Colonel John St. Clair, the British army's Deputy Quartermaster General and chief logistician for Forbes's campaign. St. Clair's role is discussed in Forbes to Henry Bouquet, 6, 23 July 1758; Forbes to Pitt, 10 July 1758, in *Writings of Forbes*, pp. 128–30, 156, 141. On the economic benefits that use of Brad-

dock's Road would bring, see Louis K. Koontz, "Washington on the Frontier," *VMHB* 36 (October 1928), p. 323; Norkus, "Virginia's Role in the Capture of Fort Duquesne, 1758," p. 301; Baker-Crothers, *French and Indian War*, pp. 132–33; Freeman, *Washington*, 2:323; Gipson, *The Victorious Years*, p. 264. Bernhard Knollenberg suggests that personal economic interests influenced George Washington's strong advocacy of the old Braddock Road (see Knollenberg, *George Washington: The Virginia Period, 1732–1775* [Durham, N.C., 1964], pp. 65–66. Concern about the military implications of using the Pennsylvania route is expressed in Robert Rutherford to Washington, 31 July 1758, in *Letters to Washington*, 3:3–4. For Washington's criticism of the Pennsylvania route see, for example, Washington to Halkett, 2 August 1758; Washington to Fauquier, 5 August 1758; Washington to Bouquet, 6 August, 18 August, 28 August, 2 September 1758, in *Writings of Washington*, 2:260–61, 261–62, 263, 269–70, 275–76, 284–86. Fed up with Washington's foot dragging, the exasperated Forbes at last raged that Washington's "behavior about the roads, was no ways like a Soldier," Forbes to Bouquet, 4 September 1758, in *Writings of Forbes*, p. 199.

34. Forbes to Pitt, 6 September 1758, in *Writings of Forbes*, p. 203; William Denny to Fauquier, 23 November 1758; Forbes to Fauquier, 26 November 1758, in *Fauquier Papers*, 1:113–14. On the Treaty of Easton and its long-range significance, see also Gipson, *The Victorious Years*, pp. 274–79, and Leach, *Arms for Empire*, pp. 441–44. Among its other advantages, the shorter route leading west from Raystown linked Forbes's army with the rich farm country of middle and eastern Pennsylvania, a far more bountiful source of supply than anything Virginia had to offer.

35. Washington to Robinson, 1 September 1758, in *Writings of Washington*, 2:227. For other examples of Washington's doleful reports on the prospects of the Forbes expedition, see ibid., Washington to Fauquier, 5 August, 2 September, 25 September 1758; and Washington to Thomas Walker, 11 August 1758, pp. 261–62, 278–83, 219, 266.

36. Robinson to Washington, 13 September 1758, in *Letters to Washington*, 3:94; the military bill of September 1758 is reprinted in Hening, *Statutes*, 7:171–79. Two weeks after the autumn session began, Fauquier warned the Board of Trade that Virginia's participation in the Forbes expedition had become jeopardized because members of the assembly were "so much soured" by its slow progress (Fauquier to the Board of Trade, 23 September 1758, in *Fauquier Papers*, 1:76). Just how "soured" was indicated by a motion calling for the immediate dissolution of the First Virginia Regiment. Since enlistments in the Second Virginia Regiment expired on 1 December, the sponsors of this proposal aimed at nothing less than the near-term abolition of the entire provincial army. They almost had their way. In the end, the "old and judicious" members of the lower house defeated the dissidents' motion, but only by a slim margin of five votes. Dissident influence so far prevailed, however, that the final bill granting fifteen thousand pounds for the provincial army stipulated that future support was contingent on the return of Washington's regiment from Pennsylvania by 1 December (the date on which Byrd's regiment would cease to exist). The dissidents' motion and its narrow defeat are discussed in Ramsay to Washington, 17 October 1758, in *Letters to Washington*, 3:117.

37. Events surrounding the capture of the turncoat Englishman and "French" Indians and the final push to the Ohio are discussed in Gipson, *The Victorious Years*, pp. 282–83; Leach, *Arms for Empire*, pp. 443–44; and Freeman, *Washington*, 2:358–64. As Washington and other Virginians had predicted, the business of cutting a road through the Alleghenies was laborious and slow. In all, it took Forbes almost four months to cut and fill his way from Raystown to Fort Duquesne.

38. McIlwaine, *Burgesses, 1758–1761*, pp. 49, 52; Hening, *Statutes*, 7:252–53; Fauquier to Byrd, 12 November 1758, in *Fauquier Papers*, 1:104–5.

39. Washington to Fauquier, 28 November 1758, in *Writings of Washington*, 2:308.

### 6. "FINE REGIMENT": SOLDIERS WHEN THEY CHOSE TO BE SO

1. Forbes sternly reprimanded both Major Grant and Grant's immediate superior, Colonel Henry Bouquet, for the embarrassing defeat of 14 September, see Forbes to Bouquet, 23 September 1758, in Alfred Procter James, ed., *Writings of General John Forbes Relating to His Service in North America* (Menasha, Wis., 1938), pp. 218–20; see also Forbes to Abercromby, 21 September, 8 October 1758, in ibid., pp. 215–16, 225. For Washington's sarcastic report on Grant's defeat, see Washington to Fauquier, 25 September 1758; Washington to Mrs. George William [Sally Cary] Fairfax, 25 September 1758, in *The Writings of George Washington from the Original Manuscript Sources, 1745–1799*, ed. John C. Fitzpatrick, 39 vols. (Washington, D.C., 1931–44), 2:290, 292. The Virginia provincials lost five officers and sixty-two men killed, missing, or captured in the engagement on 14 September. These losses are discussed in Washington to George William Fairfax[?], 25 September 1758, in Peter Walne, ed., "George Washington and the Fairfax Family: Some New Documents," *Virginia Magazine of History and Biography* (hereafter cited as *VMHB*), 77 (October 1969): 454–56. Grant's defeat is described in Lawrence Henry Gipson, *The British Empire before the American Revolution*, vol 7: *The Great War for Empire: The Victorious Years, 1758–1760* (New York, 1949), pp. 268–70 and Douglas Edward Leach, *Arms for Empire: A Military History of the British Colonies in North America, 1607–1763* (New York and London, 1973), p. 442.

2. Bouquet to Amherst, 17 September 1758; Forbes to Pitt, 6 September 1758, in *Writings of Forbes*, p. 205; Washington to Fairfax[?], 25 September 1758, in "George Washington and the Fairfax Family: Some New Documents," p. 455; Washington to Fauquier, 25 September 1758, in *Writings of Washington*, 2:290–91.

3. Stanwix to [Governor of South Carolina] William H. Lyttelton, 4 February 1760, in William H. Lyttelton Papers, 1756–1760, MSS, original in the Clements Library, University of Michigan (microfilm copy in Colonial Williamsburg Foundation Research Archives; hereafter cited as CWFRA); Murray to Amherst, 20 October 1762, Amherst Papers MSS, W.O. 34/2, ff. 129–31 (Colonial Virginia Records Project microfilm copy in CWFRA). The derogatory references to Virginia troops from the period of the Braddock expedition are in John St. Clair to Braddock, [February 1755]; Braddock to Robert Napier, 8 June 1755, in *Military Affairs in North America, 1748–1765: Selected Documents From the Cumberland Papers in Windsor Castle*, ed. Stanley Pargellis (New York, 1936; reprint, New York, 1969), pp. 64, 84.

4. Fauquier to Byrd, 23 January 1759, in *The Official Papers of Francis Fauquier, Lieutenant Governor of Virginia, 1758–1768*, ed. George Reese, 3 vols. (Charlottesville, 1980–83), 1:158–59. The sequence of events in the immediate aftermath of the capture of Fort Duquesne is summarized in Richard Lee Morton, *Colonial Virginia*, 2 vols. (Chapel Hill, 1960), 2:726–28, and in *The Correspondence of the Three William Byrds of Westover, Virginia, 1684–1776*, ed. Marion Tinling, 2 vols. (Charlottesville, 1977), 2:668, n. 1. When the assembly reconvened in February 1759, Governor Fauquier, well aware that the reduction of Fort Duquesne had diminished the assembly's enthusiasm for military undertakings, assured the members of his own desire "to lessen the Expences of the Country as much as possible." To that end, the lawmakers learned that Fauquier already had sent home those militiamen who had been stationed on the frontier while the provincials were away campaigning with Forbes. Their places in Hampshire, Frederick, and Augusta counties had been taken by six companies of provincials lately returned from Fort Duquesne. Four companies of rangers were patrolling Bedford and Halifax counties on Virginia's southwestern frontier. These troop dispositions were outlined in Fauquier's opening speech to the assembly session of February 1759 (see Henry Read McIlwaine, *Journals of the House of Burgesses of Virginia, 1758–1761* [Richmond, 1909], pp. 55–56). The remaining four companies of the (First) Virginia Regiment had been retained by General Forbes, who feared a French counterattack on Fort Pitt, the new stronghold he was erecting on the

ruins of Fort Duquesne (see Forbes to Pitt, 27 November 1758, in Gertrude Selwyn Kimball, ed., *Correspondence of William Pitt When Secretary of State with Colonial Governors and Military and Naval Commissioners in America*, 2 vols. (New York and London, 1906), 1:406–9; Forbes to Fauquier, 26 November 1758, 11 January 1759; Fauquier to Forbes, 24 January 1759, in *Fauquier Papers*, 1:114, 154, 162).

5. On the Virginia provincials' role in the taking of the remaining French posts in the Ohio country, see Byrd to Fauquier in *Fauquier Papers*, 1:234. On the other uses to which the Virginians were put, see Stanwix to Byrd, 23 July 1759, in *Byrd Correspondence*, 2:674–75, and "Return of the Effective Rank and File of the Western Army[,] Fort Loudoun, 16 June 1760," in Amherst Papers MSS, W.O. 34/43, f. 44 (microfilm copy in CWFRA). Reports of the growing Cherokee threat are in Fauquier to Robert Monckton, 17 October 1760, in *Fauquier Papers*, 1:419–20; Monckton to Bouquet, 30 October 1760, in Bouquet Papers MSS, British Museum, Add. MSS. 21638, ff. 161–62 (microfilm copy in CWFRA); Monckton to Amherst, 20 November, 4 December 1760, in Amherst Papers MSS, W.O. 34/43, ff. 95–96, 100 (microfilm copy in CWFRA). His health broken by a severe case of camp dysentary he had contracted in July 1758, Brigadier General Forbes died in Philadelphia in March 1759. Command of British forces in the southern colonies (from Pennsylvania southward) passed to Brigadier General (later Major General) John Stanwix the same month. Stanwix, in turn, was succeeded by Brigadier General Robert Monckton in May 1760. Major General Jeffery Amherst assumed overall command of British forces in North America in December 1758. The shuffling of generals is discussed in *Letters to Washington and Accompanying Papers*, ed. Stanislaus Murray Hamilton, 5 vols. (Boston and New York, 1898–1902), 3:6, n. 1; circular letter from Major General Jeffery Amherst to the governors of New York, New Jersey, Connecticut, Rhode Island, Massachusetts Bay, New Hampshire, Pennsylvania, Maryland, and Virginia, 13 December 1758; Amherst to Fauquier, 22 March 1759; Monckton to Fauquier, 8 May 1760, in *Fauquier Papers*, 1:133, 191, 354.

6. Strains in the alliance between Virginia and the Cherokees were discussed in chapter 4 above. Anglo-Cherokee relations during the mid-eighteenth century are given detailed coverage in David H. Corkran, *The Cherokee Frontier: Conflict and Survival, 1740–1762* (Norman, Oklahoma, 1962), especially chapters 11–18; the complex social and political structure of the Cherokee nation is analyzed in Fred Gearing, "Priests and Warriors: Social Structures for Cherokee Politics in the Eighteenth Century," *American Anthropologist* 64 (October 1962): 1–124. For contemporary reports of growing hostility between Virginians and Cherokees, see Dinwiddie to [Clement] Read, 15 April 1757, in *The Official Records of Robert Dinwiddie, Lieutenant-Governor of the Colony of Virginia, 1751–1758, Now First Printed from the Manuscript in the Collections of the Virginia Historical Society*, ed. Robert A. Brock, 2 vols. (Richmond, 1883), 2:612–13; Washington to Dinwiddie, 30 May 1757, 10 June 1757, 5 November 1757, in *Writings of Washington*, 2:40–41, 48, 157–58.

7. On the large numbers of Cherokees arriving in Winchester in March and April 1757, see Washington to Stanwix, 10 April 1758; Washington to William Henry Fairfax, 23 April 1758, in *Writings of Washington*, 2:173, 181, and Forbes to Pitt, 1 May 1758, in *Pitt Correspondence*, 1:237–38. Forbes noted that the Cherokees were "rather offended at not seeing our Army and Artillery assembled, which I am afraid they had reason to expect." Washington's troubles with the Cherokees are discussed in Washington to Blair, 9 April 1758; Washington to St. Clair, 12 April 1758; Washington to Halkett, 11 May 1758, in *Writings of Washington*, 2:171–72, 175, 198. Clashes between Cherokee warriors and residents of Bedford, Augusta, and Halifax counties are reported in William Callaway to Washington, 15 May 1758; Blair to Washington, 24 May 1758; "Depositions and Letters in Regard to Behavior of Friendly Cherokees," in *Letters to Washington*, 2:296, 305, 307–11, 316.

8. McIlwaine, *Burgesses, 1758–1761*, pp. 133–34; William Waller Hening, ed., *The Statutes at Large: Being a Collection of All the Laws of Virginia from the First Session of the Legislature, in the Year 1619*, 13 vols. (Richmond and Philadelphia, 1808–23), 7:332; Fauquier to Lyttelton, 21 October 1759; Fauquier to William Bull, 24 May 1760, in *Fauquier Papers*, 1:254–55, 365. At this time an additional four hundred Virginia provincials still were serving in and around Fort Pitt.

9. On Lyttelton's appeal for Virginia's help, see McIlwaine, *Burgesses, 1758–1761*, p. 171; the Old Dominion's response is noted in Hening, *Statutes*, 7:358. Because of the threatening situation with the Cherokees, the Virginia assembly had earlier agreed to continue the Virginia Regiment until November 1760. At the governor's option, the three hundred men defending the colony's southwest frontiers could be continued in service until April 1761; the details are in Hening, *Statutes*, 7:348–49. Fauquier explained his decision to recall the Virginia Regiment after Montgomery's withdrawal in Fauquier to the Board of Trade, 17 September 1760, in *Fauquier Papers*, 1:411.

10. The British side of the campaign of 1761 is discussed in Leach, *Arms for Empire*, pp. 491–92.

11. The Virginia Regiment's mission and contributions in the campaign of 1761 are discussed in McIlwaine, *Burgesses, 1758–1761*, pp. 267–70, and in Fauquier to Amherst, 15 December 1760, 13 March 1761, in *Fauquier Papers*, 1:443; 2:487–88. The regiment's part in the successful outcome of the Cherokee War is also addressed in Morton, *Colonial Virginia*, 2:735, and in W. Stitt Robinson, *The Southern Colonial Frontier, 1607–1763* (Albuquerque, 1979), p. 222. Lieutenant Henry Timberlake, a young provincial subaltern who had marched on the Byrd-Stephen expedition to the Great Island of the Holston, visited the Cherokee towns immediately after the Indians sued for peace in mid-November 1761. The record of his experiences is in *The Memoirs of Lieut. Henry Timberlake* (London, 1765).

12. Fauquier to Amherst, 17 November 1761, in *Fauquier Papers*, 2:591; John Pendleton Kennedy, ed., *Journals of the House of Burgesses of Virginia, 1761–1765* (Richmond, 1909), p. 26; Hening, *Statutes*, 7:463–65. The peace treaty with the Cherokees was ratified on 18 December 1761; a copy has been reprinted in *Fauquier Papers*, 2:685–88. Fauquier ordered Colonel Adam Stephen to disband the regiment in a now missing letter written on or about 2 February 1762. The governor informed Jeffery Amherst of his action on 3 February; see Fauquier to Stephen, [2 February(?) 1762]; Fauquier to Amherst, 3 February 1762, in *Fauquier Papers*, 2:671–73. On the assembly's call to disband the provincial army, see Hening, *Statutes*, 7:463–65; Kennedy, *Burgesses, 1761–1765*, pp. 8, 26, 33–34, 36. William Byrd III resigned his colonelcy in the Virginia Regiment in September 1761. He was offered, but declined, command of the provincial army in 1762. Byrd was succeeded by Adam Stephen, long the Virginia Regiment's second-ranking officer; see Fauquier to Amherst, 21 May 1762, in *Fauquier Papers*, 2:739; Kennedy, *Burgesses, 1761–1765*, p. 6.

13. Fauquier to Amherst, 1 April 1762, in *Fauquier Papers*, 2:703–4. The 268 recruits the assembly agreed to raise for the British army represented a quota requested earlier by Jeffery Amherst (see ibid., Amherst to Fauquier, 21 February 1762, pp. 689–90). The Bourbon rulers of France and Spain had signed the so-called Family Compact on 15 August 1761, some six months after the French had initiated peace negotiations with Great Britain. The compact contained a secret proviso in which Spain agreed to enter the war by May 1762 unless Britain and France had already concluded peace. Pitt anticipated Spain's belligerency and pressed the Cabinet for a declaration of war. He failed to get his way and resigned his office in October 1761. Spain's hostile intentions subsequently became more apparent, and on 4 January 1762 the British issued a declaration of war; the Spanish reciprocated on 18 January. The British declaration is reprinted in ibid., pp. 649–51; the events leading up to and immediately following Spain's entry into the war are discussed in Leach, *Arms for Empire*, pp. 493–94 and

Gipson, *The British Empire before the American Revolution*, vol. 8: *The Culmination, 1760–1763* (New York, 1953), pp. 247–53.

14. On the decision to base the regiment at Fredericksburg, see Amherst to Fauquier, 10 April 1762; Fauquier to Amherst, 21 May 1762; Amherst to Fauquier, 5 June 1762; Amherst to Stephen, 5 June 1762; Fauquier to Amherst, 12 June 1762, in *Fauquier Papers*, 2:716, 739, 741, 744, 747. Richard P. Morton mistakenly claims that the Virginia Regiment "remained on the frontier until disbanded in May 1763" (Morton, *Colonial Virginia*, 2:736.). Small detachments apparently were maintained during 1762 at Fort Cumberland and at Redstone Creek (thirty miles south of Fort Pitt), but the main body of provincial troops was stationed at Fredericksburg until the end of the year. The record is also clear that the regiment ceased to exist in December 1762 (see Stephen to Fauquier, [4 December 1762]; Fauquier to Amherst, 15 December 1762; in *Fauquier Papers*, 2:847, 854; "A Memorial of the Officers of the Virginia Regiment" and Governor Fauquier's "Address" to the House of Burgesses, 3 December 1762, in McIlwaine, *Burgesses, 1761–1765*, pp. 124–25, 133). An interesting glimpse of camp life during the regiment's sojourn at Fredericksburg is in the "Orderly Book for the Virginia Regiment, May–September 1762," original in the Huntington Library Miscellaneous MSS (microfilm copy in CWFRA). Governor Fauquier learned early in February 1763 that a cessation of hostilities had been proclaimed; on 23 May 1763 Williamsburg received word that a "Definitive Treaty of Peace had been signed in Paris" (see Fauquier to the earl of Egremont, 4 February 1763; earl of Egremont to Fauquier, 18 February 1763, in *Fauquier Papers*, 2:904–5, 917).

15. On the eve of the Revolution, one Virginian offered the following grandiloquent account of the part played by the Old Dominion and her sister colonies during the French and Indian War:

> Witness the exertions of America in the last war. Need I particularize them? Whether I look towards the place of the unhappy, but brave Braddock's fall, or turn my eyes to the northern theater of operations, my admiration, my countrymen, of your valor, intrepidity, and bravery, is still the same. Conspicuous in every scene, you have demonstrated what a love for your country . . . can effect.

Written by "Virginius," this paean appeared in the *Virginia Gazette* (Rind) on 16 June 1774.

16. Beverley to John Bland, 5 April 1763, in Robert Beverley Letterbook, original in the Library of Congress (microfilm copy in CWFRA); see also Washington to Stewart, 2 May 1763, in *Writings of Washington*, 2:399–400. The Board of Trade's demands are in Board of Trade to Fauquier, 7 February 1763, in *Fauquier Papers*, 2:909–10. The complex squabble over Virginia's paper currency is summarized in Morton, *Colonial Virginia*, 2:745–49, and in Gwenda Morgan, "Virginia and the French and Indian War: A Case Study of the War's Effect on Imperial Relations," *VMHB* 81 (January 1973): 43–45; a more thorough discussion is in Joseph Albert Ernst, "Genesis of the Currency Act of 1764: Virginia Paper Money and the Protection of British Investments," *William and Mary Quarterly*, (hereafter cited as *WMQ*), 3d ser., 23 (January 1965): 33–74.

17. On the renewed but ultimately unsuccessful lobbying by the Ohio and Loyal companies following the expulsion of the French from the Ohio country, see Morton, *Colonial Virginia*, 2:739–41, and Lois Mulkearn, comp. and ed., *George Mercer Papers Relating to the Ohio Company of Virginia* (Pittsburgh, 1954), pp. 150–52; the Board of Trade explained the reasons for its opposition to further western expansion in Board of Trade to Fauquier, 13 June 1760, in *Fauquier Papers*, 1:376–77. On this subject, see also Eugene M. Del Papa, "The Royal Proclamation of 1763: Its Effect upon Virginia Land Companies," *VMHB* 83 (October 1976): 406–11.

18. "Memorial of George Washington, Adam Stephen, and Andrew Lewis" [1762], in *Fauquier Papers*, 2:744–75; the "Memorial" was enclosed with a letter from Fauquier to the Board of Trade dated 10 July 1762; see ibid., pp. 769–71. The uneventful fate of the "Memorial" is discussed in ibid., p. 776, n. 1, and in Morgan, "Virginia and the French and Indian War," p. 43. On the mustering out pay voted by the assembly for the officers and men of the Virginia Regiment, see Hening, *Statutes*, 7:464, 493.

19. Monckton to Amherst, 9 July 1760, in Amherst Papers MSS, W.O. 34/43, ff. 69–71 (microfilm copy in CWFRA); Stewart to Washington, 12 March 1761, in *Letters to Washington*, 3:205. The esteem in which the Virginia Regiment came to be held also was reflected in private and favorable references to Virginia officers made by their British counterparts. In a letter to Colonel Henry Bouquet written early in 1759, Major General Jeffery Amherst praised Lieutenant Colonel George Mercer of the Virginians for "his zeal and attachment to the King[']s Service and his Judgement and alacrity in executing whatever may tend to the honour of His Majesty's arms" (see Amherst to Bouquet, 5 March 1759, in Bouquet Papers MSS, British Museum, Add. MSS. 21634, ff. 73–78 [microfilm copy in CWFRA]). Bouquet praised another Virginia officer in a letter written to his immediate superior, Brigadier General Robert Monckton, in December 1760. Of Captain Robert Stewart, Bouquet said: "I was happy to have him there [at the former French fort at Venango], For People who have any Head at all, and can act of themselves, according to the times, and circumstances, are not very common here" (Bouquet to Monckton, 20 December 1760, in Bouquet Papers MSS, British Museum, Add. MSS. 21638, ff. 173–74 [microfilm copy in CWFRA]). On this subject, see also: Major Samuel Zobel to Colonel William Amherst, 24 January 1763, in [Jeffery] Amherst Papers MSS, W.O. 34/94, f. 19; [Jeffrey] Amherst [to the East India Company], "Statement regarding the character and services of Mr. [Robert] Stewart, an officer in the Virginia Provincial Reg't," in Amherst Papers MSS, W.O. 34/100, f. 206; Thomas Gage to William Ellis, 23 February 1765, War Office, In Letters, America and the West Indies, 1764–1765, W.O. 1/6, ff. 124–25 (microfilm copy in CWFRA).

20. On the Virginia Regiment's generally high enlistment rate during the years after 1758, see "Extract of a Letter from Virginia," 19 April [1759], in the *Pennsylvania Gazette*, 26 April 1759; Fauquier to the Board of Trade, 9 May 1759; 2 June 1760, in *Fauquier Papers*, 1:215, 372; Fauquier to Amherst, 11 May 1762, in *Fauquier Papers*, 2:734. On the good quality of provincial recruits for the 1759 campaign, see Fauquier to the Board of Trade, 9 June 1759, in *Fauquier Papers*, 1:219.

21. The continued high caliber of provincial recruits is mentioned in Stewart to Washington, 16 September 1759, in *Letters to Washington*, 3:165; see also "Dispatch from Savannah," 7 August 1760, in the *Pennsylvania Gazette*, 4 September 1760. For Fauquier's comments about the recruiting situation in 1762 and the reenlistment of many provincial veterans, see Fauquier to Amherst, 11 May, 14 May 1762, in *Fauquier Papers*, 2:734–35. Concerning the provincials' steady performance in the field, see the *Pennsylvania Gazette*, 17 April 1760. The Virginians' courageous deeds are also mentioned in Amherst to Fauquier, 21 January 1761; 11 May 1761; 28 May 1761, in *Fauquier Papers*, 2:465, 522, 529–30. The endurance of Virginia soldiers during the hard campaigning that followed the fall of Fort Duquesne is noted in Captain Richard Mather to Bouquet, 13 February 1761, in *The Papers of Colonel Henry Bouquet*, ed. Sylvester K. Stevens and Donald H. Kent (Harrisburg, Pa., 1941), series 21646, p. 33; and in Andrew Burnaby, *Travels through the Middle Settlements in North-America in the Years, 1759 and 1760* (London, 1775), p. 34. On the use of Virginia provincials for running down deserters, see Mather to Bouquet, 23 August 1760; Captain Henry Woodward to Bouquet, 4 December 1760, in *Bouquet Papers*, series 21645, pp. 143, 208.

22. Fauquier's order to buy convicts is in Fauquier to Byrd [April 1759], in C.O. 5/1329, ff. 354–55. A detailed study on the use of convict labor in the Old Dominion takes note of Fauquier's order to Byrd but concludes that "the evidence is not certain that any convict was imported directly into military conscription" (see Frederick Hall Schmidt, "British Convict Servant Labor in Colonial Virginia" (Ph.D. diss., College of William and Mary, 1976), pp. 116–17. Fauquier's observation about the "Military Ardor" of young Virginians is in Fauquier to the Board of Trade, 9 May 1759, in *Fauquier Papers*, 1:215.

23. On the relative financial attraction of a ten-pound enlistment bounty, see Land, "Economic Behavior in a Planting Society: The Eighteenth Century Chesapeake", p. 483, and the same author's "Economic Base and Social Structure: The Northern Chesapeake in the Eighteenth Century," in Gary B. Nash, ed., *Class and Society in Early America* (Englewood Cliffs, 1970), p. 121; see also Jackson Turner Main, *The Social Structure of Revolutionary America* (Princeton, 1965), pp. 77–78, 156. The Reverend Devereux Jarratt, the product of eighteenth-century Virginia yeoman stock, in later life recalled that by his nineteenth year he "had never owned five shillings cash in all my life"; Jarratt, *The Life of the Reverend Devereux Jarratt* (Baltimore, 1806), pp. 25–26.

24. The near-classic case study of small-unit cohesion as the sine qua non of combat effectiveness is Edward A. Shils and Morris Janowitz, "Cohesion and Disintegration in the German Wehrmacht in World War II," *Public Opinion Quarterly* 12 (Summer 1948): 280–315; see also S. L. A. Marshall, *Men Against Fire* (New York, 1947), especially chapter 10. The costs of waging war when unit cohesion is lacking is the theme of Paul L. Savage and Richard A. Gabriel, "Cohesion and Disintegration in the American Army in Vietnam," *Armed Forces and Society* 2 (May 1976): 340–76. Probably the best-known study of the emergence of a new class of essentially noncombatant "military managers" in the heavily bureaucratized armies of the twentieth century is Morris Janowitz, *The Professional Soldier: A Social and Political Portrait* (Glencoe, Il., 1960).

25. The part played by Washington's rigorous training program in stimulating pride, cohesion, and "a professional ethic" within the Virginia Regiment is expertly analyzed by Don Higginbotham in *George Washington and the American Military Tradition* (Athens, Ga., 1985), especially pp. 32–33.

26. Descriptions of the monument at Fort Cumberland are in *Washington Papers*, 4:163, n. 1; and Will H. Lowdermilk, *History of Cumberland (Maryland)* (Washington, 1878), pp. 266–67. Two of the five soldiers to whom the monument was dedicated, Sergeants William Shaw and Joseph Fent, actually survived their supposedly fatal skirmish in the Allegheny outback.

27. The altercation between Sergeant Hughes and the Winchester innkeeper is described in Robert Stewart to Washington, 20 June 1756, in *Letters to Washington*, 1:280–83.

28. Stephen to Washington, 20 August 1757; Mercer to Washington, 17 August 1757, in *Letters to Washington*, 2:180, 177–78.

29. This point is made repeatedly in Shils and Janowitz, "Cohesion and Disintegration in the German Wehrmacht"; see especially pp. 284, 287, 295–97.

30. For details on combat fatalities among provincial officers during this period see W. W. Abbot et al., eds., *The Papers of George Washington: Colonial Series*, 4 vols. to date (Charlottesville, 1983–    ), 2:24–25n; 109, n. 1; 113, n. 1; 150, n. 1; 3:43, n. 7. In his highly acclaimed study of the provincial army of Massachusetts, Fred Anderson makes clear that the Bay Colony's enlisted men also had settled views on the subject of proper officer behavior; that is, they expected their officers to lead by example. As Anderson puts it: "leadership among the [Massachusetts] provincials was

physical and personal" (see Anderson, *A People's Army: Massachusetts Soldiers and Society in the Seven Years' War* (Chapel Hill, 1984), pp. 155–60).

31. Command appointments are discussed in Dinwiddie to Washington, 4 June 1754, in *Washington Papers*, 1:126–27; Fauquier to Byrd, 23 January 1759, in *Fauquier Papers*, 1:158–59; Fauquier to Amherst, 21 May 1762, in *Fauquier Papers*, 2:739. Changes in regimental command also are noted in Morton, *Colonial Virginia*, 2:645, 652, 726, 735.

32. Details regarding the military careers of individual provincial officers, including length of service, are available in the rich notes that accompany W. W. Abbot's new edition of the Washington papers. Interestingly, beginning in May 1757, the Virginia Regiment's three senior officers, Washington, Stephen, and Major Andrew Lewis, also served simultaneously as company commanders (see Dinwiddie to Washington, [16 May 1757], in *Washington Papers*, 4:153–54, n. 2).

33. Information concerning "veteran" enlisted men in the Virginia Regiment was derived from the George Washington Papers (MSS, Library of Congress, Washington, D.C.), ser. 4, 4: items 424–25, 428–30, 434–35, 452, 461, 463; 6: items 722, 733, 756, 778.

34. Washington to Stephen, [9 January 1756], in *Washington Papers*, 2:264; Washington Papers MSS, ser 4., 6: item 756. Brief sketches of John Sallard and Reuben Vass are in *Washington Papers*, 2:61n, 354n. Sallard, in particular, came highly recommended (see Landon Carter to Washington, 25 September 1755; John Tayloe to Washington, 27 September 1755; William Brokenbrough to Washington, 29 September 1755, in *Letters to Washington*, 1:97–98, 100–01).

35. For a suggestive comment about the battlefield role of noncommissioned officers in the War of Independence, see Robert Middlekauff, "Why Men Fought in the American Revolution," *Huntington Library Quarterly*, 43 (1980): 138.

36. Davies, "The Curse of Cowardice," in *Sermons on Important Subjects. By the Late Reverend and Pious Samuel Davis, A. M. Sometime President of the College of New Jersey*, 5 vols. (Philadelphia, 1818), 5:277; on this theme see also Maury to John Fontaine, 15 June 1756, in Ann Maury, ed. and trans., *Memoirs of a Huguenot Family: Translated and Compiled from the Original Autobiography of the Rev. James Maury* (reprint, Baltimore, 1967), p. 404.

37. Reports concerning mistreatment of provincial soldiers are discussed in ibid., p. 281; Washington to Dinwiddie, 8 September 1756; Washington to Loudoun, 10 January 1757, in *Washington Papers*, 3:399; 4:80–81.

38. That the institution of slavery was charged with political symbolism for white men living in eighteenth-century Virginia is one of the central arguments in Edmund S. Morgan's *American Slavery, American Freedom: The Ordeal of Colonial Virginia*. According to Morgan, the principal beneficiaries of the perverse symbiosis between black slavery and white freedom were men of the "middling sort," the smaller planters who made up the largest single element in white society. Morgan also contends that as the eighteenth century progressed, the yeomanry and the gentry became more closely linked by common economic interests and—as they became surrounded by increasing numbers of black slaves—a growing regard for their own freedom. (As votaries of liberty, white Virginians were also, Morgan claims, a receptive audience for the ideas of radical Whig thinkers such as John Trenchard, Thomas Gordon, and Robert Molesworth.) See Morgan, *American Slavery, American Freedom*, chapter 18, especially pp. 369–70, 376–78, 380–82.

## EPILOGUE

1. The provincial government's efforts to excite a war spirit were limited, to say the least. In October 1754 Governor Dinwiddie asked a convention of Anglican clergy to "inculcate into the People the great dangers we are Expos'd to." The following month

the governor requested that members of the assembly use their influence in their home counties to drum up volunteers for the Virginia Regiment. Dinwiddie's last apparent attempt at wooing public opinion came in the autumn of 1755 when he proclaimed 24 September as a day of general fasting "for the Preservation of us from the Hands of our Enemies" (see "Governor Dinwiddie's Reply to the Commissary and Clergy," [October 1754]; "Address of Governor Dinwiddie to the General Assembly," 2 November 1754, in *The Official Records of Robert Dinwiddie, Lieutenant-Governor of the Colony of Virginia, 1751–1758, Now First Printed from the Manuscript in the Collections of the Virginia Historical Society,* ed. Robert A. Brock, 2 vols. [Richmond, 1883], 1:361–62, 380); the governor's proclamation of a general fast was published in the *Virginia Gazette* (Hunter) of 29 August 1755. Of the surviving contemporary accounts of the "Associators," the most descriptive are in the *Pennsylvania Gazette* for 10 May and 3 June 1756; see also Dinwiddie to Washington, 8 May 1756, in *Dinwiddie Papers,* 2:406. The "Associators'" brief sojourn on the frontier is discussed in Douglas Southall Freeman, *George Washington: A Biography,* 7 vols. (New York, 1948–57), 2:198. Rhys Isaac argues that the Associators self-consciously set out to provide "an example to the common people" (see Isaac, "Religion and Authority: Problems of the Anglican Establishment in Virginia in the Era of the Great Awakening and the Parson's Cause," *William and Mary Quarterly,* 3d ser., 30 (January 1973): 30.

2. On the low regard in which poor Virginians were held, see, for example, Dinwiddie to Arthur Dobbs, 17 July 1755, in *Dinwiddie Papers,* 1:468; Dinwiddie to Washington, 19 August 1756; Robert Stewart to Washington, 31 December 1758, in *Letters to Washington and Accompanying Papers,* ed. Stanislaus Murray Hamilton, 5 vols. (Boston and New York, 1898–1902), 1:343; 3:149; Jack P. Greene, ed., *The Diary of Colonel Landon Carter of Sabine Hall, 1752–1778,* 2 vols. (Charlottesville, 1965), 2:795.

3. The record brims with charges that during the French and Indian War, Virginia militiamen were militarily useless and that even as rudimentary draft boards, the performance of militia units ranged from barely adequate to totally ineffective; see, for example, Dinwiddie to John Buchanan, 11 August 1755; Dinwiddie to the Lords of Trade, 23 February 1756; Dinwiddie to the earl of Loudoun, 9 August 1756, in *Dinwiddie Papers,* 2:154–55, 344, 476; Washington to Loudoun, 10 January 1757; Washington to Dinwiddie, 27 June 1757; Washington to John Stanwix, 15 July 1757, in W. W. Abbot et al., eds., *The Papers of George Washington: Colonial Series,* 4 vols. to date (Charlottesville, 1983–     ), 4:87–88, 265, 306; Charles Smith to Washington, 2 December 1758, in *Letters to Washington,* 3:132. This interpretation of the militia follows the argument laid down in Richard H. Kohn, *Eagle and Sword: The Federalists and the Creation of the Military Establishment in America, 1783–1802* (New York and London, 1975), pp. 6–9. One study finds that the Virginia militia was serving as a rudimentary selective service system by the middle of the seventeenth century (see William L. Shea, *The Virginia Militia in the Seventeenth Century* [Baton Rouge, 1983], p. 52).

4. This conclusion coincides with that reached by Stanislaw Andrzejewski in his now classic study, *Military Organization and Society* (London, 1954).

5. This argument is developed most fully in Edmund S. Morgan, *American Slavery, American Freedom: The Ordeal of Colonial Virginia* (New York, 1975). Morgan places almost exclusive stress on slavery's impact on the political thinking and emotions of the "better" and "middling" sorts of men; see especially pp. 369–70, 376–78, 380–82. The political symbolism that slavery held for Virginians in the late colonial period is discussed as well in Jack P. Greene, "Society, Ideology, and Politics: An Analysis of the Political Culture of Mid-Eighteenth Century Virginia," in Richard M. Jellison, ed., *Society, Freedom, and Conscience: The Coming of the Revolution in Virginia, Massachusetts, and New York* (New York, 1976), pp. 67–69. Even more than Morgan, Greene fixes on slavery's influence on the thinking of men belonging to the

upper crust. The potency of slavery as a source of political imagery in prerevolutionary political thought is also discussed in Bernard Bailyn, *The Ideological Origins of the American Revolution* (Cambridge, Mass., 1967), pp. 232–46, and to a lesser extent in Gordon S. Wood, *The Creation of the American Republic, 1776–1787* (New York, 1969), pp. 23, 34, 39.

6. Thomas Jefferson to John Adams, 16 May 1777; Adams to Jefferson, 26 May 1777, in Lester J. Cappon, ed., *The Adams-Jefferson Letters: The Complete Correspondence Between Thomas Jefferson and Abigail and John Adams*, 2 vols. (Chapel Hill, 1959), 1:4–5.

7. John F. Smyth, *A Tour in the United States of America*, 2 vols. (London, 1784), 1:356, quoted in Robert E. and B. Katherine Brown, *Virginia, 1705–1786: Democracy or Aristocracy?* (East Lansing, 1964), p. 33.

8. That the nature of Virginia society underwent a profound change during the second half of the eighteenth century is Rhys Isaac's main point in *The Transformation of Virginia Society, 1740–1790* (Chapel Hill, 1982). Isaac's analysis is confined primarily to the religious and political confrontations that constituted popular challenges to the traditional social order. Nothing is said of the "lesser sort's" successful challenge to an elitist military policy during the French and Indian War. A suggestive consideration of the origins of a less deferential order in one outlying region of colonial Virginia is in Albert H. Tillson, Jr., "The Militia and Popular Political Culture in the Upper Valley of Virginia, 1740–1775," *Virginia Magazine of History and Biography*, 94 (July 1986): 285–306.

# BIBLIOGRAPHY

**PRIMARY SOURCES**

## 1. Manuscript Collections

### Colonial Williamsburg Foundation Research Archive
(Williamsburg)

Allason Letter Book. Microfilm copy of the Letter Book of William Allason, 1757–1770, in the Virginia State Library.

Amherst Papers. Microfilm copies of the Jeffery Amherst Papers in the British War Office.

Beverley Letter Book. Microfilm copy of the Robert Beverley Letter Book in the Library of Congress.

Bouquet Papers. Microfilm copies of the Henry Bouquet Papers in the British Museum.

Gooch Papers. Typescript copies of the William Gooch Papers in the British Public Record Office.

America and the West Indies. Typescript copies of Colonial Office Papers, Class 5, vols. 211, 1322, 1325, 1326, 1327, 1367. Public Record Office. London.

Great Britain. Public Record Office. High Court of Admiralty, vol. 30. Miscellaneous Papers, 1750–1756.

Great Britain. Public Record Office. War Office Papers, Classs 4, Out Letters, Secretary at War, 1755–1757.

Great Britain. Public Record Office. War Office Papers, Class 1, In Letters, America and the West Indies, 1764–1765.

Jerdone Letter Book. Microfilm copy of the Letter Copy Book of Francis Jerdone, 1756–1763, in the Swem Library, College of William and Mary.

Lyttelton Papers. Microfilm copies of the William H. Lyttelton Papers, 1756–1760, in the Clements Library, University of Michigan.

Orderly Book for the Virginia Regiment. Microfilm copy of the Orderly Book for the Virginia Regiment, May-September 1762, in the Henry E. Huntington Library.

Shelburne Papers. Microfilm copies of the earl of Shelburne Papers in the Clements Library, University of Michigan.

Virginia Colonial Papers. Microfilm copies of the Virginia Colonial Papers, 1762–1767, in the Virginia State Library.

### Library of Congress (Washington, D.C.)
Washington Papers

## 2. Printed Materials

Abbot, W. W. et al., eds. *The Papers of George Washington: Colonial Series.* 4 vols. to date. Charlottesville, 1983–.

Brock, Robert A., ed. *The Official Records of Robert Dinwiddie, Lieutenant-Governor of the Colony of Virginia, 1751–1758.* 2 vols. Richmond, 1883–84.

Burnaby, Andrew. *Travels through the Middle Settlements in North America in the Years 1759 and 1760.* London. 1775.

Cappon, Lester J., ed. *The Adams-Jefferson Letters: The Complete Correspondence Between Thomas Jefferson and Abigail and John Adams.* 2 vols. Chapel Hill, 1959.

Davies, Samuel. *Sermons on Important Subjects. By the Late Reverend and Pious Samuel Davies.* Philadelphia, 1818.

Davis, Richard Beale, ed. *The Colonial Virginia Satirist; Mid-Eighteenth Century Commentaries on Politics, Religion, and Society.* Philadelphia, 1967.

Farish, Hunter Dickinson, ed. *Journal and Letters of Philip Vickers Fithian, 1773–1774: A Plantation Tutor in the Old Dominion.* Charlottesville, 1957.

Fitzpatrick, John C., ed. *The Diaries of George Washington, 1748–1799.* 4 vols. Boston, 1925.

———. *The Writings of George Washington from the Original Manuscript Sources, 1745–1799.* 39 vols. Washington, D.C., 1931–44.

Greene, Jack P., ed. *The Diary of Colonel Landon Carter of Sabine Hall, 1752–1778.* 2 vols. Charlottesville, 1965.

Hamilton, Charles, ed. *Braddock's Defeat: The Journal of Captain Robert Cholmley's Batman; The Journal of a British Officer; Halkett's Orderly Book.* Norman, Okla., 1959.

Hamilton, Stanislaus Murray, ed. *Letters to Washington and Accompanying Papers.* 5 vols. Boston and New York, 1898–1902.

Hening, William Waller, ed. *The Statutes at Large: Being a Collection of All the Laws of Virginia.* 13 vols. Richmond and Philadelphia, 1809–23.

Jackson, Donald, ed. *The Diaries of George Washington, 1748–1799.* 6 vols. Charlottesville, 1976–79.

James, Alfred Proctor, ed. *Writings of General John Forbes Relating to his Service in North America.* Menasha, Wis., 1938.

Jarratt, Devereux. *The Life of the Reverend Devereux Jarratt.* Baltimore, 1906.

Jones, Hugh. *The Present State of Virginia From Whence Is Interred A Short View of Maryland and North Carolina.* Edited by Richard L. Morton. Chapel Hill, 1956.

"Journal of Captain Charles Lewis, October 10 - December 10, 1755." *Proceedings* of the Virginia Historical Society, 11 (1891): 203–16.

Kennedy, John Pendleton, ed. *Journals of the House of Burgesses of Virginia, 1761–1765.* Richmond, 1907.

Kimball, Gertrude Selwyn, ed. *Correspondence of William Pitt When Secretary of State With Colonial Governors and Military and Naval Commissioners in America.* 2 vols. New York and London, 1906.

"[Lieutenant Thomas] Morton's Diary." *The Virginia Historical Register and Literary Note Book,* 4 (January 1851): 143–47.

Livingston, William. *A Review of the Military Operations in North America.* Dublin, 1757.

Maury, Ann, ed. and trans. *Memoirs of a Huguenot Family: Translated and Compiled from the Original Autobiography of the Reverend James Maury.* New York, 1853; reprint, Baltimore, 1967.

Mays, David John, ed. *The Letters and Papers of Edmund Pendleton, 1743–1803.* 2 vols. Charlottesville, 1967.

McIlwaine, Henry Read, ed. *Journals of the House of Burgesses of Virginia, 1752–1755, 1756–1758.* Richmond, 1909.

———. *Journals of the House of Burgesses of Virginia, 1758–1761.* Richmond, 1908.

Mulkearn, Lois, comp. and ed. *George Mercer Papers Relating to the Ohio Company of Virginia.* Pittsburgh, 1954.

"Observations in Several Voyages and Travels in America." *London Magazine,* July 1744; reprinted in the *William and Mary Quarterly,* 1st ser., 15 (January 1907), 147–48.

Palmer, William P., ed. *Calendar of Virginia State Papers and Other Manuscripts, 1652–1781, Preserved in the Capital at Richmond.* Richmond, 1875; reprint, New York, 1968.

Pargellis, Stanley M., ed. *Military Affairs in North America, 1748–1765: Selected Documents From the Cumberland Papers in Windsor Castle.* New York, 1936; reprint, New York, 1969.

Reese, George, ed. *The Official Papers of Francis Fauquier, Lieutenant Governor of Virginia, 1758–1768.* 3 vols. Charlottesville, 1980–83.

Stephen, Adam. "The Ohio Expedition of 1754." *Pennsylvania Magazine of History and Biography,* 18 (1894), 43–44.

Stevens, S. K., and Donald H. Kent. *The Papers of Henry Bouquet.* 19 vols. Harrisburg, Pa., 1940–43.

Sumners, Louis P., ed. "Journal of Doctor Thomas Walker, 1749–1750." *Annals of Southwest Virginia, 1769–1800.* Abington Va., 1929.

Tinling, Marion, ed. *The Correspondence of the Three William Byrds of Westover, Virginia, 1684–1776.* 2 vols. Charlottesville, 1977.

Walne, Peter, ed. "George Washington and the Fairfax Family: Some New Documents." *Virginia Magazine of History and Biography,* 77 (October 1969): 454–56.

———. "A Mystery Resolved: George Washington's Letter to Governor Dinwiddie, June 10, 1754." *Virginia Magazine of History and Biography,* 79 (April 1971), 135–39.

Timberlake, Henry. *The Memoirs of Lieut. Henry Timberlake.* London, 1765.

## SECONDARY SOURCES

### 1. Books and Articles

Abernethy, Thomas Perkins. *Three Virginia Frontiers.* Gloucester, Mass., 1962.

———. *Western Lands and the American Revolution.* New York, 1937.

Adair, Douglas, ed. "James Madison's Autobiography." *William and Mary Quarterly,* 3d. ser., 2 (April 1945): 191–209.

Alden, John Richard. *John Stuart and the Southern Colonial Frontier: A Study of Indian Relations, War, Trade, and Land Problems in the Southern Wilderness, 1754–1775.* Ann Arbor, 1944.

———. *Robert Dinwiddie: Servant of the Crown.* Charlottesville, 1973.

Anderson, Fred. *A People's Army: Massachusetts Soldiers and Society in the Seven Years' War.* Chapel Hill, 1984.

Andrzejewski, Stanislaw. *Military Organization and Society.* London, 1954.

Bailey, Kenneth P. *The Ohio Company of Virginia and the Westward Movement, 1748–1792: A Chapter in the History of the Colonial Frontier.* Glendale, Calif., 1939.

Bailyn, Bernard. *The Ideological Origins of the American Revolution.* Cambridge, Mass., 1967.

Baker-Crothers, Hayes. *Virginia and the French and Indian War.* Chicago, 1928.

Baker-Crothers, Hayes, and Ruth Allisan Hudnut. "A Private Soldier's Account of Washington's First Battles in the West: A Study in Historical Criticism." *Journal of Southern History*, 8 (May 1942): 21–35.

Becker, Robert A. "Revolution and Reform: An Interpretation of Southern Taxation, 1736 to 1783." *William and Mary Quarterly*, 3d. ser., 32 (July 1975): 417–42.

Berkeley, Francis L., Jr. "The War of Jenkins' Ear." *The Old Dominion: Essays for Thomas Perkins Abernethy*. Edited by Darrett B. Rutman. Charlottesville, 1964.

Bernath, Stuart L. "George Washington and the Genesis of American Military Discipline." *Mid-America: An Historical Review*, 2 (April, 1967): 83–100.

Bliss, Willard F. "The Rise of Tenancy in Virginia." *Virginia Magazine of History and Biography*, 58 (October 1950): 427–41.

Boorstin, Daniel J. *The Americans: The Colonial Experience*. New York, 1958.

Bridenbaugh, Carl. *Myths and Realities: Societies of the Colonial South*. Baton Rouge, 1952.

Brown, Robert E., and B. Katherine Brown. *Virginia, 1705–1786: Democracy or Aristocracy?* East Lansing, 1964.

Cappon, Lester J., et al., eds. *Atlas of Early American History: The Revolutionary Era, 1760–1790*. Princeton, 1976.

Clayton, T. R. "The Duke of Newcastle, the Earl of Halifax, and the American Origins of the Seven Years' War." *Historical Journal*, 24 (September 1981): 571–603.

Clode, Charles M. *The Military Forces of the Crown: Their Administration and Government*. 2 vols. London, 1869.

Cook, Roy Bird. "Virginia Frontier Defenses, 1719–1795." *West Virginia History*, 1 (1940): 119–30.

Corkran, David H. *The Cherokee Frontier: Conflict and Survival, 1740–1762*. Norman, 1962.

Cousins, Geoffrey. *The Defenders: A History of the British Volunteer*. London, 1968.

Cress, Lawrence Delbert. *Citizens in Arms: The Army and the Militia in American Society to the War of 1812*. Chapel Hill, 1982.

De Hass, Willis. *History of the Early Settlement and Indian Wars of Western Virginia: Embracing an Account of the Various Expeditions in the West, Previous to 1795*. Reprint. Parsons, W. Va., 1960.

Del Papa, Eugene M. "The Royal Proclamation of 1763: Its Effect upon Virginia Land Companies." *Virginia Magazine of History and Biography*, 83 (October 1976): 406–11.

Egnal, Marc. "The Origins of the Revolution in Virginia: A Reinterpretation." *William and Mary Quarterly*, 3d. ser., 37 (July 1980): 401–28.

Ernest, Joseph Albert. "Genesis of the Currency Act of 1764: Virginia Paper Money and the Protection of British Investments." *William and Mary Quarterly*, 3d. ser., 23 (January 1965): 33–74.

———. "The Robinson Scandal Redivivus: Money, Debts, and Politics in Revolutionary Virginia." *Virginia Magazine of History and Biography*, 77 (April 1969): 146–73.

———. *Money and Politics in America, 1755–1775: A Study in the Currency Act of 1764 and the Political Economy of Revolution*. Chapel Hill, 1973.

Flexner, James Thomas. *George Washington: The Forge of Experience (1732–1775)*. Boston, 1965.

Flippen, Percy Scott. *The Royal Government in Virginia*. New York, 1919.

———. "William Gooch: Successful Royal Governor of Virginia." *William and Mary Quarterly*, 2d. ser., 6 (January 1926): 2–18.

Fortesque, John W. *A History of the British Army.* 13 vols. London and New York, 1899–1930.

Freeman, Douglas Southall. *George Washington: A Biography.* 7 vols. New York, 1948–57.

Fregault, Guy. *Canada: The War of the Conquest.* Translated by Margaret M. Cameron. Toronto, 1969.

─┼ Frey, Sylvia R. *The British Soldier in America: A Social History of Military Life in the Revolutionary Period.* Austin, 1981.

Gearing, Fred. "Priests and Warriors: Social Structures for Cherokee Politics in the Eighteenth Century." *American Anthropologist,* 64 (October 1962): 1–124.

Giddens, Paul H. "The Co-Operation of the Southern Colonies in the Forbes Expedition Against Fort Duquesne." *Virginia Magazine of History and Biography,* 36 (January, April 1928): 1–16, 145–61.

Gilbert, Arthur N. "The Changing Face of British Military Justice, 1757–1783." *Military Affairs,* 49 (April 1985): 80–84.

─⌐⌐ Gipson, Lawrence Henry. *The British Empire before the American Revolution.* 15 vols. Caldwell, Idaho, and New York, 1936–70.

Greene, Jack P. *The Quest for Power: The Lower Houses of Assembly in the Southern Royal Colonies, 1689–1776.* Chapel Hill, 1963.

───. "Society, Ideology, and Politics: An Analysis of the Political Culture of Mid-Eighteenth Century Virginia." *Society, Freedom and Conscience: The Coming of the Revolution in Virginia, Massachusetts, and New York.* Edited by Richard M. Jellison. New York, 1976.

Griffin, Paul F., Robert N. Young, and Ronald L. Chatham. *Anglo-America: A Regional Geography of the United States and Canada.* San Francisco, 1962.

Harrington, J. C. *New Light on Washington's Fort Necessity: A Report on the Archeological Explorations at Fort Necessity National Battlefield Site.* Richmond, 1957.

Harrison, Fairfax. "George Washington's First Commission." *Virginia Magazine of History and Biography,* 31 (July 1923): 269–80.

Henretta, James A. *The Evolution of American Society, 1700–1815: An Interdisciplinary Analysis.* Lexington, Mass., 1973.

─ Higginbotham, Don. *Daniel Morgan: Revolutionary Rifleman.* Chapel Hill, 1961.

───. *The War of American Independence: Military Attitudes, Policies, and Practice, 1763–1789.* New York and London, 1971.

───. *George Washington and the American Military Tradition.* Athens, Ga., 1985.

─ Higonnet, Patrice Louis-Rene. "The Origins of the Seven Years' War." *Journal of Modern History,* 40 (March 1968): 59–90.

Hofstader, Richard. *America at 1750: A Social Portrait.* New York, 1973.

Isaac, Rhys. "Religion and Authority: Problems of the Anglican Establishment in Virginia in the Era of the Great Awakening and the Parson's Cause." *William and Mary Quarterly,* 3d. ser., 30 (January 1973): 3–36.

───. *The Transformation of Virginia: 1740–1790.* Chapel Hill, 1982.

James, Alfred P. *The Ohio Company: Its Inner History.* Pittsburgh, 1959.

─ Janowitz, Morris. *The Professional Soldier: A Social and Political Portrait.* Glencoe, Il., 1960.

Jennings, Francis. *The Ambiguous Iroquois Empire: The Covenant Chain Confederation of Indian Tribes with English Colonies from its beginnings to the Lancaster Treaty of 1744.* New York and London, 1984.

Kegley, F. B. *Kegley's Virginia Frontier: The Beginning of the Southwest, the Roanoke of Colonial Days, 1740–1783, with Maps and Illustrations.* Roanoke, Va., 1938.

Kercheval, Samuel. *A History of the Valley of Virginia.* Edited by Oren F. Morton. 4th ed. Strasburg, Va., 1925.

Knollenberg, Bernhard. *George Washington: The Virginia Period, 1732-1755.* Durham, N.C., 1964.

Kohn, Richard H. *Eagle and Sword: The Beginnings of the Military Establishment in America.* New York, 1975.

Koontz, Louis K. *The Virginia Frontier, 1754-1763.* Baltimore, 1925.

―――. "Washington on the Frontier." *Virginia Magazine of History and Biography,* 36 (October 1928): 302-15.

―――. *Robert Dinwiddie: His Career in American Colonial Government and Western Expansion.* Glendale, Calif., 1941.

Land, Aubrey C. "Economic Behavior in a Planting Society: The Eighteenth Century Chesapeake." *Journal of Southern History,* 33 (November 1967): 469-85.

―――. "Economic Base and Social Structure: The Northern Chesapeake in the Eighteenth Century." *Class and Society in Early America.* Edited by Gary B. Nash. Englewood Cliffs, N. J., 1970.

Leach, Douglas Edward. *Arms for Empire: A Military History of the British Colonies in North America, 1607-1763.* New York and London, 1973.

―――. *Roots of Conflict: British Armed Forces and Colonial Americans, 1677-1783.* Chapel Hill, 1986.

Lowdermilk, Will H. *History of Cumberland (Maryland).* Washington, 1878.

Main, Gloria L. *Tobacco Colony: Life in Early Maryland, 1650-1720.* Princeton, 1982.

Main, Jackson Turner. *The Social Structure of Revolutionary America.* Princeton, 1965.

Marshall, S. L. A. *Men Against Fire.* New York, 1947.

Middlekauff, Robert. "Why Men Fought in the American Revolution." *Huntington Library Quarterly,* 43 (Spring 1980): 135-48.

Morgan, Edmund S. *Virginians at Home: Family Life in the Eighteenth Century.* Williamsburg, 1952.

―――. *American Slavery, American Freedom: The Ordeal of Colonial Virginia.* New York, 1975.

Morgan, Gwenda. "Virginia in the French and Indian War: A Case Study of the War's Effects on Imperial Relations." *Virginia Magazine of History and Biography,* 81 (January 1973): 23-48.

Morton, Louis. *Robert Carter of Nomini Hall: A Virginia Tobacco Planter of the Eighteenth Century.* Charlottesville, 1945.

Morton, Richard Lee. *Colonial Virginia.* 2 vols. Chapel Hill, 1960.

Mullin, Gerald W. *Flight and Rebellion: Slave Resistance in Eighteenth-Century Virginia.* New York, 1972.

Nichols, Franklin Thayer. "The Organization of Braddock's Army." *William and Mary Quarterly,* 3d. ser., 4 (April 1947): 125-47.

Norkus, Nellie. "Virginia's Role in the Capture of Fort Duquesne, 1758." *The Western Pennsylvania Historical Magazine,* 45 (December 1962): 291-308.

Osgood, Herbert L. *The American Colonies in the Eighteenth Century.* 4 vols. New York, 1924.

Pargellis, Stanley M. *Lord Loudoun in North America.* New Haven, 1933.

―――. "Braddock's Defeat." *American Historical Review,* 41 (January 1936): 253-69.

Peckham, Howard H. *The Colonial Wars, 1689-1762.* Chicago, 1964.

Pole, J. R. "Historians and the Problem of Early American Democracy." *American Historical Review,* 67 (April 1962): 626-46.

Quarles, Benjamin. "The Colonial Militia and Negro Manpower." *Mississippi Valley Historical Review*, 45 (March 1959): 643–52.

Reid, John Phillip. *In Defiance of the Law: The Standing Army Controversy, the Two Constitutions, and the Coming of the American Revolution*. Chapel Hill, 1981.

Rice, Otis. K. "The French and Indian War in West Virginia." *West Virginia History*, 1 (1940): 134–46.

Riker, Thad W. "The Politics Behind Braddock's Expedition." *American Historical Review*, 13 (July 1908): 742–52.

Robinson, W. Stitt. "Virginia and the Cherokees: Indian Policy from Spotswood to Dinwiddie." *The Old Dominion: Essays for Thomas Perkins Abernethy*. Edited by Darrett B. Rutman. Charlottesville, 1964.

———. *The Southern Colonial Frontier, 1607–1763*. Albuquerque, 1979.

Rogers, Alan. *Empire and Liberty: American Resistance to British Authority, 1755–1763*. Berkeley, 1974.

Rossiter, Clinton. "Richard Bland: The Real Whig in America." *William and Mary Quarterly*, 3d. ser., 10 (January 1953): 33–79.

Russell, Peter E. "Redcoats in the Wilderness: British Officers and Irregular Warfare in Europe and America, 1740–1760." *William and Mary Quarterly*, 3d. ser., 35 (October 1978): 629–52.

Rutman, Darrett B., and Anita H. Rutman. *A Place in Time: Middlesex County, Virginia, 1650–1750*. New York, 1984.

Sargent, Winthrop, ed. *The History of an Expedition against Fort Duquesne in 1755 under Major-General Edward Braddock*. Philadelphia, 1855.

Savage, Paul L., and Richard A. Gabriel. "Cohesion and Disintegration in the American Army in Vietnam." *Armed Forces and Society*, 2 (May 1976): 340–76.

Savelle, Max. *The Origins of American Diplomacy: The International History of Angloamerica, 1492–1763*. New York and London, 1967.

Shea, William L. *The Virginia Militia in the Seventeenth Century*. Baton Rouge, 1983.

Shils, Edward A., and Morris Janowitz. "Cohesion and Disintegration in the German Wehrmacht in World War II." *Public Opinion Quarterly*, 22 (Summer 1948): 280–315.

Shy, John W. "A New Look at Colonial Militia." *William and Mary Quarterly*, 3d. ser., 20 (April 1963): 175–85.

———. *Toward Lexington: The Role of the British Army in the Coming of the American Revolution*. Princeton, 1965.

Smith, Glenn C. "The Affair of the Pistole Fee." *Virginia Magazine of History and Biography*, 48 (July 1940): 209–21.

Sosin, Jack M. *Whitehall and the Wilderness: The Middle West in British Colonial Policy, 1760–1775*. Lincoln, Neb., 1961.

———. *The Revolutionary Frontier, 1763–1784*. New York, 1967.

Spaulding, Oliver L., Jr. "The Military Studies of George Washington." *American Historical Review*, 29 (July 1924): 675–80.

Speier, Hans. *Social Order and the Risks of War: Papers in Political Sociology*. Cambridge, Mass., 1952.

Sydnor, Charles S. *Gentlemen Freeholders: Political Practices in Washington's Virginia*. Chapel Hill, 1952.

Tillson, Albert H., Jr. "The Militia and Popular Political Culture in the Upper Valley of Virginia, 1740–1775." *Virginia Magazine of History and Biography*, 94 (July 1986): 285–306.

Van Alstyne, Richard W. *The Rising American Empire*. New York, 1960.

Waddell, Joseph A. *Annals of Augusta County, Virginia, From 1726 to 1871*. Staunton, Va., 1902; reprint, Bridgewater, Va., 1958.
Warner, Charles Willard Hoskins. *Road to Revolution: Virginia's Rebels from Bacon to Jeffeson, 1676–1776*. Richmond, 1961.
Webb, Stephen Saunders. *The Governors-General: The English Army and the Definition of Empire, 1569–1681*. Chapel Hill, 1979.
Weigley, Russell F. *History of the United States Army*. New York, 1976.
Wertenbaker, Thomas J. *Patrician and Plebian in Colonial Virginia, 1698–1750*. Charlottesville, 1910.
———. *The Planters of Colonial Virginia*. Princeton, 1922.
Western, John R. *The English Militia in the Eighteenth Century: The Story of a Political Issue*. London, 1965.
Wood, Gordon S. *The Creation of the American Republic, 1776–1787*. New York, 1969.
Wright, John W. "Pickering's Letter on Washington." *Tyler's Historical Quarterly and Geneological Magazine*, 7 (July 1925): 18–19.

**2. Unpublished Dissertations and Theses**
Aldridge, Frederick Stokes. "Organization and Administration of the Militia System of Colonial Virginia." Ph.D. diss., American University, 1964.
Lawrence, Parker King. "Anglo-American Wilderness Campaigning, 1754–1764: Logistical and Tactical Developments." Ph.D. diss., Columbia University, 1970.
Nyland, Keith Ryan. "Doctor Thomas Walker (1715–1794) Explorer, Physician, Statesman, Surveyor and Planter of Virginia and Kentucky." Ph.D. diss., The Ohio State University, 1971.
Paschall, Davis Y. "Crime and Its Punishment in Colonial Virginia, 1607–1776." Master's thesis, College of William and Mary, 1937.
Schmidt, Frederick Hall. "British Convict Servant Labor in Colonial Virginia." Ph.D. diss., College of William and Mary, 1976.
Young, Chester Raymond. "The Effects of the French and Indian War on Civilian Life in the Frontier Counties of Virginia, 1754–1763." Ph.D. diss., Vanderbilt University, 1969.

# INDEX